TEACHING CLASSROOM CONTROVERSIES

T0383131

Teaching Classroom Controversies is the essential guide for all teachers trying to navigate their way through issues of controversy in the age of 'fake news' and 'alternative facts.' Arguing that schools have a key role to help turn the tide and promote intellectual humility and openness, the book shows teachers how they can set the boundaries to ensure a purposeful learning environment that thinks about controversy in terms of evidence, reasoned argument, and critical reflection.

Drawing on the latest research, the first part of the book provides frameworks for teaching and learning about controversy, including how to facilitate respectful discussion, the biases that impact student beliefs, and the pedagogical techniques that should be applied in the classroom. The second part offers practical guidance on how to teach the most contentious issues facing young children and teenagers in society today, dealing with wide-ranging questions such as:

- Is Santa Claus real?
- Do I have a 'normal' family?
- Is the Holocaust a hoax?
- Should there be any limits on free speech?

Teaching Classroom Controversies offers teachers the tools to develop their students' critical thinking on the timely and cutting-edge issues of controversy that are shaping our world.

Glenn Y. Bezalel is Deputy Head (Academic) at City of London School, where he teaches Religion & Philosophy. Glenn is also researching the pedagogy of conspiracy theories and controversy at the University of Cambridge and has written numerous articles on a range of educational topics for both academic and professional publications. He lives in London with his wife and five children.

"In this remarkable book, Glenn Bezalel charts a path through some of the hottest and most explosive issues in contemporary discourse. Teachers are often expected to be able to discuss fraught issues, an expectation that does not match their confidence in their own knowledge and ability to do so. Despite this, we owe it to our students to be well-informed and to be able to help them delve into these topics in a non-judgmental, safe and supportive way, but until now there has been no single resource that is scholarly, meticulously well-researched and clear enough to help us do this. Bezalel's book fits this role perfectly."

Adam Boxer, *Head of Science at Totteridge Academy in London and*
Education Director for Carousel Learning

"We live in a time when social forces within and outside of our school systems push to discourage teachers from dealing with controversial subject matters in their classrooms. Yet the need for teachers to continue to do so has never been greater. Glenn Bezalel's book, *Teaching Classroom Controversies*, presents a compelling case for teaching controversial issues, and offers solid and practical advice for how to do so effectively."

Professor Nicholas Burbules, *Department of Education Policy, Organization*
and Leadership, University of Illinois Urbana-Champaign

"*Teaching Classroom Controversies* could not have arrived at a better moment in the history of classroom life. In this incisive, practical and beautifully written book for teachers, Glenn Bezalel demonstrates why critical thinking in education matters more than ever and provides the reader with a highly accessible account of how to nurture it in a time where the capacity to speak 'truth to power' and the role of the critical thinker is in crisis in modern educational institutions globally."

Professor Jo-Anne Dillabough, *Faculty of Education,*
University of Cambridge

TEACHING CLASSROOM CONTROVERSIES

Navigating Complex Teaching Issues in the Age of Fake News and Alternative Facts

Glenn Y. Bezalel

Routledge
Taylor & Francis Group

LONDON AND NEW YORK

Designed cover image: © Getty Images

First published 2024
by Routledge
4 Park Square, Milton Park, Abingdon, Oxon OX14 4RN

and by Routledge
605 Third Avenue, New York, NY 10158

Routledge is an imprint of the Taylor & Francis Group, an informa business

© 2024 Glenn Y. Bezalel

British Library Cataloguing-in-Publication Data
A catalogue record for this book is available from the British Library

ISBN: 9781032287348 (hbk)
ISBN: 9781032287331 (pbk)
ISBN: 9781003298281 (ebk)

DOI: 10.4324/9781003298281

Typeset in Interstate
by codeMantra

For Hannah, Shayna, Akiva, Jemima, and Tamara.

CONTENTS

Introduction

Why Now?

I'm offended!
I can't be friends with someone who holds such views!
I hope I'm not 'cancelled' for saying this but…

This book makes a simple claim: we can do better.

To be sure, there have always been critics of the youth of the day. "There is nothing new under the sun," the Bible tells us. An exasperated Aristotle bemoaned the teenagers of the ancient world too: "Young people are high-minded because they have not yet been humbled by life, nor have they experienced the force of circumstances… They think they know everything, and are always quite sure about it."

In our time, we teachers, parents, and grandparents of a (slightly) older generation may well wince as we're reminded of what the all-American Harry 'Rabbit' Angstrom had to say of his pitiable son, a contemporary of ours, in John Updike's classic 1981 novel, *Rabbit is Rich*:

> Spineless generation, no grit, nothing solid to tell a fact from a spook with. Satanism, pot, drugs, vegetarianism. Pathetic. Everything handed to them on a platter, think life's one big TV, full of ghosts.[1]

Indeed, there is nothing new under the sun!

And so as a teacher I'll readily admit that my biases are firmly in favour of young people and the generation of students I have the privilege to teach in my classroom.

However, there is something new, something quite disturbing, about how we deal with issues of controversy in today's world. Disagreement very quickly turns into delegitimisation and exclusion. Many young people are simply unwilling to hear the other side of the argument. And in the age of social media where privacy is a thing of the past, personal and off-the-cuff conversations can fast turn into an online storm leaving people 'cancelled' in our increasingly unforgiving world. This chilling effect leaves many unwilling to speak up and share their sincerely held views. No one, let alone a teenager, wants to be socially ostracised and to be seen as a pariah by their peers.

At the best of times, teaching (and parenting) is a difficult business. But with ever louder voices drowning each other out in our highly fractious society, those in charge of developing and nurturing the next generation are finding it increasingly difficult to find their way through. So many teachers I work with and speak to simply steer away from controversy as they want to play it safe.

Who can blame them? With weekly media reports of teachers (and students) facing sanctions for all things controversial, there is a climate of fear that what I say may go viral for all the wrong reasons.

And quite simply, there is no turning back. Social media is here to stay and controversies aren't going anywhere. And as this book will show, we are simply losing out by not equipping our students with the correct tools for thinking about controversy. I can't think of a better forum than the school to raise such issues in a purposeful and relatively safe environment. And this is necessary not just because we wish to develop our students' critical thinking skills as well as their awareness about timeless and timely issues of disagreement. It is also important because however much we try to coddle our children, they will grow up and will have to confront ideas and opinions that they disagree with and even find offensive and horrific. By exposing young people (at the appropriate age) to competing ideas, we are helping them to refine their intellectual stances so that they can enter into the debate with confidence rather than flee in fear. As David Wolpe noted, there is a paradox that as risk diminishes, fear grows. We have much to gain from bringing controversy and risky topics back into the classroom.

DOI: 10.4324/9781003298281-1

How This Book Will Help

So, this book is intended as a complete handbook for teaching and learning about controversy. It is an "Everything you always wanted to know about controversy* (*but were afraid to ask)" kind of book. Aimed at education researchers and classroom teachers, it is a story of two halves: theory and practice.

Part I: Controversy in Theory begins with Chapter 1 which sets the scene, offering three reasons as to how we got here. First, we will see that for many in our supposedly 'post-truth' world, opinions have been elevated above facts. In pursuing their righteous cause, the inconvenient truth may be set aside for the greater good. Second, where people have absolute faith in the righteousness of their cause, they often find it difficult to perceive of legitimate opposing viewpoints, leading them to fol-low the mantra of #*nodebate*. And third, there is a growing vicious cycle in that we are decreasingly meeting people unlike us. I don't just mean in identity terms, such as people mixing with people who *look* different from us; we're also not having those face-to-face conversations with people who *think* differently from us. In response to these challenges, I will introduce a concept called 'polarity' that I think can help us think our way through these problems and frame our approach to teaching and learning about controversy.

Chapter 2 discusses the controversy of controversy. With different approaches to understanding the term itself, it is vital we come to a workable definition in order to help teachers frame the topic under discussion and so decide whether to take a directive or non-directive approach. For example, if a subject is deemed controversial, such as whether to support Democrat or Republican, then the teacher might take a non-directive approach, or she would be seen as being biased or even attempting to brainwash her students. It is only for non-controversial topics that teachers should take a directive approach, explicitly teaching that there is a right and wrong answer to the question at hand, perhaps most obviously in a subject like Maths. Nevertheless, between the subjective world of politics and the objective world of logic, there is a huge grey area that might well be difficult for teachers to navigate. This chapter will consider the behavioural, political, and epistemic criteria for considering controversy through salient case studies such as the Holocaust, vaccinations, and transgender rights, to show their strengths and weaknesses. Whilst ultimately opting for the epistemic criterion, which calls on us to rely on reason and evidence for framing our teaching of controversy, I will also show its weaknesses and explain why it isn't a catch-all for every issue of controversy, most notably for religious and moral issues. Rather, this book will argue for a pluralistic outlook that takes into consideration epistemic, social, and existential concerns.

Chapter 3 provides the rules of engagement for dialogue, discussion, and debate in the classroom. To help maximise learning about controversy, rules must be in place to nurture virtuous thinking and behaviour. Most notably, we will employ the 'principle of charity,' assuming the best from your peers in the debate, especially your opponents. We will discuss the pedagogical techniques most suitable for teaching and learning about controversy. This includes creating an atmosphere where participants are all drawn in and find themselves thinking and learning together, building on each other's ideas. Nurturing such a space, predicated on respect, mutual concern, and communality, can see all involved in what is known as 'interthinking,' engaging collaboratively in a manner that goes beyond any indi-vidual student's own reasoning. Indeed, it is to be argued that dialogue, discussion, and debate are invaluable in themselves as educational goals, cultivating performance virtues, such as tenacity, con-fidence, and eloquence. This chapter will go on to explain and assess the numerous stances a teacher may take during such discussions depending on the issue at hand.

Chapter 4 closes the theory section of the book with a passionate call for promoting critical think-ing through controversy. Turning to the ground-breaking work of the behavioural sciences, still largely under-utilised in the classroom, this chapter will map out the heuristics and biases that impact young people's thinking about controversies. Just as we call for reasoned debate and evidence-led argu-ments, it behoves us to recognise our own foibles and just how 'predictably irrational' we are. Through intriguing dilemmas – from visual illusions to common yet simple misconceptions – I will highlight the virtue of intellectual humility as we learn how our 'two systems' of thinking judge issues of controversy around us. Firmly advocating that critical thinking skills can be taught, we will also offer solutions for young people to deal with these cognitive failures.

Part II: Controversy in Practice covers many of the most common controversies teachers will face in the classroom. Each controversy is dealt with comprehensively: the key arguments are explored and different pedagogical methods offered. Armed with such guidance, every teacher should feel confident about how to teach such controversies in their classrooms and beyond. Whether you have the time to explore the book fully or just a lunch break here and there to peruse one of the guides, each guide is designed with the busy teacher in mind.

To help you navigate your way through each guide, I begin the section with a template that explains exactly what you can expect from each section of the guide you turn to. Remember, to get most out of this book, the chapters in Part I will give you a comprehensive theoretical background. Nevertheless, for when you want to get straight to the practicalities, each guide will be self-contained to put you in good stead for teaching in the classroom. I aim for uniformity and consistency so that making use of the guides becomes intuitive. Here are the themes that each guide explores for a comprehensive take on the issue of controversy you want to know more about:

- **Age group** What might be appropriate for 16-18 year olds may well be inappropriate for younger children. The pitch, tone, and manner of your teaching will be crucial for a successful learning experience.
- **How explosive is this topic?** Many a teacher has innocently voiced their views on an issue only to find themselves under the spotlight. Here we explore where the fault lines may lie so that you are well-prepared for those unintended consequences.
- **How should I teach this topic?** How you frame the subject will be vital for curating the right environment for learning in the classroom. Where the issue is uncontroversial, then it should be taught in a directive way, e.g. 1 + 1 = 2 isn't up for discussion. In contrast, where we have deemed the topic controversial, such as a political disagreement, then the teacher's approach should be non-directive, offering differing sides of the debate without intending to unduly influence or even brainwash her students.
- **Key terms and necessary knowledge** This book argues that knowledge and skills go together. To be skilful in arguing your case, make sure you know your stuff. Here is the background information you'll need to teach the issue of controversy with confidence.
- **Skills: Students' Oracy and Teachers' Socratic Questioning** Complementing the content are the skills for learning and teaching about controversy. This section aims to support two corresponding skills: developing oracy for your students and nurturing questioning techniques for teachers. Insightful questioning makes for enriching classroom experiences.
- **Some theory** This section is for those teachers who want to delve a little deeper into the educational and philosophical considerations behind each debate. I cite the key thinkers who have helped shape how we think about the issue of controversy, whilst also providing guidance on how to best utilise these ideas when raising the subject in the classroom.
- **Beware!** Here we go into more depth about possible pitfalls to think about and plan for. Education isn't just about how we think but also how we feel, invariably linking the topic under discussion to our personal and social circumstances. As teachers of children, we will need to be sensitive about the emotional issues our students may be grappling with, whilst never losing sight of pursuing truth and evidence.
- **Sources and Resources** Each guide relates to a topic that could be a book in itself. Beyond the information at your fingertips in this book, I also offer links – both on and offline – so that teachers know where to turn to for increasing mastery of the subject.
- **Links to other controversies** The template concludes with subject links for each controversy to help you connect the dots and think about how one topic may impact on another.

Of course, no book can examine every issue of controversy and so it may be helpful to think about them in terms of the themes that are raised. This will help provide rules of thumb for thinking about the framework for teaching and learning about each issue of controversy. In turn, the topics are wide-ranging not only in terms of subject matter but also in terms of age group – and so there really is something for everyone. Just as teachers of young children might get caught out on questions about the reality of Santa Claus, teachers in high school are often faced with challenges regarding conspiracy theories, sex and relationships, and the culture wars.

Each comprehensive guide aims to provide a pluralist lens to the issue at hand, recognising the differing voices that may come into play for a healthy grasp of the topic. This means that cultivating understanding and identity formation must be part of the teacher's toolkit, just as the turn to proof, truth, and evidence is so critical for any educational experience. Thus, although the pursuit of rational thought and action as advocated by the epistemic criterion is indeed central, it must go hand in hand with values of empathy, tolerance, and respect.

Indeed, the moral controversies included in this book, relating to topics such as gender and sexuality, are no less contested. Through the application of hard moral cases that may be said to leave one 'morally dumbfounded,' such as sibling incest(!), I attempt to show why reason alone isn't enough to capture the complexity of such moral dilemmas. So, beyond the 'epistemic' consideration, we also need to appreciate existential and social motives which will be crucial to how young people view such debates. For example, a student in my class may be questioning their own gender identity and so it is vital that as a teacher I am sensitive to such an existential state when leading a discussion on the issue. Equally, religious and familial beliefs may provide overwhelming social considerations for many students. In turn, I argue that the classroom requires a pluralist moral framework, as exemplified by Moral Foundations Theory (MFT), developed by Jonathan Haidt. Not only does MFT consider the liberal ethic of autonomy, it also extends consideration to the ethics of community and divinity, which are crucial for meeting the broader aims of moral education, such as developing reason, identity, and cultural understanding. Furthermore, MFT offers due regard to the role of intuitions as part of our decision-making process.

Yet we will also see that a key advantage for studying controversy is to develop good citizenship, in the best traditions of liberalism and democracy. In a robust defence of freedom of expression, our consideration of controversies such as the so-called 'culture wars' will argue that schools can 'bridge' people from different cultural and political viewpoints in a purposeful environment. Whilst democracies thrive on dissent and disagreement, they flounder when peoples on different sides of the aisle raise barriers and refuse to engage with each other. Yet the aim of such debate is not in order to come to agreement. Rather, simply interacting with the 'other' is the basis for helping people understand and tolerate those they disagree with. Such values underpin the notion that schools have a role and even duty to promote good citizenship.

Finally, no account of controversy can ignore the subject of conspiracy theories. Largely dismissed and ridiculed by the establishment, conspiracy theories have come to the fore in the age of 'fake news' and 'alternative facts.' With open access to social media and the wider internet, the democratisation of knowledge has both helped and hindered young people's understanding of the world around them. Whilst conspiracy theories have become a byword for lies, propaganda, and poor thinking, what makes them particularly difficult to deal with is that some have turned out to be true: think Watergate and Wikileaks. Our treatment of conspiracy theories will include both the generalist and particularist approaches: just as the former views conspiracies through a default sceptical lens, the latter suggests each conspiracy theory needs to be judged on its own merits. Through provocative case studies, I will suggest that the latter approach may be more nuanced and helpful for educational purposes. In realising the limitations of the epistemic criterion when considering the controversies of conspiracy theories, I will also show the importance of existential and social considerations when discussing conspiracy theories such as Holocaust denial, climate change scepticism, and the anti-vax movement.

The concluding chapter of this book celebrates young people's growing interest and activism on the controversial issues of the day. Social media has brought global issues into the classroom in an unprecedented manner. Positively, this reinforces the argument for teaching controversy in the classroom, and so enhances the intellectual, moral, civic, and performance virtues of our students. Yet there is also a great urgency for teachers to step up and provide authoritative guidance as young people face an epistemological crisis in the age of 'fake news' and 'alternative facts.' The book therefore concludes with six nudges schools can undertake to ensure success when teaching about controversy. Whether we rethink the classroom, reimagine the place for oracy and critical thinking within our curriculum, recognise the potential for co-teaching and the importance of Socratic questioning, each of these makes for an exciting opportunity to reframe the educational experiences we offer at school.

Sadly, with ever-growing polarisation on the issues that count, recent years have been characterised by 'bonding' social capital, developing relationships with in-groups and thereby perpetuating the problems of epistemic bubbles and echo chambers. Rather, this book makes the claim that by offering space for students to reflect on their epistemic assumptions as well as their social ties and existential certainties, young people won't only become better thinkers but also develop those virtues fundamental to the workings of a democratic society, including tolerance and respect for the other. Through forging strong relationships with our students, schools are precisely the place for students to discuss real areas of controversy with those unlike themselves. Such a safe and purposeful forum affords the possibility of 'bridging' social capital, offering dignity and humanity to one's ideological opponent by listening to them, even while fundamentally disagreeing.

How to Use This Book

This handbook on teaching controversy is intended as a one-stop shop for grappling with the most troubling issues of the day. For those interested in the theory, simply read the book from beginning to end to understand the core issues raised by teaching controversial issues in schools. In the first half of the book, I present the main theoretical models for thinking about controversy as well as the pedagogical theories for delivering a lesson on issues of debate. And, of course, I'll offer my own take on the strengths and weaknesses of these differing approaches.

Yet the book is also aimed at the busy teacher (a tautology, if ever there was!) who simply needs an easy go-to guide. Each controversy in Part II can be viewed, studied, and used discretely to help prepare for an upcoming lesson. With each topic of controversy framed in a consistent and easy-to-read structure, teachers finally have a handbook at their disposal to confront the more contentious issues of the day. With frameworks for teaching offered for each controversy, teachers will be able to create 'rules of thumb' for those controversies not specifically covered. The skills learned really are transferable.

Postscript

At the time of writing, the 2022 Oscars have come and gone, but the memories stayed for all the wrong reasons. Will Smith, a legend for all of us who grew up on *The Fresh Prince of Bel Air*, lost his cool and slapped Chris Rock for his comedic dig at Jada Pinkett Smith, Will's wife. The commentary on Smith's behaviour has been endless and this is not the time to go over old ground. However, the manner in which the incident was reported speaks volumes about our values as a society. Pretty much every TV news network and newspaper censored the expletive that Smith shouted to Rock: "Keep my wife's name out your f****** mouth!" Yet they were all too happy to show him striking the comedian. Quite unwittingly, by censoring the words but showing the violence (repeatedly), our media was sending the subliminal message that saying "fucking" is somehow worse, more threatening than being physically violent. I believe that there is something profoundly wrong in censoring words but displaying violence. This book is a protest against that message.

Indeed, at the heart of this book is a belief in words and the power of talking: of expressing ourselves and hearing the other. In an age of heightened, self-righteous anger, it's time to relearn the art of discussion – and teach it. As Paul Ricoeur taught so poignantly: "We must have trust in language as a weapon against violence, indeed the best weapon there is against violence."[2]

Notes

1. John Updike. (1995) *Rabbit Is Rich*. London: Everyman's Library, p. 766.
2. Paul Ricoeur cited in Richard Kearney. (2004) *On Paul Ricoeur: The Owl of Minerva*. Farnham: Ashgate, p. 156.

Part I Controversy in Theory

1   Why Teach Controversy?

When it comes to teaching and learning about controversy, I think there are three major reasons why we're not getting top marks.

My Opinion, My Truth

***

In the heady days of Donald Trump's presidency, a highly intelligent 17-year-old I was teaching lamented how she missed Barack Obama. I asked her why, as I always like my students to support their views with reasons. What was it about Obama's presidency that she so admired? After she got over her shock that Obama's presidency could even be questioned, she replied that unlike the "homophobic" Trump, Obama had legalised gay marriage. I pointed out the fact that it was actually the US Supreme Court that legalised same sex marriages. Yet my student didn't flinch. Despite being informed that the key reason for her support of Obama actually had nothing to do with him, she replied indignantly: "But he was still the best president."

***

We are said to live in a *post-truth* world, where people can have *their* truth and their *alternative* facts. Indeed, Barack Obama himself has gone so far to say:

> If we do not have the capacity to distinguish what's true from what's false, then by definition the marketplace of ideas doesn't work. And, by definition, our democracy doesn't work. We are entering into an *epistemological* crisis.[1]

In 2016, the *Oxford English Dictionary* announced *post-truth* as its word of the year. *Post-truth* is an adjective defined as "relating to or denoting circumstances in which objective facts are less influential in shaping public opinion than appeals to emotion and personal belief." More Americans view fake news as a bigger problem than terrorism, illegal immigration, racism, and sexism. Additionally, nearly seven-in-ten U.S. adults (68%) say made-up news and information damages Americans' confidence in government institutions, and roughly half (54%) say it is having a major impact on our confidence in each other.[2] For educators, there can be little more frightening than this prospect. And so tackling this problem head-on is vital for the health of our society.

Schools and 'Truthtelling'

In her prophetic 1967 essay, 'Truth and Politics,' the philosopher Hannah Arendt warned that truth will face a crisis when we lose the non-political spaces to speak about politics and the world. We need to preserve room in society for the 'truthtellers,' people outside the political realm, for people who don't have a horse in the race. For Arendt,

> Outstanding among the existential modes of truthtelling are the solitude of the philosopher, the isolation of the scientist and the artist, the impartiality of the historian and the judge, and the independence of the fact-finder, the witness, and the reporter.[3]

In other words, our schools and universities need to be front and centre of 'truthtelling.' And so when it comes to issues of controversy, we must be committed to developing reasoned opinion as the key goal of education. Indeed, since the Enlightenment, the tools of scientific enquiry – evidence and reason – have

DOI: 10.4324/9781003298281-3

been the yardstick for measuring a good education. Rationality is the gift we have as humans to forge progress and reach truth.

Perhaps the greatest exponent of this idea was John Stuart Mill, the doyen of liberal thought. He warned:

> He who knows only his own side of the case knows little of that. His reasons may be good, and no one may have been able to refute them. But if he is equally unable to refute the reasons on the opposite side, if he does not so much as know what they are, he has no ground for preferring either opinion...

As we seek the truth, Mill reminds us, we must be open to hearing all sides of the debate. If we close ourselves off from other perspectives, then not only may we end up being wrong, but even if we are right, our truth becomes stale and obscure:

> ...the peculiar evil of silencing the expression of an opinion is, that it is robbing the human race; posterity as well as the existing generation; those who dissent from the opinion, still more than those who hold it. If the opinion is right, they are deprived of the opportunity of exchanging error for truth; if wrong, they lose, what is almost as great a benefit, the clearer perception and livelier impression of truth produced by its collision with error.[4]

Schools and Social Activism

Yet the zeitgeist is moving in a different direction. As the revolutionary Karl Marx famously put it: "Philosophers have hitherto only *interpreted* the world in various ways; the point is to *change* it."[5] For Marx, the goal of education is to make the world a better place.

On the surface, who could argue with that?

No school worth its salt is so narrow as to be only concerned with academic performance. Whatever one's ideological ties, the belief that schools should be in the business of character development is hardly controversial. As the oft-quoted warning from U.S. President Theodore Roosevelt puts it: "To educate a person in mind and not morals is to educate a menace to society."

And so the rich traditions of Character Education are more popular than ever. We're thinking more about the actual students in our classrooms than merely the subjects we are teaching. In a post-Covid 19 world, we are recognising just how important pastoral care is and the sort of virtues we want to promote. The Jubilee Centre's 'Framework for Character Education in Schools' provides a goal for education that few leaders and teachers could take issue with:

> Schools should consider questions about the kinds of persons their students will become, how the development of good character contributes to a flourishing life, and how to balance various virtues and values in this process.[6]

Of course, traditionalists and progressives may differ on the virtues we may wish to focus on or the causes to fight for. Different schools may well cater for different character aims and social values depending on their own ethos. Nevertheless, that all schools maintain a clear ethos on where they stand on these wider issues suggests that they have a sense of purpose beyond the mere academic.

Smart Menaces

Indeed, regular news stories bring to mind Roosevelt's warning about educating the smart menace. On one such occasion, in the summer of 2016, there were reports of 11 boys from Eton College, one of Britain's most prestigious schools, having an audience with Russian President Vladimir Putin during a visit to the Kremlin.[7] One of the boys boasted on a Facebook post:

> It took me a total of ten months, 1040 emails, 1000 text messages, countless sleepless nights, constant paranoia during A2 exam season, declining academic performance...but here we are. Guys, we truly gave Putin a deep impression of us and he responded by showing us his human face.

To be fair to Eton, the school commented that, "This was a private visit by a small group of boys organised entirely at their own initiative and independently of the college." But one cannot doubt that there seems to have been a huge educational failure. The lashings of academic brilliance no doubt dished out at such an educational establishment somehow forgot to focus on developing common decency and moral virtue on the way. To take pride in the efforts taken to meet with Putin of all people should send alarm bells to the boys' teachers and school leaders. As Martin Luther King Jr. wrote, aiming for intelligence is simply not enough: "The most dangerous criminal may be the man gifted with reason but no morals… Intelligence plus character – that is the goal of true education."[8]

We can go further. The specific school setting is often supported by a broader societal and state context. In the United Kingdom, for example, schools have a legal duty to actively promote fundamental 'British values.' These consist of democracy, the rule of law, individual liberty, and mutual respect and tolerance of those with different faiths and beliefs.[9] In the United States, many schools incorporate patriotism within their ethos, including pledging allegiance to the flag and the republic. Such civic virtues are promoted for young people to develop into responsible citizens in a liberal democratic milieu.

The case of Eton and Putin is a mere speck in the wider picture of a society where moral education hasn't caught up with intellectual advances. It was George Steiner who pinpointed the educational dilemma of modern times: education doesn't necessarily make us better people. At its most extreme, that the Holocaust was the handiwork of Europe's most enlightened of nations, the homeland of Kant and Schiller, still haunts us as we live in the shadow of industrial genocide: "We come after," Steiner declares. "We know now that a man can read Goethe or Rilke in the evening, that he can play Bach and Schubert, and go to his day's work at Auschwitz in the morning."[10]

Character counts; values matter.

Social Activism: at Any Cost?

Looking back, I believe that my Obama-supporting student was very much coming from this worldview. For her, the U.S. President embodied high ideals that were worth defending. Samantha Price, President of the UK Girls' Schools Association (GSA), captured the sentiment well:

> Black Lives Matter, the revelations of Everyone's Invited, high-profile violence against women and the sharp focus on ongoing widespread misogyny in society and the workplace – with police forces being the latest example – gender identity and climate change have all featured as the focal points for those we educate to rightly demand that we address.
>
> It is fair to say that these are themes that our students are genuinely very anxious about, that they feel a responsibility to address and expect us to lead and support them in this. There is a sense more than ever that they will be inheriting this world from our generation, and it is their responsibility to fix it.[11]

Young people want to fix the world; budding activists want to take up Marx's call and change it. Price went on to defend such a call to social action:

> We should challenge anyone who dismisses this generation as 'woke', 'cancel culture' or 'snowflakes'… What has really struck me is that this so-called 'woke' generation are actually simply young people who care about things: about causes, about the planet, about people. It ultimately comes down to something very simple: being kind.

From Malala to Greta Thunberg, young people today have fine role models to emulate. There is much to be optimistic about: outside of Eton (and within, I'm sure), few young people are looking to Putin and his ilk as their idols. Moreover, teachers in the classroom can feel relief that ignorance and apathy are dwindling in an age where young people are showing that they care, more than ever. Eighty-three per cent of young people (aged 16–25 years) agree that people have failed to care for the planet, whilst 75% view the future as frightening.[12] My own interactions with students over the last 15 years leave me with an overwhelming sense that teenagers really do care, that they are interested in the world around them, and they really want to make a change for the better.

But as my Idealistic student reminded me, there is a growing sense in which the end justifies the means. For many, in our pursuit to change the world, our cause is worth defending *no matter what*. In other words, righteous *opinion* supersedes uncomfortable *facts*.

#nodebate

***

As I was setting up for the lesson ahead, I overheard my students discussing a hot topic of controversy: JK Rowling's comments on sex and gender issues. One powerful voice in the class said: "I don't really get it. I love JK for all her Harry Potter books. But how can someone so smart be so ignorant about gender issues?" All of her peers nodded in agreement.

***

The clash between pursuing truth and social justice activism came to a head when it was widely reported that an 18-year-old pupil in the United Kingdom had been forced to leave her school after challenging a visiting speaker who claimed that biological sex does not exist.[13]

The incident happened when a female member of the House of Lords visited the private girls' school to talk about transphobia in parliament. The girl told *The Times* newspaper:

> The language she was using was implying critical theory took precedence over biological reality in defining women. When I questioned that, she said it wasn't an issue of semantics. She said trans people don't have basic human rights in this country. Afterwards I spoke to her and said, 'I'm sorry if I came across as rude.'

According to *The Times*, after the girl debated with the speaker, she was surrounded by some 60 students who "shouted, screamed and spat at her," accusing her of transphobia. She said she found it difficult to breathe and then collapsed. Although she felt teachers were initially supportive, the school went on to apologise for failing to provide a 'safe space.' Ultimately, due to bullying and social exclusion, the Sixth Form student left the school to finish her studies at home.[14]

For defenders of the girl, such as JK Rowling, her treatment was seen as "utterly shameful." On Twitter, Rowling wrote:

> Add this to the tottering pile of evidence that people in education and academia who've supposed to have a duty of care towards the young have succumbed to an outbreak of quasi-religious fanaticism," she added. "The girl's crime? Saying 'sex exists.'

Students in a previous school I taught at told me that the girl wouldn't have fared much better in their Sixth Form. Quite simply, open discussion and the willingness to listen to the other side is increasingly being replaced by the mantra *#nodebate* to shut down views that are considered beyond the pale. In this case, the girl's claim that sex exists as a biological fact was too much for her social warrior peers who interpreted this as a challenge to transgender people and those grappling with their gender identity. Shortly afterwards, Luke Pollard, a member of parliament in the United Kingdom, tweeted:

> Trans men are men, trans women are women and being non-binary is valid. It's time non-binary people had their rights respected. *And it's not a debate*. They exist, let's be kind.[15]

Censoring vs Cancelling vs Calling Out

Of course, we've been here before. In the past, when censorship was the great curb on free speech, such restrictions were top-down. In one of history's classic episodes of truth clashing with ideology, Galileo was condemned for heresy in 1632 by the Catholic Church for supporting the scientific truth of the Copernican theory that the sun was at the centre of the solar system. Remember, nothing can be more offensive to the religious believer than heresy – even if it is the truth! There really is nothing new under the sun...

And all teachers are aware that although blasphemy is no longer censored from above, there is the risk of cancel culture – and worse – for causing such offence from below. A Religious Studies teacher at Batley Grammar School in north England had to go into hiding after having shown an offensive cartoon of the Prophet Muhammad – reportedly taken from the French satirical newspaper *Charlie Hebdo*.[16] Any depiction of the Prophet Muhammad can cause serious offence to Muslims because Islamic law forbids images of both Allah (God) and Muhammad.[17] The incident led to the teacher's immediate suspension pending an investigation, with protests being held outside the school. The teacher was left fearing for his life. Although a report into the incident concluded that the teacher did not intend to cause offence by showing the image, the school apologised "unequivocally," promising more training for staff. The teacher was eventually allowed to return.[18]

Just as many Muslims are offended by images of the Prophet, so too are many social justice warriors outraged by what they see as transphobia. The #*nodebate* online motto has been used by many to argue that some issues are simply too offensive to be debated. Issues such as racism or homophobia for some, blasphemy or treason against the flag and country for others. Not only would it cause deep offence for those often considered the most marginalised in society, but it would give voice to extremists. And so supporters of the #*nodebate* mantra argue that offensive people aren't victims of 'cancel culture' but are simply facing the consequences of 'call-out' culture. If you spout hateful and bigoted views, the argument goes, then others have the right to hold you to account.

This approach to trans rights has been championed by Stonewall, a leading lesbian, gay, bisexual, and transgender rights charity in the United Kingdom. Their motto of 'acceptance without exception' has led them to state:

> We will always debate issues that enable us to further equality but what we will not do is debate trans people's rights to exist. This is not and will not ever be respectful. It is also an issue that is already settled in law: trans people's right to equality is already clear and has been since 2004. To have similar debates around any other part of a person's identity protected by law is unimaginable: debating whether gay people exist, or whether people of a certain faith should be able to access services, would rightly not be tolerated. It is the same for trans people.[19]

The Paradox of Safety

Schools have a duty to keep their children safe. Every school around the world will have policies in place with safeguarding their number one priority. This includes the fight against racism, sexism, or discrimination against any of the so-called 'protected characteristics.'[20] In the United Kingdom, government guidance is clear:

> Schools should continue to take steps to tackle racist and discriminatory attitudes or incidents - and condemn racism within the school and wider society. Challenging intolerant, racist or discriminatory views where these are shared at school should be seen as part of schools' wider anti-bullying and safeguarding duties.[21]

There is no greater instinct among parents and teachers alike than to protect our children. We all crave for our young ones to be healthy and happy. Indeed, such good intentions were behind the blanket banning of nuts in schools in the 1990s. With just 4 out of 1,000 children under the age of 8 allergic to peanuts in the mid-1990s, schools took no chances and decided to avoid risk altogether. Better safe than sorry. The result? By 2008, the rate of allergies to nuts more than tripled to 14 out of 1,000. By seeking to protect our children, we ended up contributing to the rise in peanut allergies![22] Alison Gopnick explains the paradox:

> Thanks to hygiene, antibiotics and too little outdoor play, children don't get exposed to microbes as they once did. This may lead them to develop immune systems that overreact to substances that aren't actually threatening - causing allergies. *In the same way, by shielding children from*

every possible risk, we may lead them to react with exaggerated fear to situations that aren't risky at all and isolate them from the adult skills that they will one day have to master.[23]

I have noticed such "exaggerated fears" first hand of late. In one school I taught at, I had invited a fellow colleague to deliver a lecture to our Sixth Formers (16–18 year olds) on the subject of Humanism, sharing their own beliefs and worldviews. A highly articulate and well-liked teacher, he spoke movingly about his own journey from a young Catholic altar boy to a teenager coming to terms with his homosexuality and his 'conversion' to Humanism in adulthood. As an observant Jew, married with five children, I found myself disagreeing with my colleague on issues of real importance to us both. Yet I never hesitated in calling on him to offer a worldview different from my own. After all, I was brought up on the ancient Jewish dictum: "Who is wise? One who learns from everyone."[24] Moreover, as a teacher in a British school, I am conscious of my legal duties when bringing issues of controversies for my students to consider:

> Schools should provide a safe space in which children, young people and staff can understand and discuss sensitive topics, including terrorism and the extremist ideas that are part of terrorist ideology.
> Schools can build pupils' resilience to radicalisation by providing an environment for debating controversial and sensitive issues, whilst adhering to requirements on political impartiality. This includes helping pupils understand how they can influence and participate in decision-making.[25]

In the last couple of years, however, I have noticed that in the post-lecture discussion, students have called our Humanist teacher out. They accuse him of being "offensive" to people of faith. This hadn't come up before but the change in tone was palpable: many of our students simply didn't want to hear from people with worldviews different from their own. They didn't want to be challenged and perhaps felt they shouldn't be challenged. So, at the end of the lecture, in my vote of thanks, I said to my colleague in front of 150 students:

> Your lecture made me feel deeply uncomfortable. Your ideas challenged my deepest held beliefs and will now force me to question my own worldview. Thank you for doing so. By giving space to ideas different from our own, we learn to refine our own perspectives in the hope of reaching the truth. And I hope that once I have taken in your ideas, you don't mind if I return to you and carry on the conversation.

My colleague thanked me in kind and said he looked forward to continuing the debate.

The Virtues of Heresy

In a remarkable interview, the theologian Richard Kearney talks about why he has remained a Catholic:

> …I never actually ceased to be a Catholic and one of the reasons for that was I was very fortunate in growing up that I had good teachers. I grew up with Benedictine monks in Glenstal Abbey in southern Ireland and one of the first things our religious doctrine teacher Father Andrew said to us was, "You come here and you think you know what Christianity is. Well, for the first thing I'm going to teach you is all the arguments against the existence of God." So, we read Marx and we read Simone de Beauvoir and we read Feuerbach and we read Nietzsche. And we read all these atheists who said, "God's for the birds. Religion is dogmatism and power and domination and misogyny and oppression… the opium of the people." We read all these then at the end, [our teacher said]: "Okay now, if there's anybody left in this class" – we're all 13-14 – "who still has an interest in God, we can have a discussion, we can start Christian doctrine classes…"[26]

Now there's a brave teacher! Father Andrew recognised that when we shield our students from 'harmful' viewpoints – and nothing could be more harmful for good Catholic boys than Marx, Feuerbach, and Nietzsche – we end up hurting our students. What is interesting about Kearney's life journey is how his resilience strengthened precisely because he was exposed to those heretical ideas as a teenager.

Wrestling with opposing forces, being forced to reckon with one's own certainties, has led Kearney to a life of dialogue with other religions and worldviews, whilst holding firm to his Catholicism. In a stinging rebuke to our fragile modern selves, the Benedictine monk reminds us, in the words of Nassim Nicholas Taleb, that "as with neurotically overprotective parents, those trying to help are often hurting us the most."[27]

And so providing that balance is a key challenge for teachers and parents alike. #nodebate is an understandable flight to safety. But while we don't want our children playing with saws and knives, it's not healthy to coddle them either.

'Two Nations'

***

For my research into all things controversial in the classroom, I visited a school just a mile away from where I used to teach. Unlike my own school at the time, which is a highly selective independent school for girls, this school was a comprehensive co-educational state school. While they were a world apart in terms of their student intake, teachers in both schools could rightly say how proud they were of their students. And as I discussed issues of controversy with both sets of students, it dawned on me how much they could learn from each other. And so I asked both sets of students if they ever mixed with their peers from down the road. Not one hand went up in either school: no one had ever met, let alone knew, anyone else from a school just nearby.

***

Concerns for diversity, equity, and inclusion are at the heart of every responsible school. We don't want our educational establishment to simply 'tolerate' difference but rather to 'celebrate' and 'champion' the other. We want all to feel included and welcome, especially those who have been marginalised for their protected characteristics. The fight for racial and social justice is an end in itself. It is hard to think of a more important moral calling for our time.

But in the context of this book, diversity is also an important tool in helping us think our way through issues of controversy. Reni Eddo-Lodge provides the following anecdote that helped diversify her own thinking when she started cycling part of the way to work as she was unable to afford the full train fare:

> An uncomfortable truth dawned upon me as I lugged my bike up and down flights of stairs in commuter-town train stations: the majority of public transport I'd been travelling on was not easily accessible. No ramps. No lifts. Nigh-on impossible to access for parent with buggies, or people using wheelchairs, or people with mobility issues, like a frame or a cane. Before I'd had my own wheels to carry, I'd never noticed this problem. I'd been oblivious to the fact that this lack of accessibility was affecting hundreds of people.[28]

The 'unknown unknown' that Eddo-Lodge describes is what Matthew Syed calls 'perspective blindness.'[29] As individuals, we find it difficult to step beyond our own frame of reference. "This helps explain," Syed writes, "why demographic diversity (differences in race, gender, age, class, sexual orientation, religion, and so on) can, in certain circumstances, increase group wisdom."[30] Homogeneity often reinforces our blind spots as we mirror each other and so diminish our collective intelligence.

Popping Epistemic Bubbles

Nevertheless, as Syed has shown, we also need to recognise the benefits of 'cognitive diversity,' differences in thoughts, insights, and perspectives. Nothing could be more racist than to imagine that all black people are the same, and it would be awfully misogynistic to assume all women think alike too.

Indeed, in seeking demographic diversity, many organisations are guilty of simply hiring and retaining people who think just like us, even if they don't look like us. And as individuals, we're often guilty of 'homophily': we are naturally drawn towards those who are like us.

In a thought experiment, sadly all too familiar for many teachers, Ilana Redstone, a professor of sociology, tells of the following anecdote that goes to the heart of what she calls 'the crisis of moral legitimacy':

> When I ask a room full of students why someone might support using race in determining college admissions, they usually have a few answers ready. They offer reasonable points like, "to offset historical and current disadvantage" or "because of the unique challenges that members of underrepresented groups face." But the opposite question – why someone might oppose the use of race in college admissions – often yields one response: racism. When pressed, few students can come up with alternative suggestions; they struggle to think of any principled reason why someone might take that position. The asymmetry in the students' ability to produce morally reasonable arguments for both positions is particularly notable given that, according to Pew, 73% of Americans agree with the statement that "colleges and universities should not consider race or ethnicity when making decisions about student admissions."[31]

On any number of controversial topics, our cognitively homogenous group is simply unable to articulate other perspectives. As Redstone concedes, some students may fear voicing unpopular positions. As we have seen from the young woman who challenged a guest speaker on Biology, hostile climates for opposing worldviews have had a chilling effect on many. As my own students tell me, it would be social suicide to voice opinions that cut against the grain amongst their peer group. Either way, Redstone concludes, "when we fail to recognise the moral legitimacy of a range of positions on controversial topics, disagreements about these issues inevitably become judgements about other people's character." We can't articulate other worldviews because we think they're simply not worthy of our attention.

Homogeneity, therefore, may not only lead us to become intellectually stale but also self-righteous and even bigoted. We lose out when we don't speak to the other, see the other, or even acknowledge the other. This leads us to become trapped in our own 'epistemic bubbles,' which as C. Thi Nguyen explains, "is a social epistemic structure in which some relevant voices have been excluded through omission."[32] As birds of a feather flock together, we simply avoid contact with those that make us feel uncomfortable, selecting information that confirms our worldview. As the historian Niall Ferguson pithily sums it up:

> Facebook encourages you to like or not like what you see in your news feed. Twitter allows you to retweet or like other people's tweets or block those users who offend your sensibilities. Pretty soon you are in a filter bubble inhabited exclusively by people who share your view of the world. The result is a paradise not just for fake news but also for extreme views.[33]

Of course, online or in the classroom, epistemic bubbles might well be inadvertent. In an age of information overload, it sometimes helps to filter the information coming through, whether through the company I keep or with the help of online algorithms, responding to my likes and obvious interests. But it also warps my worldview, further binding me to those like me, whilst blinding me from the worldviews of others. And, it seems, the 'choice architecture' of our schools, their 'default' position, make it increasingly unlikely for young people to meet other young people entirely unlike them.

Bonding and Bridging

In the two schools I mention in my anecdote, despite the physical proximity, the schools were worlds away in terms of social-economic diversity: affluent middle-class students simply didn't mix with working class boys and girls. I was sadly reminded that Benjamin Disraeli's observations rang true nearly 200 years later:

Two nations; between whom there is no intercourse and no sympathy; who are as ignorant of each other's habits, thoughts, and feelings, as if they were dwellers in different zones, or inhabitants of different planets... the rich and the poor.[34]

Hoorah for the 'bonding' but boo for the lack of 'bridging.' As Robert Putnam explains, 'bonding' social capital describes the relationships or associations *within* a social group or community. These are great for "getting by" and enjoying life. But for "getting ahead," we need to 'bridge' social capital, to create networks and associations *between* social groups.[35] Creating opportunities for our students to experience demographic and cognitive diversity must be central to their educational development. Such 'epistemic bubbles' are surprisingly easy to pop as we simply adapt the 'choice architecture' to expose our students to people with worldviews different from their own. In turn, we brought students together from the two schools in the vignette above through a joint debating society. This not only helps them learn about the arguments they've missed out on, but also creates a sense of humility as they recognise there are perspectives they hadn't yet considered. Such intellectual virtues are complemented by the moral virtue of tolerance as each become more *familiar* with others unlike themselves.

As Kwame Anthony Appiah points out, in tracing the growing acceptance of homosexuality in Europe and North America, reason had very little to do with it after all. Rather, the "perspectival shift" occurred as "[t]he increasing presence of 'openly gay' people in social life and in the media has changed our habits." By meeting and becoming more familiar with homosexuals, more people thought less in terms of "the private activity of gay sex," and "started thinking about the public category of gay people."[36] Quite simply, Appiah concludes, "people got used to lesbian and gay people." This is precisely why the study of controversial issues can help promote diversity, equity, and inclusion in a much more meaningful way:

> I am urging that we should learn about people in other places, take an interest in their civilisations, their arguments, their errors, their achievements, not because that will bring us to agreement, but because it will help us get used to one another. If that is the aim, then the fact that we have all these opportunities for disagreement about values need not put us off. Understanding one another may be hard; it can certainly be interesting. But it doesn't require that we come to agreement.[37]

John McWhorter, a left-leaning professor at Columbia University, wrote similarly of his intellectual development as he began to mix with more conservative students, discussing key issues of the day, such as abortion rights in America.

> I didn't become a Republican, but I considered my immersion in their worldview a part of my education. I'm glad fate threw me into getting to know them, and, indeed, it was part of why I felt comfortable being a Democrat working for a right-leaning think tank, the Manhattan Institute, in the aughts. A major lesson I took from those law students was to avoid a tempting, all-too-common misimpression: *that if people have views different from yours, then the reason is either that they lack certain information or are simply bad people – that they're either naifs or knaves.*[38]

The Vices of Echo Chambers

So far so good. Sadly though, things get a little more complicated when we think about the effects of an 'echo chamber,' which Nguyen explains, "is a social epistemic structure in which other relevant voices have been actively discredited... an echo chamber's members share beliefs which include reasons to distrust those outside the echo chamber."[39] People within echo chambers don't just ignore outsiders, they actively seek to discredit and undermine alternative worldviews. Think of cult indoctrination at its most pernicious. As Nguyen warns, the distinction between epistemic bubbles and echo chambers is crucial because they require very different educational responses.

Indeed, the problem becomes far more acute if the student's worldview is a result of his living in an echo chamber. In terms of civic virtue, a young person may lack civility and neighbourliness in the classroom as his narrow outlook on the issue at hand could lead him to actively dismiss and exclude other worldviews, especially rival epistemic sources, as illegitimate. So-called neutral evidence is dependent on deep levels of trust in the testimony of the experts. Where that trust has broken down, an appeal to so-called reason and objectivity won't work and may even simply reinforce that distrust. In rejecting any evidence that inconveniently undermines his own theory, the student, cultish or conspiratorial in his outlook, may be guilty of what Kevin deLaplante calls "self-sealing," for "[w]henever the theory is poked by some bit of countervailing evidence, it seals itself by reinterpreting that evidence as consistent with the theory after all." This is done precisely when "conspiracy theorists are dogmatically attached to an ideological worldview that is immune to rational criticism."[40] Bridging social capital, therefore, would most likely backfire as such an approach would be mere confirmation of the teacher or educational system setting out to brainwash those espousing different views.

The more effective education response is based on the old adage that prevention is always preferable to a cure. Therefore, 'presuasion' and inoculation against the vices of cult-like behaviour and conspiracism must be part of the curriculum in order to guide students how to think about conspiracy theories when they arise. For example, hearing from a Holocaust survivor or family member at a relatively young age will help inoculate against Holocaust denial later in life. However, as we will see below in our discussion on 'polarities,' once a student has gone down the rabbit hole of extremism, we need much broader educational tools at our disposal. We have to recognise that the intellectual debate can take us only so far.

Polarity Management in Education

We have seen that the educational world is locked in a battle over the overriding aim of schools: between those fighting for truth on one side and the social justice warriors on the other. With both sides battling it out, how do we respond? As an author, I want both sides to read my book and not lose half my audience. Is there a way forward that gives credence to our critical thinkers and social justice warriors? I think there is – and not just because I want to double my sales.

> Just before I suggest a way forward, let me offer you two controversial scenarios that a teacher may face in the classroom. Have a think about what would be the correct response:
> Scenario 1: In the week running up to Christmas, an eight-year-old girl asks her teacher in front of the whole class: "Is Santa Claus real?"
> Scenario 2: In a Science lesson, a 16-year-old boy asks his Science teacher:
>
> > Don't you agree that this climate change scare is a bit of a hoax? Climate change scientists get government grants to spew out their claims and so it suits them to publish such misinformation. I don't think there really is significant climate change and where it does occur, it's hardly manmade.

To help tackle such dilemmas, I want to introduce Barry Johnson's concept of 'polarity management.' This framework can help us move away from either/or thinking to both/and. The concept of polarity is explained succinctly by Shoshana Boyd Gelfand as follows: "a polarity is an ongoing problem with two correct answers that are interdependent."[41] For example, we all need to breathe, a vital function that has two correct but opposing and interdependent actions – inhale and exhale. The question is how we manage that flow: remember, too much of one without the other leads to discomfort and difficulty. Rather, breathing must work in a positive, life-enhancing fashion.

This is true too in so many aspects of our lives and, I argue here, when we educate our children.[42] As Supertramp complained back in 1979 in their stirring 'The Logical Song,' schooling for children must be more than a place where we learn to be "Oh clinical, oh intellectual, cynical." We want our children to have a sense that "life [is] so wonderful/A miracle... beautiful, magical." Yes, even magical. The sense of wonder and imagination that ties in with virtues such as hope and faith (whether in humanity, nature, or the divine) are also obvious outcomes we would want to see as teachers. And so when we think back to the Santa Claus question, it is obvious that only a clinical, intellectual, cynical grinch would answer, "There is no Santa Claus. That's the truth and that's what we're here to learn."

However wedded to facts and truth we may be (and so we should), our Santa Claus scenario shows that education must involve a careful balance of other values too. Otherwise, we end up in the cold and cynical world of Charles Dickens' Thomas Gradgrind in *Hard Times*. His school inspector colleague, also dedicated to facts, asks the class: "Suppose you were going to carpet a room. Would you use a carpet having a representation of flowers upon it?"

Little Sissy Jupe is one of the few brave enough to admit she would.

> "If you please, sir, I am very fond of flowers."
>
> "And is that why you would put tables and chairs upon them, and have people walking over them with heavy boots?"
>
> "It wouldn't hurt them, sir. They wouldn't crush and wither, if you please, sir. They would be the pictures of what was very pretty and pleasant, and I would fancy –"
>
> "Ay, ay, ay! But you mustn't fancy," cried the gentleman, quite elated by coming so happily to his point. "That's it! You are never to fancy."
>
> "You are not, Cecilia Jupe," Thomas Gradgrind solemnly repeated, "to do anything of that kind."
>
> "Fact, fact, fact!" said the gentleman. And "Fact, fact, fact!" repeated Thomas Gradgrind.
>
> "You are to be in all things regulated and governed," said the gentleman, "by fact. We hope to have, before long, a board of fact, composed of commissioners of fact, who will force the people to be a people of fact, and of nothing but fact. You must discard the word Fancy altogether. You have nothing to do with it. You are not to have, in any object of use or ornament, what would be a contradiction in fact. You don't walk upon flowers in fact; you cannot be allowed to walk upon flowers in carpets. You don't find that foreign birds and butterflies come and perch upon your crockery; you cannot be permitted to paint foreign birds and butterflies upon your crockery. You never meet with quadrupeds going up and down walls; you must not have quadrupeds represented upon walls. You must use,' said the gentleman, 'for all these purposes, combinations and modifications (in primary colours) of mathematical figures which are susceptible of proof and demonstration. This is the new discovery. This is fact. This is taste."
>
> The girl curtseyed, and sat down. She was very young, and she looked as if she were frightened by the matter-of-fact prospect the world afforded.[43]

The concept of polarity shows us that Gradgrind's telescopic focus on truth, to the exclusion of all else, leads us to a negative and destructive outcome of a young girl "frightened" of what the uncaring world has to offer. The Dickensian arrogance, cynicism, and mean-spiritedness are intellectual vices we must guard against in the classroom – even with truth on our side. If only Sissy had Tom Stoppard's philosophy professor in the play *Jumpers* to come to her aid. As George says in response to the claim that "the Church is a monument to irrationality":

> The National Gallery is a monument to irrationality! Every concert hall is a monument to irrationality! – and so is a nicely kept garden, or a lover's favour, or a home for stray dogs!... If rationality were the criterion for things being allowed to exist, the world would be one gigantic field of soya beans![44]

Truth + Character

Just as life is more than soya beans so too schooling is more than the mere epistemic pursuit of truth. For example, in the immediate aftermath of a tragedy, no teenager wants to hear a teacher analyse the reasons and causes of what happened; they need comfort and care. The concept of polarity reminds us that we needn't settle for either/or in the classroom. There is a time to pursue truth *and* moral values to achieve Luther King's goals of intelligence plus character (Figure 1.1).

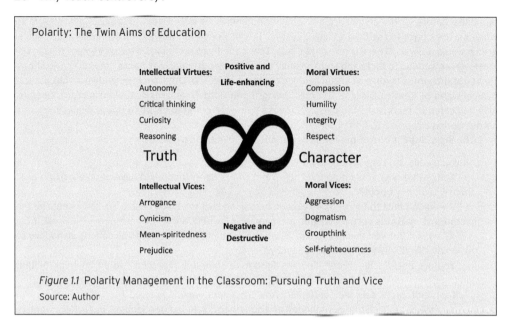

Polarity: The Twin Aims of Education

Intellectual Virtues:
Autonomy
Critical thinking
Curiosity
Reasoning

Truth

**Positive and
Life-enhancing**

Moral Virtues:
Compassion
Humility
Integrity
Respect

Character

Intellectual Vices:
Arrogance
Cynicism
Mean-spiritedness
Prejudice

**Negative and
Destructive**

Moral Vices:
Aggression
Dogmatism
Groupthink
Self-righteousness

Figure 1.1 Polarity Management in the Classroom: Pursuing Truth and Vice
Source: Author

And so as we flow to a classroom displaying moral virtues such as compassion, humility, and respect, we give a nod to the teacher who helps feed her students' imagination about Santa Claus and the wonders of Christmas. Richard Attenborough's Santa put it best in *Miracle on 34th Street*:

> I'm not just a whimsical figure who wears a charming suit and affects a jolly demeanour. You know, I'm a symbol. I'm a symbol of the human ability to be able to suppress the selfish and hateful tendencies that rule the major part of our lives.

But, as teachers, can we remain in the pure realm of values for long? Remember, the concept of polarity helps me to recognise that I must flow back to my twin aim of Truth before my focus on values becomes uncomfortable and destructive.

Let's now turn to Scenario 2: our 16-year-old climate change denier or sceptic. He has challenged his teacher on the anthropogenic cause of climate change, opining that it pays for scientists to whip up a storm. Assuming the boy is sincere in his beliefs, he may also be turning to 'The Logical Song' for inspiration, fearful that "they'll be calling you a radical/Liberal, oh fanatical, criminal/Won't you sign up your name, we'd like to feel you're acceptable."

Should the teacher give credence to such a viewpoint? The problem is that if we stay in the realm of values, we soon begin to promote moral vices such as dogmatism and groupthink. In extreme circumstances – as we saw them above with regard to charges of blasphemy and transphobia – there is a very short journey towards self-righteousness and aggression. As Steven Pinker has warned, "we have seen that when a creed becomes attached to an in-group, the critical faculties of its members can be disabled, and there are reasons to think that has happened within swaths of academia."[45]

So, two cheers for Gradgrind as such issues propel us to flow to the realm of truth and teach key intellectual virtues, such as critical thinking, curiosity, and reasoning. Quite simply, not all opinions are equal. Teachers have a duty to uphold reason and the scientific method when a person's 'values' become dogmatic to the point that their ideology clashes with the evidence. Specifically in this scenario, a teacher will need the confidence and wherewithal to counter the claim that there is no real evidence for anthropogenic climate change. Neutrality simply isn't an option when it leads to negative and destructive outcomes through spreading misinformation that undermine democratic values such as truth and evidence.

The Epistemic, The Existential, and The Social

To be sure, teachers need a rich toolbox of strategies to deal with such controversial challenges in the classroom. Even when ostensibly dealing with issues of fact and truth, we have to recognise that it's not only epistemic considerations we need to teach about, but that existential and social considerations often come into the mix. We don't merely teach "students" but whole human beings with all the baggage and biases we all bring. Perversely, simply focusing on facts may well prove to be an own goal, and so teachers need to think carefully about which strategies will help promote the truth and the associated virtues of autonomy and reasoning. This is especially true when our students might already be trapped in their echo chambers.

Thus on key controversies of the day – climate change, evolution, and Covid vaccines – teachers might be tempted to think that sceptics or deniers suffer from bad thinking and intellectual vices such as gullibility, carelessness, and close-mindedness.[46] In turn, it is perfectly natural for teachers to assume the "cures" for such "crippled epistemologies" lie within education as "most people lack direct or personal information about the explanations for terrible events."[47] Our 16 year old is brainwashed and so needs the facts to correct his misunderstandings.

Dan Kahan has labelled this educational approach the 'science comprehension thesis,' which holds that, "[a]s members of the public do not know what scientists know, or think the way scientists think, they predictably fail to take climate change as seriously as scientists believe they should" – or indeed similar controversies. So, the Biology teacher could be forgiven for thinking that going through the data on vaccines should do the trick. Sadly, it's a little more complicated and that's why we need the concept of polarity guiding us in the classroom.

Rather, Kahan's research has demonstrated that climate change sceptics are actually no less scientifically literate than climate realists. And where a student is all set on their outlook, it turns out that additional education will only serve to reinforce their worldview! 'Doing a Gradgrind' on them isn't going to work. This is why Pinker argued that by taking up the environmental cause, Al Gore "may have done the movement more harm than good, because as a former Democrat vice-president and presidential nominee he stamped climate change with a left-wing seal."[48] Pinker thus echoes Kahan's guidance that climate realists would be better off "[r]ecruiting conservative and libertarian commentators who have been convinced by the evidence and are willing to share their concern... than recruiting more scientists to speak more slowly and more loudly."[49]

Rather, Kahan's findings supported the 'cultural cognitive thesis' (CCT), which posits that "individuals, as a result of a complex of psychological mechanisms, tend to form perceptions of societal risks that cohere with values characteristic of groups with which they identify." Rather than "bad thinking," CCT showed that the range of approaches towards climate change were intuitive, with people on both sides of the aisle fitting their interpretations of scientific evidence into their competing cultural philosophies. This means that better education will only serve to justify one's own worldview.

This is an example of what's known as 'myside bias.' Next time you sit down to watch a game of football with a friend supporting the opposing team, ask yourself when you argue over whether the penalty awarded was fair whether your support for one side might be impacting your judgement. In a fascinating study, Kahan's team showed a recording of protests in front of a building. When the scene was labelled a protest outside an abortion clinic, conservatives saw a peaceful gathering, whilst liberals focused on the protestors blocking the entrance and intimidating those entering. However, when it was labelled as a protest against excluding gay people at a military recruitment centre, the conservatives saw red, whilst the liberals praised the heartening scenes.[50]

The lesson is clear: the concept of polarity calls upon us as teachers to champion the twin educational aims of truth and character. The continual flow between these two poles will help ensure that we nurture virtuous students dedicated to the truth. Yet it also shows that our teaching methods will be crucial to the success of teaching controversy in our classrooms. This is often difficult to navigate and so this handbook will provide both the theoretical underpinnings for thinking about controversy as well as practical guidance for doing controversy in the classroom.

Notes

1. Jeffrey Goldberg. (16 November 2020) 'Why Obama Fears for Our Democracy,' *The Atlantic*. Retrieved from: https://www.theatlantic.com/ideas/archive/2020/11/why-obama-fears-for-our-democracy/617087/?utm_source=newsletter&utm_medium=email&utm_campaign=atlantic-daily-newsletter&utm_content=20201116&silverid-ref=MzM1MDQ4NjU4NTk5SO.
2. Amy Mitchell et al. (5 June 2019) 'Many Americans Say Made-Up News Is a Critical Problem That Needs to Be Fixed,' Pew Research Centre. Retrieved from: https://www.pewresearch.org/journalism/2019/06/05/many-americans-say-made-up-news-is-a-critical-problem-that-needs-to-be-fixed/.
3. Hannah Arendt. (17 February 1967) 'Truth and Politics,' *The New Yorker*. Retrieved from: https://www.newyorker.com/magazine/1967/02/25/truth-and-politics.
4. J.S. Mill. (1992) *On Liberty*. London: Everyman, p. 19.
5. Karl Marx. (1845) *Theses on Feuerbach*. Retrieved from: https://www.marxists.org/archive/marx/works/1845/theses/index.htm.
6. Jubilee Centre. (2017) 'A Framework for Character Education in Schools.' Retrieved from: https://www.jubileecentre.ac.uk/userfiles/jubileecentre/pdf/character-education/Framework%20for%20Character%20Education.pdf.
7. BBC News. (1 September 2017) 'Eton Boys Given Private Audience with Vladimir Putin.' Retrieved from: https://www.bbc.co.uk/news/world-europe-37242146.
8. Martin Luther King, Jr. (1947) 'The Purpose of Education.' Retrieved from: https://kinginstitute.stanford.edu/king-papers/documents/purpose-education#:~:text=The%20function%20of%20education%2C%20therefore,reason%2C%20but%20with%20no%20morals.
9. Home Office. (2011) 'Prevent Strategy.' Retrieved from: https://assets.publishing.service.gov.uk/government/uploads/system/uploads/attachment_data/file/97976/prevent-strategy-review.pdf.
10. George Steiner. (1998). *Language and Silence*. London: Yale.
11. Samantha Price. (22 November 2021) 'Don't Call Our Young People "Woke," Says GSA President.' Retrieved from: https://gsa.uk.com/2021/11/dont-call-our-young-people-woke-says-gsa-president/.
12. Caroline Hickman et al. (December 2021) 'Climate Anxiety in Children and Young People and their Beliefs about Government Responses to Climate Change: A Global Survey,' *The Lancet*. Retrieved from: https://reader.elsevier.com/reader/sd/pii/S2542519621002783?token=E1DC-1CE95D440E0FA5195E8A3DC4708B9BDB13078F8C155B25B47B2C090190530AF3535D-F38E4A7974F862960B12D49E&originRegion=eu-west-1&originCreation=20220428194119.
13. See, for example, 'Nadhim Zahawi Backs Schoolgirl Forced Out after Trans Row' (2022). Retrieved from: https://www.thetimes.co.uk/article/nadhim-zahawi-backs-schoolgirl-forced-out-after-trans-row-jwwz22z8n.
14. Nicola Woolcock. (2022) 'JK Rowling Defends Girl "Driven Out of School for Questioning Trans Ideology."' Retrieved from: https://www.thetimes.co.uk/article/girl-driven-out-of-school-for-questioning-trans-ideology-ls790krdh.
15. Luke Pollard. (2022) 'I Wasn't Able to Attend the Debate on Non-binary People Today....' Retrieved from: https://twitter.com/LukePollard/status/1528787053365932032. Emphasis added.
16. Tom Airey. (2021) 'Batley Grammar School: Blasphemy Debate Leaves Town "at crossroads."' Retrieved from: https://www.bbc.co.uk/news/uk-england-leeds-56590417.
17. Although not explicitly forbidden in the Quran, Islamic tradition believes that images can give rise to idolatry and so any attempt to capture God or his Prophet Muhammad through imagery is considered an insult. For a helpful guide, see BBC News, 'Why Does Depicting the Prophet Muhammad Cause Offence?' Retrieved from: https://www.bbc.co.uk/news/world-europe-30813742.
18. Some may point to the more extreme case of Samuel Paty. Mr Paty, a teacher in Conflans-Sainte-Honorine, a north-west suburb of Paris, was beheaded in a gruesome attack by an 18-year-old Islamist after he showed cartoons of the Prophet Muhammad during a class about freedom of speech in October 2020. As he had done in similar lessons in recent years, Mr Paty, a history and geography teacher, advised Muslim students to leave the room if they thought they might be offended. An

online campaign was launched against Mr Paty, ultimately culminating in his brutal murder. Whilst this case is testimony to how real the threats against free speech and civil discourse are, I don't believe that readers of this book will be dwelling on any arguments that endorse violence against teachers or anyone else for views they oppose. Let's remain focused on our question of whether some views are so offensive that they are not up for debate.

19. Ruth Hunt. (2018) 'Our Work for Trans Equality is at the Heart of Our Mission for Acceptance without Exception.' Retrieved from: https://www.stonewall.org.uk/node/100426.

20. Under UK law, for example, "It is against the law to discriminate against anyone because of:

- age
- gender reassignment
- being married or in a civil partnership
- being pregnant or on maternity leave
- disability
- race including colour, nationality, ethnic, or national origin
- religion or belief
- sex
- sexual orientation

People are protected from discrimination in all areas of life, included "at work" and "in education."

21. Department for Education. (2022) 'Political Impartiality in Schools.' Retrieved from: https://www.gov.uk/government/publications/political-impartiality-in-schools/political-impartiality-in-schools.

22. Greg Lukianoff and Jonathan Haidt. (2018) *The Coddling of the American Mind*. London: Allen Lane.

23. Alison Gopnick. (2016) 'Should We Let Toddlers Play with Saws and Knives?' Retrieved from: https://www.wsj.com/articles/should-we-let-toddlers-play-with-saws-and-knives-1472654945. Emphasis added.

24. Ethics of the Fathers 4:1.

25. Department for Education. (2022) 'Political Impartiality in Schools.' Retrieved from: https://www.gov.uk/government/publications/political-impartiality-in-schools/political-impartiality-in-schools.

26. Richard Kearney. 'Why Remain Catholic?' Retrieved from: https://www.youtube.com/watch?v=s3SI-jWz7Ud8.

27. Nassim Nicholas Taleb. (2012) *Antifragile*. New York: Random House, p. 5.

28. Reni Eddo-Lodge. (2017) *Why I'm No Longer Talking to White People About Race*. London: Bloomsbury, p. 88.

29. Matthew Syed. (2021) *Rebel Ideas*. London: John Murray, p. 20.

30. Ibid., p. 23.

31. Ilana Redstone. (2022) 'The Crisis of Moral Legitimacy,' *Tablet*. Retrieved from: https://www.tablet-mag.com/sections/news/articles/crisis-moral-legitimacy.

32. C. Thi Nguyen. (2020) 'Echo Chambers and Epistemic Bubbles,' *Episteme*, 17(2): 141-161.

33. Nial Ferguson. (2017) 'Speak Less Softly but Do Not Forget the Big Stick.' Retrieved from: https://www.thetimes.co.uk/article/speak-less-softly-but-do-not-forget-the-big-stick-qkrntdc6h.

34. Benjamin Disraeli. (2017) *Sybil*. Oxford: Oxford World's Classics.

35. Robert D. Putnam. (2000) *Bowling Alone: The Collapse and Revival of American Community*. New York: Simon & Schuster.

36. Kwame Anthony Appiah. (2007) *Cosmopolitanism: Ethics in a World of Strangers*. London: Penguin, p. 77.

37. Ibid., p. 78.

38. John McWhorter. (2022) 'I'm Pro-Choice. But I Don't Think Pro-Lifers Are Bad People.' Retrieved from: https://www.nytimes.com/2022/05/06/opinion/roe-supreme-court.html. Emphasis added.

39. Nguyen, p. 142.

40. Kevin deLaplante. (2014) 'Critical Thinking About Conspiracies.' Retrieved from: https://kevindelaplante.com/wp-content/uploads/2020/07/Critical-Thinking-About-Conspiracies.pdf.

41. Shoshana Boyd-Gelfand. (2013) 'The Power of Polarities.' Retrieved from: https://www.youtube.com/watch?v=Jqd4-eemoAw.

42. For a defence of Truth in university education, see Jonathan Haidt. (2016) 'Why Universities Must Choose One Telos: Truth or Social Justice.' Retrieved from: https://heterodoxacademy.org/blog/one-telos-truth-or-social-justice-2/. Haidt writes there that "a university must have one and only one highest and inviolable good" – and between Truth and Justice, Haidt persuasively argues, universities must choose Truth. The controversies at the heart of the university life are beyond the remit of this book but I am making the point that when we educate children, there are different factors at play.

43. Charles Dickens. (1992) *Hard Times*. London: Everyman's Library, pp. 6–7.

44. Tom Stoppard. (1986) *Jumpers*. London: Faber and Faber, p. 30.

45. Steven Pinker. (2018) *Enlightenment Now*. London: Allen Lane, p. 373.

46. For example, see Qassim Cassam. (2015) 'Bad Thinkers,' *Aeon*. Retrieved from: https://aeon.co/essays/the-intellectual-character-of-conspiracy-theorists.

47. Cass Sunstein and Adrian Vermeule. (2009) 'Conspiracy Theories: Causes and Cures,' *Journal of Political Philosophy*, 17: 202–227.

48. Pinker (2018), p. 382.

49. We will explore in various scenarios when one might wish to consider bringing an external expert to teacher the topic under scrutiny. Like it or not: the messenger does count when trying to change beliefs.

50. Kahan, D.M., Hoffman, D.A., Braman, D., Evans, D. and Rachlinski, J.J. (2012). '"They Saw a Protest": Cognitive Illiberalism and the Speechconduct Distinction.' *Stanford Law Review*, p. 864.

2 The Controversy of Controversy

Defining controversy is, well, controversial. According to the Oxford English dictionary, 'controversy' is defined as a "prolonged public disagreement or heated discussion." Just a moment's reflection leads us to recognise that this definition applies to a lot of topics:

- Are transgender women, women?
- Are vaccinations safe?
- Did Lee Harvey Oswald really assassinate President John F. Kennedy?
- Is it acceptable to poke fun at different religions?
- Do aliens exist?
- Should recreational drugs be legalised?
- Is Earth flat?
- Did the Holocaust happen?
- Is climate change a result of human activity?
- Are people really equal?

Think about these questions and tick each of those that you find controversial. As you look at the unticked questions (if there are any), ask yourself if you know anyone else who would find those remaining questions controversial and up for discussion.

Like it or not, these are topics that people really do argue about. Check in to social media at any time and you'll see raging debates about these issues of controversy and so much more. The same is true of the sort of debates our students are having. As teachers, we get a real thrill when we pass teenagers in the school corridors and overhear them debating global issues of the day with passion – rather than simply wondering where to meet up on Saturday night.

And yet, there is surely something that makes us feel uneasy about all of this. I'm not sure most teachers would get a buzz out of students debating whether the Holocaust really happened. (I certainly hope not!) I also think many teachers would be somewhat concerned if students were debating whether people are equal or not. I also can't imagine a responsible Physics teacher being open to a discussion on whether Earth is flat. In fact, I think many of us would be proud of our students if they stood up to racists in the playground and say in no uncertain terms that discrimination isn't up for debate.

So, as teachers, how do we unpack these issues of controversy?

Where do we draw the line?

How can we ensure that what we teach and learn about controversy actually enhances the educational aims we discussed in our introduction, including advancing rationality, developing critical thinking, and nurturing our students' character?

To help think about these questions, let's explore three major approaches toward understanding controversy and consider their relative merits and pitfalls.

Controversy under the Behavioural Criterion

Perhaps the most common approach to thinking about controversy is known as the 'behavioural criterion,' which is to say that something is controversial as soon as any number of people disagree about the issue at hand – just like any of the topics listed above. As Charles Bailey, put it:

> Controversies are largely social phenomena: that is, they are those topics and issues about which numbers of people are observed to disagree. Controversies, seen like this, can occur in any area

DOI: 10.4324/9781003298281-4

of knowledge and experience. There can be controversies about scientific matters, aesthetic matters, historical matters, controversies about religion and about cosmology as well as about morals, society, and politics.[1]

(Bailey, 1971: 69)

Supporters of the behavioural criterion will point to a very powerful benefit that is at the heart of a liberal democratic society: the value of free speech. As Bertrand Russell memorably taught: "Do not fear to be eccentric in opinion, for every opinion now accepted was once eccentric."[2] If tolerance is a key civic virtue, which enhances societal cohesion, so too is humility a moral virtue, as we would do well to recognise that the zeitgeist may change. Mill put it best when he warned that the "silencing of discussion is an assumption of infallibility."[3] We are all fallible – even teachers – and so none of us has the authority "to decide the question for all mankind, and exclude every other person from the means of judging" (ibid.). As Jordan Peterson, a Canadian psychologist, forcefully argued: "Who is going to regulate it? Who is going to define it?"[4]

For advocates of free speech, this argument comes at a particularly important time amidst what some have referred to as 'cancel culture.' Of course, public outrage and shutting down people's opinions has always been around, even in liberal democracies. We all lost out when pious disdain ostensibly led Thomas Hardy to stop writing novels after outcries over the themes that he explored in classics like *Tess of the D'Urbervilles* and *Jude the Obscure*. Many worry that such puritanism – from both the non-liberal left and right – is spoiling our public discourse across all disciplines. In a public missive called 'A Letter on Justice and Open Debate' published in Harper's Magazine in 2020, a group of leading intellectuals from across the political spectrum decried what they saw as "a new set of moral attitudes and political commitments that tend to weaken our norms of open debate and toleration of differences in favour of ideological conformity." Free speech advocates ranging from Noam Chomsky to David Brooks, and including prominent figures like JK Rowling and Salman Rushdie, felt that "the free exchange of information and ideas, the lifeblood of a liberal society, is daily becoming more constricted." In upholding "the value of robust and even caustic counter-speech from all quarters," they argue that "the way to defeat bad ideas is by exposure, argument, and persuasion, not by trying to silence or wish them away." The classroom, it may be argued, is the litmus test for such exposure to different arguments, for as they conclude, "[t]he restriction of debate, whether by a repressive government or an intolerant society, invariably hurts those who lack power and makes everyone less capable of democratic participation." [5]

In historical terms, let's take the 'controversy' of slavery. Long ago, Aristotle had provided the intellectual justification for what was seen as a natural part of human relationships: "From the hour of their birth, some are marked out for subjection, others for rule."[6] It is difficult for us to appreciate that Aristotle's position was very much the norm for most societies throughout history. It took the "eccentric" ideas of so-called radical abolitionists to turn the tide of public opinion thousands of years later. One such free spirit was a heroic teacher called Anthony Benezet. Born in France in 1713, he had himself suffered religious persecution as a Huguenot (French Protestant) and fled with his family to London before moving on to Philadelphia to join a Quaker community. Counter to the orthodoxies of 18th century America, the outspoken Benezet set up America's first public girls' school. Yet he also took up the fight against slavery and anti-black racism, teaching night classes for slaves in 1750 before founding the so-called 'African School' in Philadelphia in 1770 to educate the children of slaves. In contrast to the mainstream racist culture of the day, he wrote:

> I have found amongst the negroes as great a variety of talents as amongst a like number of whites; and I am bold to assert, that the notion entertained by some, that the blacks are inferior in their capacities, is a vulgar prejudice, founded on the pride of ignorance of their lordly masters, who have kept their slaves at such a distance, as to be unable to form a right judgement of them.[7]

Of course, with hindsight, Benezet's actions seem remarkably *un*controversial. This is why for liberals there are no 'sacred cows' except free speech itself: everything should be up for debate. Just as the morality of slavery was finally challenged, so too should we appreciate that ideas we accept today may well flip tomorrow. As Russell wrote:

> The essence of the liberal outlook in the intellectual sphere is a belief that unbiased discussion is a useful thing and that men should be free to question anything if they can support their questioning by solid arguments. The opposite view, which is maintained by those who cannot be called liberals, is that the truth is already known, and that to question it is necessarily subversive.[8]

Bertrand Russell's Ten Commandments of Education

A famous critic of religion, Russell came up with his own Ten Commandments that he thought teachers would do well to promote:

1. Do not feel absolutely certain of anything.
2. Do not think it worthwhile to produce belief by concealing evidence, for the evidence is sure to come to light.
3. Never try to discourage thinking, for you are sure to succeed.
4. When you meet with opposition, even if it should be from your husband or your children, endeavour to overcome it by argument and not by authority, for a victory dependent upon authority is unreal and illusory.
5. Have no respect for the authority of others, for there are always contrary authorities to be found.
6. Do not use power to suppress opinions you think pernicious, for if you do, the opinions will suppress you.
7. Do not fear to be eccentric in opinion, for every opinion now accepted was once eccentric.
8. Find more pleasure in intelligent dissent than in passive agreement, for, if you value intelligence as you should, the former implies a deeper agreement than the latter.
9. Be scrupulously truthful, even when truth is inconvenient, for it is more inconvenient when you try to conceal it.
10. Do not feel envious of the happiness of those who live in a fool's paradise, for only a fool will think that it is happiness

---

We should therefore adopt the liberal virtue of humility through Russell's first commandment that we shouldn't feel absolutely certain of anything. Rather, by accepting that we might be wrong, we open the opportunity to learn, which any responsible teacher should aim to promote. Teachers should therefore take a 'non-directive' approach when teaching controversy and remain neutral to allow students to fully explore and tease out the issue under debate. Nothing should be taught "as settled," certainly not on the basis of authority, for "a victory dependent upon authority is unreal and illusory." For very practical reasons, Russell fears that simply suppressing the opposing side will ultimately backfire and not convince anyone. A sceptical student witnessing a teacher striking down a potential debate may reasonably ask: what does the teacher have to hide?

TEACHING CONTROVERSIES

Directive approach: when a topic is considered *uncontroversial*, teaching should aim to provide students with the correct answer, e.g. 1 + 1 = 2; Paris is the capital city of France.

Non-directive approach: when a topic is considered *controversial*, teaching should be balanced with the aim to provide students with a range of conflicting viewpoints, e.g. an exploration of the concept of justice; whether artificial intelligence will be beneficial or harmful to our planet.

Moreover, of the controversial topics I listed above, think about how many we are really 'expert' in to make that call. As knowledge is being 'democratised' through AI platforms and websites such as Wikipedia, where just a click away an interested student has access to the world's literature on any given topic, we might even be forced to admit to ourselves that there are controversies where our students are more tuned in than we are – as the Greta Thunbergs and Malalas of this world have shown.

This leads us to the next justification for the 'behavioural criterion' and that's the problem of what Keith E. Whittington calls "the argument from conviction." By holding on to our received beliefs, which may be central to our core identity, such as our religious or political values, we may simply take it for granted that they're true. They become, as J.S. Mill put it, "dead dogma." In turn, Whittington explains:

> if we want to have real confidence in our beliefs as individuals, but also as a society, that we should be particularly willing to expose our ideas to the harshest critics we can find because those critics will help us, and they will help us be more confident in the strength of our own ideas. And sometimes they will also show us the weaknesses of our ideas and force us, then, to think more carefully about them and force us to build better and more robust supports for those ideas. So we will come away more sophisticated thinkers with more carefully held and carefully considered ideas than we went into those conversations with.[9]

Supporters of this approach therefore call on teachers to remain balanced and offer a range of perspectives in order to promote student autonomy. Take the highly controversial subject of politics and current affairs. Differing views may well be expressed in the classroom and we all want our students to engage with the issues of the day to help them grow into responsible citizens, nurturing civic virtues like civility and awareness. They may express a range of perspectives, including conservative, liberal, or socialist sensibilities. Some may be feminists, libertarians, or anarchists. A teacher leading a debate on the rights and wrongs of different conceptions of the state and society would on principle and on pragmatic grounds encourage their students to consider and discuss contrasting views. To simply shut down the debate and teach only one perspective hardly helps students' thinking on the issues at hand. Russell's commandment that we must "never try to discourage thinking, for you are sure to succeed," serves as a healthy warning to teachers considering teaching such issues of controversy as settled and not up for debate.

Yet how far are we willing to go with all this?

For example, in July 2019, William Latson, the headteacher of the Spanish River Community High School in Boca Raton, Florida, told a parent that he would remain neutral on whether or not the Holocaust happened. Latson reasoned that because we do not all have the same beliefs on the subject, it should be taught as controversial in a non-directive teaching manner. He said: "I do allow information about the Holocaust to be presented and allow students and parents to make decisions about it accordingly."

However, as Deborah Lipstadt, a leading historian of the Holocaust, candidly tweeted: "This principal – who's neutral on whether the Holocaust happened – should be fired because he's an idiot. The Holocaust has the dubious distinction of being the best documented genocide in the world." As the oft-quoted adage has it: "Don't so open-minded that your brains fall out!" Latson was duly sacked from his position.

Relying on the behavioural criterion and suggesting that even the Holocaust should be taught as controversial because not everyone believes the genocide happened is patently absurd when one appreciates the weight of evidence against this position. To doubt the Holocaust, or even remain neutral on it, flies in the face of basic educational norms, and is a result of bad thinking and most probably anti-Semitism. Where does it end? To be in doubt about the Holocaust pretty much throws everything up into the air.

Thus, in dismissing the behavioural criterion, Robert Dearden, a professor of education, observed:

> If all that is needed is for a number of people to assert a counter-opinion for the matter to become controversial, regardless of that counter-assertion's ungroundedness, inconsistency, invalidity or mere expressiveness of a vested interest, then even the shape of the earth becomes at once controversial.[10]

Entertaining ideas such as flat earth theory and Holocaust denial is hardly in keeping with developing key intellectual virtues such as critical thinking, reasoning, and reflective judgement. In turn, there is a real concern that classroom debates under the behavioural criterion threaten to collapse into relativism and nihilism as no norms of reasoning and evidence are agreed upon. We don't want an Orwellian nightmare in our classrooms.

To be fair to liberals like Russell, they are certainly not advocating a free for all. U.S. Senator Daniel Patrick Moynihan put it best: "You're entitled to your own opinions, but you're not entitled to your own facts." In succinctly capturing the limits of tolerance, he pinpoints for us the central problem of the 'behavioural criterion': it simply lets in too much.

Controversy under the Political Criterion

Just as the behavioural criterion lets in too much, we will see that the so-called 'political criterion' can be somewhat ambiguous. Yet many policy makers are partial to the political criterion and so we must take it seriously.

Michael Hand helpfully explains that this approach advocates that questions "should be counted as controversial when answers to them are not entailed by the public values of the liberal democratic state."[11] Therefore, on grounds of efficacy the political criterion seems an attractive option, as Hand has observed:

> Teachers using this criterion are... spared the onerous task of deciding whether a moral question is such that contrary views can be held on it without those views being contrary to reason; all they need do is check whether more than one view on it is compatible with a commitment to basic rights and liberties.[12]

This is due to the distinction liberal philosophers make "between *public* values, which the state is entitled or obliged to uphold, and *private* values, which the state has no mandate to enforce." Concern for the state of the former, was precisely Tony Blair's reasoning behind the promotion of 'British' values in the aftermath of the 7/7 terror bombings in 2005:

> Integration, in this context, is not about culture or lifestyle. It is about values. It is about integrating at the point of shared, common unifying British values. It isn't about what defines us as people, but as citizens, the rights and duties that go with being a member of our society.
> ...when it comes to our essential values - belief in democracy, the rule of law, tolerance, equal treatment for all, respect for this country and its shared heritage - then that is where we come together, it is what we hold in common; it is what gives us the right to call ourselves British. At that point, no distinctive culture or religion supersedes our duty to be part of an integrated United Kingdom.[13]

Therefore, as for the behavioural criterion above, when discussing current affairs, such as conservative vs liberal ideals on any given issue, the teacher must take a non-directive approach "with a view to maximising the future citizen's autonomy."[14] Indeed, in the United Kingdom, this is a legal requirement, as the Education Act 1996 states: "where political issues are brought to the attention of pupils... they are offered a balanced presentation of opposing views."

FUNDAMENTAL BRITISH VALUES

Democracy
The rule of law
Individual liberty
Mutual respect and tolerance of different faiths and beliefs

Source: *Prevent* Strategy 2011.

Under the Education Act 2002, schools are required to actively promote fundamental British values, including democracy, the rule of law, individual liberty, and mutual respect and tolerance of different faiths and beliefs. Quite simply, these concepts must be taught as uncontroversial and settled. At face value, these liberal democratic principles seem, indeed, uncontroversial. If a teacher is walking down the corridor and overhears students calling for the expulsion of Muslim or Hindu peers, it is to be hoped that the teacher would be deeply troubled by such views and that she would seek to counter such perspectives in an unapologetic manner – whatever pedagogical form that may take. It would be grotesque to treat bullying or racism as issues that are worthy of debate. Such behaviour lacks 'mutual respect and tolerance' and so should be rejected.

However, while the values that Blair promoted are very much within the core aims of a successful liberal education, their framing as 'British' rather than 'liberal' values may well be counterproductive. As John Beck has argued, "for some UK citizens, growing cultural and ethnic diversity is in itself re-sponsible for eroding a clear sense of national identity and social cohesion."[15] On the other hand, the rise of the Black Lives Matter movement has seen many directly point the finger at Britain's alleged historic role in promoting prejudice and discrimination. With such continuing divides in liberal demo-cratic societies today, it is difficult to defend values such as tolerance and equal treatment as our own national values as an uncontroversial claim. Thus, as Beck concludes, the legal imperative for schools to actively promote 'British values' is educationally problematic, suggesting indoctrination, rather than promoting "reasoned analysis and open and critical discussion."[16]

At the same time, the political criterion becomes notoriously difficult to apply when dealing with controversies like conspiracy theories that seek to challenge the foundations of liberal democratic societies. Let's look at some examples:

- Do our political leaders lie and conspire to get what they want?
- Is the system 'rigged' against some in society?
- Were vaccinations and lockdowns in the time of Covid yet another method of governmental control?

As Charles Pigden notes, scepticism surrounding conspiracy theories may entail a "claim that we should not believe or investigate conspiracy theories involving evil plots by government agents if this contradicts official opinion," thus consigning the investigations into Watergate, Iran-Contra, and Wikileaks as 'unAmerican' and 'anti-democratic.'[17] Meanwhile, protests in the United Kingdom against the U.S.-U.K. invasion of Iraq led the then British Prime Minister Tony Blair to retort: "The very reason why we are taking the action that we are taking is nothing to do with oil or any of the other conspiracy theories put forward."[18] Yet with nearly a third of Brits at the time believing that the key reason for in-vading Iraq was precisely "to secure and control oil supplies from the Middle East," such a conspiracy theory was indeed widely believed by a sceptical public.[19]

In turn, to justify shutting down debate in the classroom which seeks to question the basis of the power structure by appealing to the very values of that power structure is clearly problematic. For the establishment to protect its way of life and silence dissenters, including conspiracy theorisers, would surely go against the very democratic values schools are meant to promote.

The political criterion thus begins to unravel when both sides of the debate can use its principles to justify whether the topic under discussion is controversial or not.[20] The singular challenges of conspiracy theorising really put the political criterion to the test. On the one hand, for those opposed to conspiracy theories, there is nothing more damaging to the liberal democratic enterprise than at-tacking its very foundations. Barack Obama, perhaps the most articulate spokesman for liberal values, has gone as far as to label conspiracy theories as "the biggest threat to democracy." Similarly, Angela Merkel, another former world leader who represents the liberal democratic consensus, dedicated part of her final address as Chancellor of Germany to the fragility of democracy, which she said, "depends on solidarity and trust, including the trust in facts." She was very clear about the forces that are threats to the liberal democratic consensus:

Wherever scientific insight is denied and conspiracy theories and hatred are spread, we need to resist. Our democracy also depends on the fact that where hatred and violence are seen as a legitimate means to force through certain interests, our tolerance as democrats must find its limits.[21]

Many liberals now fear that conspiracism has moved from the margins to the mainstream and is "delegitimising the democratic state." They are now seen as pervasive in an age of 'post-truth,' 'fake news,' and 'alternative facts,' spurred on by the rise of the internet, proliferation of 24-hour news outlets, and social media. For example, at the time of writing, there are growing fears over the public's exposure to 'anti-vax' messages proliferating on social media, with a King's College London and Ipsos MORI study showing that "one in three people in the UK (34%) say they've seen or heard messages discouraging the public from getting a coronavirus vaccine." Whilst "one in seven (14%) believe the real purpose of a mass vaccination programme against coronavirus is simply to track and control the population. This rises to a quarter (27%) of 16- to 24-year-olds." It is precisely due to young people's exposure to the internet for their news intake that helps explain their vulnerability to 'fake news,' with the study showing that:

> People who get a great deal or fair amount of information on Covid-19 from WhatsApp (42%) and YouTube (39%) are around three times as likely to believe this. Those who use Twitter (29%) and Facebook (28%) in this way are also more likely to think it is true.

With young people especially receiving their news and information increasingly from unregulated websites and social media outlets, critics of conspiracy theories may well point to the importance of developing a pedagogy of conspiracy theories to inoculate students from believing in them or even developing a conspiracist mindset. For example, a recent Economist Educational Foundation resource defined a conspiracy theory as follows:

> A conspiracy theory is when someone *falsely* believes that a particular group of people are hiding the truth about how an event happened. For example, that the government lied and people didn't really land on the moon. When conspiracy theories are spread, they become fake news.[22]

Of course, the move to shut down conspiracy theories can also claim strong grounding in the liberal democratic tradition. In contrast to the open-ended claims of free speech advocates, there are many who support limits to free speech precisely in order to protect democracy. This approach was perhaps most strongly formulated by Karl Popper, a giant of 20th century intellectual thought. Having witnessed the rise of Nazism in his native Vienna, Popper fled to England to escape anti-Semitism in 1937. No doubt with an eye on the rise of Nazi totalitarianism, Popper explained the necessity of the 'paradox of tolerance,' in one of his most celebrated and controversial passages:

> Unlimited tolerance must lead to the disappearance of tolerance. If we extend unlimited tolerance even to those who are intolerant, if we are not prepared to defend a tolerant society against the onslaught of the intolerant, then the tolerant will be destroyed, and tolerance with them.–In this formulation, I do not imply, for instance, that we should always suppress the utterance of intolerant philosophies; as long as we can counter them by rational argument and keep them in check by public opinion, suppression would certainly be unwise. But we should claim the right to suppress them if necessary even by force; for it may easily turn out that they are not prepared to meet us on the level of rational argument, but begin by denouncing all argument; they may forbid their followers to listen to rational argument, because it is deceptive, and teach them to answer arguments by the use of their fists or pistols. We should therefore claim, in the name of tolerance, the right not to tolerate the intolerant.[23]

And Popper had real ire for what he dismissed as the "conspiracy theory of society."[24] Seen as the chief critic of conspiracy theories, Popper argued that conspiracy theorists simply mischaracterised the reality of democratic decision-making processes. In his highly influential writing on the subject, he rejected conspiratorial thought as "a theory which I think implies exactly the opposite of the true aim of the social sciences." Accepting that "the conspiracy theory of society" was widespread, Popper argued that it has "very little truth in it." This is because "one of the striking things about social life is that nothing ever comes off exactly as intended" (ibid.). As Popper wrote:

> I think that the people who approach the social sciences with a readymade conspiracy theory thereby deny themselves the possibility of ever understanding what the task of the social sciences is, for they assume that we can explain practically everything in society by asking who wanted it, whereas the real task of the social sciences is to explain those things which nobody wants.[25]

On the other hand, for those defending conspiracy theorisers, there can be nothing more important than upholding 'the rule of law' and aiming to hold those in power to account. As scholars such as David Coady argue, "conspiracy theories do not deserve their bad reputation," criticising those "excessively unwilling to believe conspiracy theories."[26] By dismissing all conspiracy theories as a class of explanation, we may be guilty of bias, misleading students into assuming that belief in conspiracy theories is irrational. Surely this sweeping approach is too simplistic.

Indeed, recent scholarship has seen the rise of the 'particularist' project which "is predicated on the acceptance that as conspiracies occur, we can only dismiss particular instances of them if someone does the investigative work to check that they are actually unwarranted." Contra to the Economist Educational Foundation resource's claim that conspiracy theories are "false" beliefs, history shows that some do turn out to be true: from the assassination of Julius Caesar to the Gleiwitz false flag attack on Nazi Germany in the 1930s, to Watergate and Iran-Contra in the modern United States. Particularists such as Charles Pigden have therefore concluded that, "it is perfectly reasonable to look for conspiracies in the explanation of events... Sometimes they work and sometimes they don't. It is a case of suck it and see." Lee Basham goes further and writes that a wholesale rejection of conspiracy theories, known as 'generalism,' "is not a morally appropriate attitude in an open society... It ignores the key role conspiracy theorists play in securing our democracy." From Watergate to the Volkswagen Emissions Scandal of 2015, the 'conspiracy theorists' who uncovered these conspiracies should hardly be seen as a threat to democracy. For example, Edward Snowden's leaking of the National Security Agency's mass surveillance programme in 2013 reminded us that even in democracies conspiracies really do happen. We know that governments and powerful corporations have sought to cover up conspiratorial behaviour, sometimes resorting to extreme and even illegal measures. And so the suggestion that conspiracy theories can be dismissed based on the political criterion is too simplistic, highlighting the unique challenge conspiracy theories present. One is left in the impossible position of wondering which side is really naïve and which side healthily sceptical. With the political criterion falling short, we now need to consider controversy in light of the epistemic criterion.

Controversy under the Epistemic Criterion

If we step back for a moment, we would do well to revisit what all of this is for. Why teach controversy and why teach at all? Interestingly, the question itself contains a hint of the answer. We surely wouldn't want an answer that requires no justification, that is imposed upon us because of authority. Answering "it's the law!" simply won't do. Any answer worth consideration must offer *reasons* to win us over. (And if you disagree, remember that you need to provide *reasons* too. Hopefully, the irony isn't lost on you...)

And so Hand puts it succinctly as follows: "the central aim of education is to nurture rational thought and action."[27] There may well be other reasons to educate – and we will consider complementary aims below – but developing the intellectual virtues of critical thinking and reasoning have been part and parcel of education across time and cultures in a rather uncontroversial manner. This approach is also supported by Amartya Sen in his discussion on the goals of education:

> Education is about helping children to develop the ability to reason about new decisions any grown-up person will have to take. The important goal... [is] what would best enhance the capability of children to live 'examined lives' as they grow up in an integrated country.[28]

Indeed, whether one aligns with traditionalists or progressives, it would be fair to assume that developing our students' character attributes and learner habits so that they can flourish in the world, is a key educational aim we can all champion. In turn, by framing a debate through a rational lens, teachers will encourage students to develop their beliefs on the basis of reasoning and critical thinking, in the best tradition of a liberal education.

Dearden provides a helpful definition of the epistemic criterion of controversiality that seeks to do precisely that:

> A matter is controversial if contrary views can be held on it without those views being contrary to reason. By 'reason' here is not meant something timeless and unhistorical but the body of public knowledge, criteria of truth, critical standards and verification procedures which at any given time has been so far developed.[29]

As Hand explains, each view needs to be judged by the evidence or reasoned arguments in their support. Where only one view enjoys such support, the teacher should take a directive approach, teaching that racial prejudice, for example, is wrong – no matter how many people may disagree. 'Opinionation' is thus rejected as champions of the epistemic criterion proudly state that "not all opinions are equal." While there may well be Holocaust deniers or flat earth theorists, schools must reject those rejectionist views that fly in the face of overwhelming historical or scientific evidence.

Rather, students should only be taught in a directive manner when the evidence is overwhelming, i.e. the Holocaust did happen and Earth isn't flat. Note that the epistemic criterion tracks the best available evidence, not the truth, recognising that evidence and truth may come apart. This encapsulates the best of the scientific method, upholding the intellectual virtue of humility that we may be proven wrong in the future by subsequent evidence that overturns our current thinking. At the same time, even with regard to the most egregious of controversial claims – that of Holocaust denial amid the backdrop of alleged Jewish global domination – Deborah Lipstadt's prime charge is epistemic: the conspiracist claims are absurd precisely because the Holocaust is the most documented genocide in world history.

This approach is crucial because, as Barack Obama recently warned, democratic societies are facing an "epistemological crisis" as young people are struggling to distinguish between fact and fiction. Teachers therefore have a clear duty to help guide their students through the minefield of competing narratives from a largely unregulated social and news media. Even where teachers lack direct expertise in the subject matter at hand, they may be able to guide students on how to think about controversy in epistemic terms, which this book will provide guidance for. It is to be shown that teachers can set the boundaries to ensure a purposeful learning environment that thinks about controversy in terms of evidence, reasoned argument, and critical reflection.

Easy, isn't it?

Well, not so fast.

Let's try out these moral dilemmas (and I apologise in advance if you're a little squeamish):

- A few friends go off hiking in the mountains before stopping to fish in a lake. As they're about to fish, one of them notices the body of a young dead woman. They carry on fishing before telling the police of their discovery.
- A woman is cleaning out her bedroom, and she finds her old American flag. She doesn't want the flag anymore, so she cuts it up into pieces and uses the rags to clean her bathroom.
- A family's dog was killed by a car in front of their house. The family had heard that dog meat is delicious, and so the family members all agree to cut up the dead dog, cook it, and eat it for dinner.
- A man goes to the supermarket once a week and buys a dead chicken. But before cooking the chicken, he has sexual intercourse with it. Then he thoroughly cleans it, cooks it well, and eats it.
- A brother and sister – 22 years old and 20 years old respectively – like snogging each other. When nobody is around, they often kiss each other on the mouth.[30]

I'll give you time to get a glass of water (or something a little stronger) to help calm your nerves.

Are you back?

If you're ready for the next round, I have two simple questions that may make you feel a little uneasy:

1.   Do *you* think these behaviours – in and of themselves – are *uncontroversially* acceptable?
2.   Now apply the epistemic criterion to each of them and think about how it would suggest we teach any of these scenarios:

•   In a directive way: it should be taught as uncontroversially wrong
•   In a non-directive way: it should be taught as controversial
•   In a directive way: it should be taught as uncontroversially right.

When these dilemmas are put to people, most of us sense *intuitively* that there is something obviously and self-evidently wrong. Yet epistemically, one would be hard-pressed to justify these intuitions on rational grounds. As Jonathan Haidt described it, we are left 'morally dumbfounded,' as we hold on to what we *know* to be right despite our inability to reason why. "It just is!" or "I just do!" we might hear a student respond in exasperation as to why siblings snogging is wrong, or why they consider eating one's dead pet as repulsive. Indeed, they may even go on to snap that if someone can't see what's wrong with the behaviour in these scenarios, then perhaps something is wrong with them! That sense of disgust was powerfully captured by the ethicist Leon Kass:

> Repugnance, here as elsewhere, revolts against the excesses of human wilfulness, warning us not to transgress what is unspeakably profound. Indeed, in this age in which everything is held to be permissible so long as it is freely done, in which our given human nature no longer commands respect, in which our bodies are regarded as mere instruments of our autonomous rational wills, repugnance may be the only voice left that speaks up to defend the central core of our humanity. Shallow are the souls that have forgotten how to shudder.[31]

Perhaps then these cases suggest that whilst the epistemic criterion is necessary, it is not enough to fully consider moral controversies. Rather, we should recognise the interplay of intuition and reason to take full account of human sentiment in the decision-making process.[32] While the former affords the necessary heuristics (mental rules of thumb) to help provide a framework for life, the latter provides the equally necessary critical reflection to help ensure that we don't blindly follow our intuitions into barbarism. Even Steven Pinker, the doyen of reason, conceded: "Whatever its ontological status may be, a moral sense is part of the standard equipment of the human mind. It's the only mind we've got, and we have no choice but to take its intuitions seriously."[33]

'Moral Foundations Theory': A Call for a Pluralist Criterion

To be clear, I am not seeking to reject the epistemic criterion outright but rather to argue for the need to broaden the range of considerations relevant to deciding whether a moral judgement is justified or not. Hand's reasoning is driven by his "central aim of education" which is "to equip students with a capacity for, and inclination to, rational thought and action."[34] This underlying assumption highlights why his approach to matters of controversy is too restrictive as he fails to consider other central aims to education important for spiritual, moral, social, and cultural debates.

If we rely only on the narrow epistemic criterion, then we are tied to a style of thinking that hinges on Western thinking. 'People like us' think primarily in terms of what is known as the 'ethic of autonomy,' where the individual is prime and we live through a harm-rights-and-justice code. Although this has become the basis for Western thinking since the Enlightenment, it cannot deal effectively with the 'morally confounding' scenarios we brought above.[35] Beyond the liberal "no harm to others" mantra, we need to look to other 'moral languages' (ibid.) to fully understand our own deep-seated repugnance in such scenarios. This means opening up towards a more pluralistic mindset and appreciating different modes of thinking from around the world. A second type of moral language is called the 'ethic of community,' which relies on concepts such as duty, respect, and loyalty, that aims to preserve institutions and social order. This helps explain our loyalties to family structures and social traditions – helping explain why many of us cringe at the thought of snogging our sibling. The third is called the 'ethic of divinity,' which relies on concepts such as purity, sanctity, and sin, that protects the 'divinity' inherent in each of us – helping explain why fishing close to a dead body is deeply disrespectful even though there is no harm done.

It is only an appeal to a plurality of ideals that include sanctity and degradation, so instinctive in moral communities that we can articulate why those behaviours in the 'moral dumbfounding' scenarios above elicit our disgust. There is a real sense in which the five controversial situations desecrated someone or something many of us hold dear: the sanctity of a human body – dead or alive, the flag we love, or the boundaries of family relationships. MFT also helps explain concepts like dignity and holiness, and our very natural instinct for rituals such as prayer or ceremonies.

Shweder's discovery of 'moral languages' beyond the narrow 'ethic of autonomy' gives voice to what is so intuitive to most moral communities that grant importance to concepts like purity, sanctity, and sin. Insofar as the Western conception of ethics relies on concepts such as harm, rights, and justice, it remains difficult to reason what was wrong about our 'moral dumbfounding' dilemmas. Based on a rational moral education model, we are prevented from objecting to such behaviours, leading us to call on teachers to assign the decisions made as 'justified,' which would be absurd for most of us. It is only by extending our moral understanding to the ethics of divinity and community, that we can now articulate our intuitive repugnance at the insensitivity and, at the very least, class their behaviour as controversial if not outright uncontroversially wrong.

And so a pluralist outlook, one that balances reason with intuition, is required to appreciate the nuance and subtleties of peoples' differing beliefs and practices that topics of controversy require us to engage with. For example, Mary Earl frames religious education through three 'lenses' or modes of interpretation:

1. **Cultural understanding** to help us "understand how beliefs and practices form traditions and how there can be continuity and change within those traditions"
2. **Identity formation** "cherishes the 'I' at the centre by seeing it in relationship, always, with the other, with the environment, and with ideas about the existence (or not) of the divine"
3. **Issues of proof, truth, and evidence** "tell us what has formed the creeds, texts, ethical practices and philosophies which believers of any kind adhere to. It also, as school students grow older, helps them to see how difference and diversity often arise around foundational truth, proof and evidence issues – and how scholars deal with this developing discourse."[36]

This pluralistic approach allows us to educate the whole student. When a student denies the Holocaust, it would be naïve to think the educational response can be limited to epistemic considerations only. To be sure, bad thinking is going on. But we cannot educate epistemic weakness in isolation. Any responsible teacher will also be wondering what is happening at the individual and social levels that led a student to think – and *feel* – in such a way. We belittle our students when we view them as purely thinking-machines and teach them only in terms of facts and evidence. Foremost, they are human with a range of influences and pressures that will impact their approaches to topics of controversy.

Earl's three-pronged approach broadens school students' exposure to meaning in terms of culture, identity, and belief and practice. Although the pursuit of "rational thought and action" is indeed central, it must go hand in hand with educational values of empathy, tolerance, and respect. In an increasingly globalised world, with ever-growing fissures in society along cultural, religious, and ethnic lines, the need for cultural understanding has never been greater in order to help foster "tolerance, respect and, eventually recognise the 'otherness' of the other."[37] We must be wary of only advocating a narrow WEIRD (Western, Educated, Industrialised, Rich, and Democratic) style of thinking when dealing with controversies of global importance.[38]

Foundation	Care/harm	Fairness/cheating	Loyalty/betrayal	Authority/subversion	Sanctity/degradation
Adaptive challenge	Protect and care for children	Reap benefits of two-way partnerships	Form cohesive coalitions	Forge beneficial relationships within hierarchies	Avoid communicable diseases
Original triggers	Suffering, distress, or neediness expressed by one's child	Cheating, cooperation, deception	Threat or challenge to group	Signs of high and low rank	Waste products, diseased people
Current triggers	Baby seals, cute cartoon characters	Marital fidelity, broken vending machines	Sports teams, nations	Bosses, respected professionals	Immigration, deviant sexuality
Characteristic emotions	Compassion for victim; anger at perpetrator	Anger, gratitude, guilt	Group pride, rage at traitors	Respect, fear	Disgust
Relevant virtues	Caring, kindness	Fairness, justice, trustworthiness	Loyalty, patriotism, self-sacrifice	Obedience, deference	Temperance, chastity, piety, cleanliness

Figure 2.1 The Original Five Foundations of Intuitive Ethics[39]
Jonathan Haidt went on to suggest that Liberty/oppression should be considered a sixth foundation. See his The Righteous Mind.

Yet it is important to note that the adoption of 'plural' values is not a 'free for all' of relativistic values, as feared under the behavioural criterion, but may rather be grounded within the pluralism of Haidt's 'Moral Foundations Theory' and its consideration of the ethics of autonomy, community, and divinity through its foundation of intuitive ethics (Figure 2.1).

Indeed, in extolling the value of 'a plurality of ideals,' the Oxford philosopher Isaiah Berlin explained why they are objective and why they are crucial for human understanding:

I came to the conclusion that there is a plurality of ideals, as there is a plurality of cultures and of temperaments...

I think these values are objective – that is to say, their nature, the pursuit of them, is part of what it is to be a human being, and this is an objective given... I can enter into a value system which is not my own, but which is nevertheless something I can conceive of men pursuing while remaining human, while remaining creatures with whom I can communicate, with whom I have some common values – for all human beings must have some common values or they cease to be human, and also some different values else they cease to differ, as in fact they do. That is why pluralism is not relativism – the multiple values are objective, part of the essence of humanity rather than arbitrary creations of men's subjective fancies.[40]

Berlin's search for common values gets to the heart of what it means to be human and the idea of human nature. As EO Wilson observed, ethicists who use pure reasoning to reach moral truths are the secular counterparts to religious transcendentalists who use sacred texts to find their moral truths.[41] To brush aside human nature, as expressed through one's intuitions, in the belief that moral reasoning transcends human nature, is a secular form of transcendentalism. As Haidt put it, "the worship of reason...is a delusion. It is an example of faith in something that does not exist."[42] Rather, as David Hume warned, the 'moral science' must begin with careful inquiry into what humans are really like, which means appealing to one's sentiments rather than one's reasoning when it comes to moral truths: "Morals and criticism are not so properly objects of the understanding as of taste and sentiment. Beauty, whether moral or natural, is felt, more properly than perceived."[43] Only a pluralist ethic can take these diverse human values into full account.

As we go on to consider different controversies and how we should deal with them in the classroom, we will broaden our considerations, and draw on a 'plurality of ideals' so that we can help students not only sharpen their own views on the matter of controversy but also help them better understand other viewpoints.

Summary of Controversy Frameworks

	Behavioural criterion	Political criterion	Epistemic criterion	Moral foundations theory: a plurality of ideals
Definition of controversy	When contrary views can be held about the topic under discussion	When contrary views can be held without contradicting the public values of the liberal democratic state	When contrary views can be held without those views being contrary to reason	When contrary views can be held without those views being contrary to reason, cultural understanding, and identity formation
Strengths	Freedom of speech; Develops virtue of humility	Upholding liberal and democratic ethos; Tolerance	Advances critical thinking and reasoning	Advances critical thinking and reasoning; Tolerance: extends consideration to existential and social motivations
Weaknesses	Lets too much in	Ambiguous	Too narrow to consider moral controversies	Arguably ambiguous

Notes

1. Charles Bailey. (1971) 'Rationality, Democracy and the Neutral Teacher,' *Cambridge Journal of Education*, 1(2): 69.
2. Bertrand Russell. (1951) 'The Best Answer to Fanaticism – Liberalism: Its Calm Search for Truth, Viewed as Dangerous in Many Places, Remains the Hope of Humanity.' Retrieved from: https://timesmachine.nytimes.com/timesmachine/1951/12/16/issue.html.
3. John Stuart Mill. (1992) *On Liberty*. London: Everyman's Library, p. 19.
4. Jordan Peterson. (2018) 'Free Speech & the Right to Offend.' Retrieved from: https://www.youtube.com/watch?v=44pERGAaKHw.
5. See the letter in full at: https://harpers.org/a-letter-on-justice-and-open-debate/.
6. Aristotle, *Politics*, Bk1.
7. Cited in W. Kashatus. (2004) 'A Friend among Quakers.' Retrieved from: http://paheritage.wpengine.com/article/friend-among-quakers/#:~:text=%E2%80%9CI%20have%20found%20amongst%20Negroes,masters%2C%20who%20have%20kept%20their.
8. Russell (1951).
9. K.E. Whittington, 'John Stuart Mill's Big Idea: Harsh Critics Make Good Thinkers.' Retrieved from: https://bigthink.com/neuropsych/john-stuart-mill/. Last accessed: 12 January 2022.
10. Robert Dearden. (2012) *Theory and Practice in Education*. London: Routledge & Kegan Paul, p. 85.
11. Michael Hand. (2007) 'Should We Teach Homosexuality as a Controversial Issue?' *Theory and Research in Education*, 5(1): 71.
12. Michael Hand. (2008) 'What Should We Teach as Controversial? A Defense of the Epistemic Criterion,' *Educational Theory*, 58(2): 221.
13. Tony Blair. (2008) 'Speech on Multiculturalism and Integration.' Retrieved from: http://englischlehrer.de/texts/blair.php.
14. David Archard. (1998) 'How Should We Teach Sex?' *Journal of Philosophy of Education*, 32(3): 447.
15. John Beck. (2018) 'School Britannia? Rhetorical and Educational Uses of "British Values,"' *London Review of Education*, 16(2): 232.

16. Ibid., p. 234.
17. Charles Pigden. (2007) 'Conspiracy Theories and the Conventional Wisdom,' *Episteme*, 4(2): 229.
18. Tony Blair (2003), cited in Hansard. Retrieved from: https://hansard.millbanksystems.com/commons/2003/jan/15/engagements.
19. YouGov Survey. (2003) 'The War on Iraq.' Retrieved from: http://cdn.yougov.com/today_uk_import/YG-Archives-Ira-itn-WarIraq-030113.pdf.
20. Michael Hand noted a similar problem for issues of sexual controversies, which we will explore in Part II. It isn't clear whether the political criterion would support a neutral stance on activities in the bedroom or advocate a libertarian "no harm to others" approach. Moreover, what does this criterion have to say on extra-marital affairs that while most of us would consider immoral are hardly matters of "public values" of the liberal democratic state?
21. Katrin Bennhold. (2021) 'Angela Merkel's Parting Message to Germany: Trust One Another,' *The New York Times*. Retrieved from: https://www.nytimes.com/2021/12/02/world/europe/angela-merkel-fare-well-germany.html.
22. Economist. (2020) 'Conspiracy Theories in the News.' Retrieved from: https://talk.economistfoundation.org/headlines/conspiracy-theories-in-the-news/resources/.
23. Karl Popper. (2012) *The Open Society and Its Enemies*. Oxford: Routledge, p. 581.
24. Karl Popper. (2002) 'Towards a Rational Theory of Tradition.' In *Conjectures and Refutations*. Oxford: Routledge, p. 167.
25. Ibid., pp. 166–167.
26. David Coady (ed.). (2006) 'An Introduction to the Philosophical Debate about Conspiracy Theories.' In *Conspiracy Theories: The Philosophical Debate*. Farnham: Ashgate, p. 9.
27. Michael Hand. (2008) 'What Should We Teach as Controversial? A Defense of the Epistemic Criterion,' *Educational Theory*, 58(2): 219.
28. Amartya Sen. (2006) *Identity and Violence: The Illusion of Destiny*. London: Allen Lane, p. 160.
29. Robert Dearden. (2012) *Theory and Practice in Education*. London: Routledge & Kegan Paul, p. 86.
30. The first of these scenarios is taken from Raymond Carver's classic short story, *So Much Water So Close to Home*. The others are variations of Jonathan Haidt's 'moral dumbfounding' dilemmas in *The Righteous Mind*.
31. Leon Kass. (1997) 'The Wisdom of Repugnance,' *The New Republic*, 216(22): 20.
32. For more on this interplay between intuition and reason, see Daniel Kahneman's *Thinking, Fast and Slow* (2011), Jonathan Haidt's *The Righteous Mind* (2013), and Joshua Greene's *Moral Tribes* (2014).
33. Steven Pinker. (2003) *The Blank Slate*. London: Penguin.
34. Michael Hand. (2008) 'What Should We Teach as Controversial? A Defense of the Epistemic Criterion,' *Educational Theory*, 58(2): 218.
35. Richard A. Shweder. (1997) 'The "Big Three" of Morality (Autonomy, Community, Divinity) and the "Big Three" Explanations of Suffering.' Retrieved from: https://humdev.uchicago.edu/sites/humdev.uchicago.edu/files/uploads/Shweder/ShwederBig3Morality-min.pdf.
36. Mary Earl. (2016) *Re-Framing Education about Beliefs and Practices in Schools: A Lens and Tools (Concept Based) Approach*. Cambridge: Woolf Institute, University of Cambridge, p. 11.
37. Ibid.
38. See Joseph Henrich. (2020) *The WEIRDist People in the World*. New York: Farrar Straus & Giroux.
39. Jesse Graham et al. (2013) 'Moral Foundations Theory: The Pragmatic Validity of Moral Pluralism.' Retrieved from: https://cpb-us-e2.wpmucdn.com/sites/uci.edu/dist/1/863/files/2020/06/Graham-et-al-2013.AESP_.pdf.
40. Isaiah Berlin. (2003) My Intellectual Path. In Rorty, A.O. (ed.) *The Many Faces of Philosophy: Reflections from Plato to Arendt*. Oxford: Oxford University Press, p. 489.
41. E.O. Wilson. (1999) *Consilience: The Unity of Knowledge*. New York: Vintage Books, p. 271.
42. Jonathan Haidt. (2013) *The Righteous Mind*. London: Penguin, p. 107.
43. David Hume. (1993) *An Enquiry Concerning Human Understanding*. Indianapolis, IN: Hackett Publishing, p. 114.

3 The Rules of Engagement

Getting Comfortable

Clasp your hands together. Be sure that your fingers are interlaced. Now look down and check which thumb is naturally on top. If it's the right thumb, then you are part of the phenotype *R* (right) family along with 44% of the population. If the left thumb comes out on top, then together with 55% of the population, you're a phenotype *L* (left). OK, feel free to separate your hands and give them a short break.

Now, I'm going to ask you to do something radical. Something that I know that 99% of my readers will feel uncomfortable experiencing. Many of you will think that something is wrong even. This time, I would like you to clasp your hands together but be sure to put the other hand on top in opposition to your natural clasp. So, if your left thumb came out on top naturally, be sure to have your right thumb on top this time, and vice versa.

How do you feel?

Are you experiencing any discomfort?

If you do this little exercise with one or more friends and notice that they naturally rest their opposite thumb on top, you may be tempted to feel that they are a little weird (at best). How could anyone think that it's normal to do such a thing? And yet, as I wrote above, we're split quite evenly across the world. Can it be that the other half are really so strange?

Before you reconsider your friendships, let me put your mind at ease. We begin clasping our hands together as babies. As our fingers meet for the first time, half of us tend to one way and half tend to the other. We then repeat these actions over time until one side becomes *familiar* and even *natural* to us. If we were so minded (and perhaps a little weird ourselves), we could start to familiarise ourselves the other way and after thousands of goes over the next year or two, we will probably feel that clasping our hands with the opposite thumb on top isn't so weird after all!

Before We Begin

As we have seen, a major problem for teaching and learning about controversy is that many of us are unwilling to hear the other side. Many of us may even put opposing viewpoints down to ignorance or self-interested motives. "If only they know what I know" or "they're only saying that because..." It's shocking to even think that there might actually be legitimate and well-reasoned arguments on different sides of the divide on the most controversial issues of the day: think abortion, how we self-identify, and the legality of guns. There is an increasing sense in which issues are so clear cut that we lock ourselves into a mindset of #nodebate. Oddly enough, we feel about an opposing viewpoint quite similarly to how we feel when we put our opposite thumb on top: it's just wrong!

And so before I start teaching about a topic of real controversy, one that I will know will face resistance among my students, I start out with the hands-clasping exercise. Not only is it fun and always elicits strange faces and wonderful sounds, it makes a point that all teenage students grasp quickly: don't reject something simply because it's *unfamiliar*. Just because something doesn't *feel* right, doesn't necessarily mean it's wrong.[1]

Indeed, having our students step back about the issue at hand and consider controversy in a broader sense brings this point home. Throughout history, what may seem obvious to one group of people is anything but to another group. It is only by familiarising ourselves with other ways of doing things can we scrutinise them and hold them to account in a fair and open way. Perhaps even more importantly, we can then reflect and hold our own values to account in light of what we have learned about the other.

DOI: 10.4324/9781003298281-5

Try the following task out yourself

What do many of us believe is good or right today that in the past our ancestors considered evil or wrong?

Attempt the following task which simply reverses the question:

What do many of us believe is wrong or even evil today that in the past our ancestors had no problem with or perhaps even thought was the right thing?

Finally, try this one out - perhaps a little more difficult:

What do many of us believe is acceptable today that 100 years from now our descendants may consider to be wrong and even evil?

Honouring Parents: Bury, Cremate, or Eat?

A potent example of considering the other side was told by Herodotus, the great Greek chronicler in the 5th century BCE, whose work *The Histories* records some of the great clashes of cultures in the ancient world: both physical and intellectual. One such clash was engineered Darius I of Persia:

> Darius, after he had got the kingdom, called into his presence certain Greeks who were at hand and asked - "What he should pay them to eat the bodies of their fathers when they died?" To which they answered, that there was no sum that would tempt them to do such a thing. He then sent for certain Indians, of the race called the Callatians, men who eat their fathers, and asked them, while the Greeks stood by, and knew by the help of an interpreter all that was said - "What he should give them to burn the bodies of the fathers at their decease?" The Indians exclaimed allowed, and bade him forbear such language.[2]

I could bring in a third group of Muslims and Jews who would be horrified by both practices. For them, burying the dead as soon as possible after death is considered a sacred requirement. There is little more disrespectful to one's parents than burning or eating their bodies among these religious groups.

Yet before you throw your hands up and think that all this shows is that there is no right answer after all, that it's all subjective, it's important to realise that all the above groups agree on one thing: we should respect "the bodies of our fathers." The question is simply how best to respect them. Every culture has its own taboos and every culture has its own rituals surrounding death.[3] While this creepiest of topics may bring out strong views amongst us and our students, we would do well to recognise such feelings exist for our classmates and peers too. Yes, we think very differently about how to respect the dead (though few of us eat our fathers anymore!) but we do think seriously and feel sincerely about such issues - whatever our viewpoint. And so it wouldn't be a leap to suggest that this is true of other topics of controversy too.

Cancel Ourselves?

I think it would be fair to say that many of us do act with revulsion when we hear that the Callatians ate their dead parents out of respect. This is something that our ancestors may have done once but many of us now feel is quite wrong.[4] Indeed, this is just one example among many that might make us a little embarrassed about how our forebears behaved.

Before we get too self-righteous though, let's now turn to the third question in the task above: "What do many of us believe is acceptable today that one hundred years from now our descendants may consider to be wrong and even evil?"

Just as we may look back with horror when we learn about how women were burned for being witches, what do we do now that will cause our descendants to look upon us with disgust? My guess is that we'll be 'cancelled' for eating meat. And I say this heavy-heartedly as a lover of meat (albeit a guilt-ridden carnivore even as I write this). We can imagine that in 100 years from now, people who we consider as heroes will have their statues pulled down and their books taken off the shelves because they ate meat.

Here's another sin we may be judged for: spending money on things we don't really need when so many people are still dying from preventable and treatable causes. Indeed, I'm sure many readers can come up with their own suggestions, all of which are very humbling for us to think about as we prepare to debate important controversies with others.

So beware of what C.S. Lewis called "chronological snobbery." It's easy to think we're so much better than those who came before us. But simply ask yourself if you would have behaved differently had you lived in those times. What if you were born and brought up in a culture very different from your own even in the world today? If history teaches us anything, the chances are we would have gone for the ride like nearly everyone else.[5]

The Principle of Charity

Before we even begin teaching controversy, we therefore need to curate a classroom environment that avoids the pitfalls of "chronological snobbery" or indeed any other type of narcissism. If the discussions are going to be fruitful, our students must be open to new ideas. J.S. Mill warned that one of the worst ways to chill freedom of speech is "to stigmatise those who hold the contrary opinion as bad and immoral men."[6] Just as humility is a moral virtue we'd like to develop for our students, so too are reflection and critical thinking important intellectual virtues for a purposeful classroom culture.

Fortunately, I believe we have a model for teaching and learning about controversy that nurtures such character attributes from the people who loved arguing most: the rabbis of the Talmud. For most of my life, I have dedicated much time to the study of the Talmud. As the vast and central text of Rabbinic Judaism, the Talmud is a unique work and so difficult to define. A compendium of rabbinic debates over hundreds of years on anything and everything, the main version was compiled in Babylon in 500 CE. Having studied at two theological seminaries, poring over the Hebrew and Aramaic texts from morning to night, I am part of a Jewish culture that pursues life-long study of the Talmud and its related commentaries for their own sake. Devotees do this because, as Rabbi Adin Steinsaltz, a leading modern Talmudic commentator describes it, the Talmud is "a book of holy intellectualism."[7] And for anyone engaged in its study, it becomes quite obvious that if the Talmud teaches you anything, it is the value of debate and discussion. Just as the Bible is replete with episodes of the prophets arguing with God, so too does the Talmud celebrate controversy. Chief Rabbi Jonathan Sacks captured the Talmudic ethos well: "argument and the hearing of contrary views is the essence of the religious life."[8] Nothing is off limits in this collection of Jewish thought, law, and legend. Arguments rage over the most minute theoretical issues, with no assumptions allowed as each viewpoint is forensically examined.

As part of my studies, I was raised on the following story that helps frame the Talmudic mindset. I think we have much to learn from the debates of the two leading Talmudical academies and how they reached their conclusions. The Talmud tells us:

> For three years the Academy of Shammai and the Academy of Hillel debated. One side said that the law is in accordance with our opinion, and the other side said that the law is in accordance with our opinion.
>
> Ultimately, a Divine Voice emerged and proclaimed: Both these and those are the words of the living God. However, the law is in accordance with the opinion of the Academy of Hillel.
>
> The Talmud asks: Since both these and those are the words of the living God, why was the Academy Hillel privileged to have the law established in accordance with their opinion?
>
> The reason is that they were *agreeable and humble, showing restraint when affronted*. Moreover, when they taught the law, they would teach both their own viewpoint *and the viewpoint of the Academy of Shammai*. Even further, when they formulated their teachings and cited a dispute, they *prioritised the viewpoint of the Academy of Shammai* over their own statements, in deference to the House of Shammai.[9]

There is much to unpack here in a narrative that is the epitome of what's known as 'the principle of charity.' First, is the delightful matter-of-fact way in which we're told that these two leading academies debated a topic for three years! In Judaism, this is known as "an argument for the sake of heaven," where the desire is to discover the truth rather than win the argument. In this vein, arguing is indeed the essence of the religious life – in Judaism at least.

Second, from the objective divine perspective, both opinions are correct. According to Talmudic logic, two diametrically opposed viewpoints can both be true. This is based on the notion that there are "seventy faces to Torah,"[10] which means that there are numerous legitimate pathways to the truth. It may be the case that one side doesn't have a monopoly on the truth: the world is complex and there might well be more than one reasonable way of seeing things.

For those of us raised on Western logic, this seems impossible. After all, Aristotle taught us long ago the proposition of 'Noncontradiction': A and not A cannot both be the case. In other words, a proposition and its opposite cannot both be true! Compare that with the Zen Buddhist teaching that "the opposite of a great truth is also true." We can see very clearly the movement away from either/ or thinking that is necessary in formal logic towards both/and thinking that we saw played out through the concept of polarity: recognising that a problem can have two (or more) correct answers that are interdependent.

Indeed, Kaiping Peng and Richard Nisbett[11] succinctly spell out the three principles that underlie Eastern dialecticism that can help show how the art of dialogue can help us move forward:

1. *Principle of change:*
      Reality is a process of change.
      What is currently true will shortly be false.
2. *Principle of contradiction:*
      Contradiction is the dynamic underlying change.
      Because change is constant, contradiction is constant.
3. *Principle of relationships (and holism):*
      The whole is more than the sum of its parts.
      Parts are meaningful only in relation to the whole.

Of course, we can see strong similarities between this approach and the Socratic dialogues in Western thought. All these rich ancient traditions suggest that only through the cut and thrust of arguing do we draw such viewpoints out, each side with their own fragment of truth. The question is whether we are open to listening to the other side.

Third and perhaps most importantly, it is for this reason that the law goes according to the House of Hillel: they were willing to listen to the other side. In other words, the Talmud is teaching us that Hillel won the debate because of their intellectual and moral virtues. It wasn't that they necessarily had the *better* argument but rather because they *argued* better. Not only did they hear the other side, but they even prioritised teaching their opponent's view over their own.

This is the celebrated 'principle of charity' that may be traced back to Rabbi Meir, another major figure of the Talmud, who said, "A person does not say things without reason."[12] And so when we debate any matter of controversy, an important skill to nurture in our students is the ability to articulate the other side. As we saw from Ilana Redstone's hapless students, it is easy to build a straw man and knock him down. Rather, the aim must be to construct a steel woman, offering the best arguments you can for the other side – and only then aim to knock her down. This not only demonstrates to all that you take other ideas seriously, but that by doing so, you reflect on your own ideas in order to reach the truth – not in order to win the argument. As Arthur Martine in the 19th century put it so beautifully:

> In disputes upon moral or scientific points, let your aim be to come at truth, not to conquer your opponent. So you never shall be at a loss in losing the argument, and gaining a new discovery.[13]

Even more, by listening to the other view, you may even discover that you got it wrong! As we have seen, what may be orthodoxy today may well become obsolete tomorrow. After thousands of years of certainty, who could have predicted that slavery is wrong after all? Certainly not the likes of Aristotle (and nearly all those who came after). For the 12th–13th-century Talmudic commentator, Samson of Sens, this was the key reason for the Talmud including and teaching the dissenting opinion, for although their reasoning may not be accepted in one generation, things may change for the next.[14] Underlying this rationale is the liberal tradition that the "silencing of discussion is an assumption of infallibility."[15] As we are all fallible, JS Mill tells us, none of us have the authority "to decide the question for all mankind, and exclude every other person from the means of judging."[16]

The Talmud is therefore helping us frame our rules of engagement. *How* we teach controversy will be crucial to the success or otherwise of our endeavours. By fostering a school culture that "argues for the sake of Heaven," we will help our students recognise that the goal of teaching and learning about controversy is to enhance understanding and move towards the truth(s), not to win and malign our opponent. Indeed, once we recognise that we are all endeavouring to climb the same mountain – albeit from different sides – then we will seek to help each other and find out about each other's pathways in a collegiate fashion.

It's Good to Talk

In studying controversy, we are therefore moving away from a lesson plan that seeks *convergence* at its aim. It may well be that in many disciplines, such as Maths or Science, the teacher wishes to develop convergent thinking, working out a clear solution to the problem at hand. As we saw in the previous chapter, such topics are *un*controversial and so require the teacher to take a directive approach, explicitly teaching that there are right and wrong answers to the question at hand. Quite simply, the view that $1 + 1 = 3$ is not "the word of the living God." It's simply wrong! This is epistemically uncontroversial and only one answer will do. This is where logical thinking is crucial to help us think our way through scientific dilemmas.

Yet, in the study of controversy, as the Talmudic debates above suggest, we are doing something quite different. In recognising that "these and those are the words of the living God," we are seeking *divergence*, welcoming the fact that there might be multiple solutions to a problem or various reasonable ways to think about a controversy. We may sometimes also seek a "middle way" between viewpoints, appreciating that contradiction is the dynamic underlying change. In matters of controversy, therefore, this is where dialectic or dialogic reasoning is often more helpful.

As teachers, we need to think carefully about the pedagogies of controversy. As you may have guessed, based on the concept of polarity, I'm suggesting there's more than one right way of doing this. Nevertheless, there are rules of thumb that will be helpful to frame our teaching and learning of controversy in the classroom.

Pedagogies of Controversy

Teacher Stance

Little can be more undermining for a good game than to know that the referee is biased. So too with a debate or discussion. Students pick up on their teacher's stance very quickly, and any hint of bias can be the subject of playground talk or WhatsApp messaging for days to come. Teachers therefore need to think carefully about the stance they will take which would be most conducive to their students' learning.

In a seminal paper on the teacher's role in discussing controversial issues, Thomas E. Kelly[17] offered four models of teaching for us to consider. First, is the not uncommon view that we should avoid issues of controversy altogether and stick to the narrow curriculum. Whether we are supporters of Mr Gradgrind or simply teachers trying to get through the syllabus in time for the exam, many teachers support 'exclusive neutrality' in the classroom. They have enough to teach without getting into this mess and being exposed for muttering the 'wrong' opinion. Of course, this book's raison d'être is to oppose this perspective, however much I may empathise with my exhausted colleagues. As we have explained, all schools in the United Kingdom are legally bound to promote British values, while all schools around the world have an ethos they will want to promote. At a minimum, 'exclusive neutrality' often isn't an option. In reality, very few teachers want to avoid the global issues that impact the lives of their students: schools need to deal with them head on.

Second, is 'exclusive partiality': we know those teachers, don't we? Just before election time, they're preaching their political views to their students, hoping to start the revolution from the school playground. There was no better example than Muriel Spark's *Miss Jean Brodie* (both novel and film a must for all teachers) whose motto sends a shiver down the spine of ethically responsible teachers everywhere – however attracted we are to the charismatic teacher in her prime: "Little girls, I am in the business of putting old heads on young shoulders, and all my pupils are the crème de la crème. Give me a girl at an impressionable age, and she is mine for life." Even though it is Miss Brodie herself who declares that the point of education is "to lead out" rather than to "intrude," her own teaching does precisely the opposite as she builds her own set of devoted students around her own worldview. The challenges of the charismatic teacher are obvious for all. At the same time, in contrast to 'exclusive neutrality,' we can imagine times when we would want teachers to persuade students to take a view on a matter of controversy, such as opposing racism or fighting against misogyny. Religious schools may have an ethos that is centred on faith in Jesus or adherence to the Muslim way of life. Surely, teachers are right to uphold their school's ethos with parents implicitly accepting such an education by sending their children to that school.

Third is 'neutral impartiality,' which seems instinctively most popular among teachers. This is where a teacher will lead a debate on a matter of controversy without disclosing her own view. Remember, this approach differs from 'exclusive neutrality' in that the teacher sees the benefit in holding the discussion. And so, in playing the scrupulous referee, she is in a strong position to lead things as she ostensibly gives each side a fair hearing. This approach certainly promotes the search for truth as the teacher is open to hearing all perspectives in the classroom and, where appropriate, may wish to play devil's advocate to draw out the weaknesses of an expressed opinion. Of course, she should aim to do this in a fair and considered way to uphold her stance. There is a real sense in which this is the liberal democratic option, with the figure of authority remaining neutral as participants work things out for themselves, enjoying their autonomy in the process. It is felt that due to the power imbalance at play here, as soon as the teacher gives her opinion on the topic under discussion, e.g. her view in favour of abortion rights for women, then this will have a chilling effect on those students who disagree with her viewpoint. Even if unintentional, the very status of the teacher means that giving her opinion may well skew the debate. This approach also guards against accusations of Miss Jean Brodie-esque brainwashing and indoctrination – precisely the opposite of a good democratic education. Just as we want our journalists neutral on the issues they're reporting on, so too do we expect our teachers to leave their views at home. Again though, is this realistic? With students exposed to a whole host of influences, claims of neutrality in the marketplace of ideas ring hollow. Teachers are respected as authority figures, and so surely, we would like them to help guide our students on issues of real concern for our students. Just as war reporters won't remain neutral when one side is the clear aggressor in a conflict, so too, it may be argued, should our teachers weigh in on the controversial issues under scrutiny.

Fourth is the curiously named approach called 'committed impartiality.' This teacher stance, supported by Kelly himself, entails two beliefs. On the one hand, the teacher should state rather than conceal their own belief on the controversial issue being taught. On the other hand, the teacher "should foster the pursuit of truth by ensuring that competing perspectives receive a fair hearing through critical discourse."[18] As Kelly explains, the teacher should 'own' her view: explicitly share her perspective rather than simply play devil's advocate as may be employed in the 'neutral impartiality' stance. Nevertheless, when disclosing her view, it is crucial that the teacher doesn't do so in order to win her students over towards her perspective. This is why the principle of charity is employed: the teacher must provide the best versions of competing viewpoints as part of the 'impartiality' that she is pursuing. If executed successfully, the argument goes, students are exposed fairly to the differing perspectives and so empowered to decide for themselves. For Kelly, this teacher stance is commendable as the teacher gets to model her passion for the issue, supporting civic virtues such as good citizenship and community awareness. Moreover, by presenting opposing views as well as her own, she celebrates democratic authority, emphasising the importance of remaining open to other perspectives no matter how passionately one believes in the issue under discussion. Finally, by revealing her own view, the teacher lowers the barrier to become a collegial mentor. This enriches the classroom dynamic as the teacher demonstrates respect towards her students by being open about her views and being willing to be challenged for them. As teachers, if we are promoting the notion of 'hearing the other side,' we must show a willingness to do so ourselves. Modelling such behaviour sends a powerful message to our students that we're in this together: even teachers are willing to admit they are fallible, that they are still wishing to learn from others – including their students. This benefit of mutuality is described powerfully by John Hattie:

> What is most important is that teaching is visible to the student, and that the learning is visible to the teacher. The more the student becomes the teacher and the more the teacher becomes the learner, then the more successful are the outcomes.[19]

With the teacher entering into the debate herself, whilst modelling the principle of charity, students will benefit greatly from the *process* of the discussion, as well as the *content*.

I would add a note of caution, however, for particularly divisive issues, such as the Israeli-Palestinian conflict. With passions running high, I think there is a real concern that a teacher will alienate students of the opposing view. Such issues may be so visceral that they will inevitably impact on any student with skin in the game. Such conversations are rarely if ever purely epistemic, discussed only at the rational level. They often hit home in very personal and social ways. For example, can you imagine how a newly arrived immigrant in your class would feel if you the teacher expressed your sincerely held view that this country should close its doors to immigrants? Whilst this view may have coherent arguments in support, every teacher needs to be sensitive to existential and social considerations as well. The flow between the polarities of seeking truth and promoting character values remains unremitting.

Notwithstanding the benefits Kelly describes for the committed impartiality stance, I think that on such particularly controversial red-hot issues, more creative teaching mechanisms can be found:

- two or more teachers can debate the red-hot issue so that students feel that all sides of the debate have been explored fairly, without charges of bias levelled at just one teacher in control of the discussion. Such an approach still reaps the same benefits as the committed impartiality approach whilst protecting teachers from charges of alienating their students
- external organisations representing different perspectives may be invited in a bid to hear from experts in the field about the issue. By inviting speakers from both sides of the divide, the school can demonstrate a willingness to be open to different viewpoints whilst distancing themselves from any potential fallout – as long as they conduct the event with skill and sensitivity. Remember though, there is nothing stopping a student attempting to continue the debate in a follow-up lesson with their teacher, and so this approach may simply just delay the inevitable.

Ultimately, the teacher will need to decide which stance to take. As long as she thinks carefully about which approach will help bring her the outcomes she desires, she can then model the teaching process to her students. It is crucial that the teaching and learning about controversy doesn't simply focus on the *content* of the argument but also the *process*. Just as the Academy of Hillel won the day because they abided by the principle of charity, teachers have much to gain by explicitly taking their students through their chosen teaching method.

Teacher Stances for Teaching Controversy

	Exclusive neutrality	Exclusive partiality	Neutral impartiality	Committed impartiality
How does it work?	Avoid issues of controversy altogether and stick to the narrow curriculum	Teacher discloses her view with the aim to persuading her students to adopt her point of view	Teacher fosters a discussion of controversy without disclosing her own view	Teacher discloses her view but with the aim of modelling how to argue for one's perspective rather than persuading her students to adopt her point of view
Strengths	• Saves time • Protects teacher	• Lends humanity to teacher – helps connect to student • No such thing as neutrality: help counter negative influences	• Principle of charity • Democratic values • Upholds autonomy of students • Fair and balanced management of discussion	• Principle of charity • Lends humanity to teacher – helps connect to students • No such thing as neutrality: help counter negative influences • Model civic responsibility in sharing one's view
Weaknesses	• Miss out on core aspect of education	• Charges of brainwashing and indoctrination • Undermines autonomy and democratic values	• No such thing as neutrality • Some issues deserve a clear teacher view, e.g. racism • Asking students to give their views without offering yours smacks of hypocrisy	• Could alienate students in a particularly divisive subject • May lead to charges of bias by some
When to use	• Avoid potential time-wasting	• Upholding legal duties, e.g. promoting British values • Supporting the school's ethos	• Extremely contentious issues whereby giving one's view may alienate students and expose the teacher	• Nearly all areas of controversy • Beware of particularly divisive issues

A time for direct, explicit instruction...

Now that the teacher has adopted a clear stance, she needs to think about the pedagogies to adopt to make the most out of the ensuing lesson on controversy. As anyone with an even cursory interest in education knows, pedagogy has been dominated by what Guy Claxton has aptly called a 'Punch and Judy' show between the 'trads' and the 'progs.'[20] Claxton himself pithily sums up the views of each pedagogical school in this table below:

Points of Difference between Traditional and Progressive Approaches to Education[21]

Traditional	Progressive
Emphasis on knowledge	Emphasis on whole child development
Preparation for further study	Preparation for life
Motivated by grades/rewards/punishments	Motivated by intrinsic love of learning
Character = good behaviour	Character = adventurous spirit
Focus on achievement	Focus on development
Content is predetermined and scheduled	Content can be opportunistic/responsive
Little choice/control by learner	Significant choice/control by learner
Little space for learners' own interests	Considerable space for learners' own interests
Disembedded from real-life concerns/contexts	Embedded in real-life concerns/contexts
Major emphasis on reading and writing	Emphasis on talk
Understanding demonstrated by explanation	Understanding shown by making and creating
Learning is (primarily) individual	Learning is (equally) social and discursive
Time to practise skills	Time to experiment and investigate
Teaching by informing and explaining	Teaching encourages grappling and thinking
Learning is memorising	Learning is exploring

So, who is right? As you may have guessed by now, I will take a both/and approach to glean the best from these two legitimate pathways in learning. I just can't believe the typically brilliant teacher out there isn't making the best of both worlds – often dependent on what they are trying to achieve. And when it comes to teaching and learning about controversy, we can show precisely how much both sides of the debate have to offer as we adopt different pedagogical techniques – traditional and progressive – side by side.

Let's return to the inspiring Father Andrew we met in Chapter 1. In order to teach Christian doctrine fully, he first taught the arguments *against* the existence of God. This meant reading the great atheists: Marx, Beauvoir, Feuerbach, and Nietzsche. Father Andrew guided his students carefully, determining a comprehensive and clear syllabus, informing and explaining the complex and nuanced ideas for his students. He built up their knowledge carefully so that they could be fully informed about all sides of the debate. This is the best of explicit instructional guidance, so well explained by Kirschner and Hendrick:

> Explicit instructional guidance is when teachers *fully explain* the concepts and skills that students are required to learn. The provided guidance can be achieved through a variety of media, such as lectures, modelling, videos, computer-based presentations, and realistic demonstrations. *It can also include class discussions and activities – if the teacher ensures that through the discussion or activity, the relevant information is explicitly provided and practised.* [emphasis added]

In order to have a fruitful debate that spirals upwards in terms of quality and understanding, the participants must know what they are talking about. A debate marked by students simply asserting their view or giving opinions without the requisite knowledge or understanding only belittles the subject matter at hand. Our students must be keenly aware of the mastery required to fully grasp complex controversial issues. This often requires a master teacher to provide the necessary curriculum and help frame their students' understanding. As Kirschner has famously shown, minimally guided instruction – sadly still seen all too often in the classroom – leads to serious misconceptions as learners are expected to discover the (hopefully difficult) concepts on their own.[22] As the debate goes in circles, students often come to the awful conclusion that all opinions are equally legitimate. It may sound harsh but indulging ignorance is not a virtue! Remember, whilst everyone is entitled to their own opinion, they're not entitled to their own facts. And so opinions formed on the basis of ignorance or erroneous understanding simply isn't acceptable in the classroom.

Note too that explicit instructional guidance boasts a range of pedagogical tools to bring real excitement to the classroom. Just as Kearney remembers his lessons so fondly all those years later, I'm sure we can all remember those brilliant teachers, with real mastery and passion for their subject, imparting intellectual gold to us. We would be much poorer without such brilliant minds supporting effective and efficient learning.

...and a time for dialogic education

But I wouldn't leave it there. Just as we have built up our knowledge, so too do we need to talk – and listen. Yes, learning is about memorising but it's also about exploring. And exploring through dialogue is a nod to the best of ancient traditions dating back to Socrates and Plato as well as the Talmudic sages.

'Dialogue' is a word we have from the Greek, meaning a *conversation*. Of course, this can take place through many forms of communication, including writing and even music. The point is that through dialogue, we are *exchanging ideas* and so building on what the other is saying. As Mikhail Bakhtin, a 20th-century Russian philosopher of language, defined it: "If an answer does not give rise to a new question from itself, it falls out of the dialogue."[23] Importantly, we can therefore exclude 'conversations' that don't meet this requirement. We've all been there or observed as bewildered onlookers: those 'conversations' which are anything but dialogues. Rather, they are a series of *monologues* as each side aims to win the battle. With neither side listening, participants are instead thinking how to defeat their opponent. Social media quarrels often have this predictable gamesmanship feel until at some point *reductio ad Hitlerum* kicks in. This is the worst and most common form of the *ad hominem*, delegitimising your opponent by saying they have the same views as Hitler. (This is usually the weapon of those who really have nothing left to say...[24]) And so be on your guard that the dialogue you are promoting really does support the participants exploring and building on others' ideas.

Robin Alexander, a pioneer of dialogic education, helpfully explains related terms that feed into the dialogue we do want to see:

- *Discussion*: literally 'shaking up' in Latin, denotes an investigation or examination, as the participants are searching, digging deeper
- *Deliberation*: wearing its heart on its sleeve, this is when the discussion is considered and attentive, as participants carefully weigh up the ideas
- *Argumentation*: when deliberation marshals reasons or evidence in its quest to build, assess, or defend a case.[25]

Now, with controversial issues, we want to promote all three elements to enrich our students' learning, to create what may be called a 'shared dialogic space.'[26] This is where interesting things start to happen, with Maurice Merleau-Ponty, a philosopher, writing that when dialogue works, it is no longer possible to say who is thinking because we find ourselves thinking together. For this to happen, the environment must be *deliberative* rather than *disputational*, predicated on respect, mutual concern, and communality. As the class explores together and engages collaboratively, the learning will go beyond any individual student's own reasoning, leading to what Neil Mercer has labelled, 'interthinking.'[27]

Of course, there may be times when the teacher may wish to set up a *debate*, aiming towards an outright winner, perhaps through a class vote, based on the arguments that have been heard. This is a *disputational* method where the aim is to win rather than explore. Such debates are enjoyable and help test the presentation skills and knowledge of our participants, drawing out the key arguments they may be expected to articulate. In such a framework, the teacher may look towards a *convergent* outcome, wishing for a conclusive argument to win the day. Either way, teachers should again remember to explicitly model their approach and explain to the class the purpose of any such *deliberative* or *disputational* dialogue they undertake.

Nurturing Critical Friends

Let me conclude with the story of Rabbi Yochanan and Resh Lakish, two of the greatest Talmudic sages celebrated for their dialogic partnership. Whilst the former was a leading rabbinic intellectual, the latter started out his adult life as a bandit. Through a chance meeting, Resh Lakish agreed to give up his criminal lifestyle and come under the pupillage of Rabbi Yochanan. Their friendship soon turned them into family as Resh Lakish went on to marry Rabbi Yochanan's sister. They developed a learning partnership, a Hevruta, that became legendary. Day and night, year after year, they would challenge each other over all aspects of Jewish law, on which they were both the leading lights. Whilst their arguments were ferocious, they were always *deliberative*, aiming for the truth rather than to win.

Sadly though, their final study session took on a dark and fateful twist. Debating an intricate area of ritual law, their subject touched on the status of purity for metal objects, including knives and spears. When Resh Lakish gave his opinion, Rabbi Yochanan made a dig: "A thief knows best about the tools of stealing." This led to a falling out between the two, with Resh Lakish so hurt by his study partner's mockery of his past that he fell ill and died.

Rabbi Yochanan was grief stricken. He knew he could never find someone to replace Resh Lakish in terms of his friendship and his intellectual brilliance. After a while, the sages recommended a Rabbi Eliezer ben Pedat, known for his sharp mind. As they studied and Rabbi Yochanan gave his opinion, Rabbi Eliezer would strengthen his study partner's argument by providing sources to support his claims. Rabbi Yochanan's stinging rebuke is instructive:

> He said, "You think you're on the level of Resh Lakish?!" When I would give my opinion on any matter, Resh Lakish would challenge me with 24 objections! I would then respond with 24 answers. Our debates led to a fuller understanding of the law. And all you have to say for yourself is, "there is a source that supports you?!" Don't you think I already know how strong my argument is?![28]

Tragically, Rabbi Yochanan left the study hall tearing his clothes in a sign of mourning, screaming out, "Where are you, Resh Lakish? Where are you?" The Talmud tells us he never recovered and died soon afterwards. Without his critical friend, Rabbi Yochanan just couldn't continue.

This tragic tale has much to teach us and our students about how we debate and discuss ideas of controversy. First, in the lovely phrase of Paul A. Kirschner and Carl Hendrick, the narrative shows that a "novice is not a little expert."[29] Rabbi Yochanan took Resh Lakish under his wing and taught him, regulating his learning. It was only when Resh Lakish became a master, a real expert, that they became study partners, interthinking through their dialogue. As we saw before, the study of controversial topics without the prerequisite knowledge, framed by minimal intervention and teacher guidance, often leads to a lesson where all are going in circles with none the wiser.

Second, Rabbi Yochanan's failure was 'playing the man,' ridiculing his intellectual sparring partner rather than sticking to the argument. This is the most grotesque of logical fallacies known as the *ad hominem* attack – and cost them both their lives! We must never allow our students to argue against an opponent by attempting to discredit the person rather than the argument itself (however much our politicians may model this in public). Outbursts such as:

Well, you would say that wouldn't you?
It's because you're so biased that you think that way...
They only think that because they're so ignorant.

These are pitfalls in arguing that must be avoided. After Resh Lakish gave his view, it was for Rabbi Yochanan to provide reasons why he might agree or disagree. As soon as someone goes for the person, alarm bells should be ringing that they have lost their way on the argument. It is also a sure indicator that they are more interested in winning than seeking the truth.

Third, the success of the study partnership was predicated on them both being each other's *critical friend*. With both participants seeking the truth, rather than being proven correct, they sought to find flaws in their opponents' arguments, forcing the other to sharpen his claim. Despite being a world away in terms of religious belief, my sense is that there would have been a great deal of mutual respect between our Talmudic sages and the consummate Cambridge atheist don, Bertrand Russell. The former lived by the latter's eighth commandment of learning: "Find more pleasure in intelligent dissent than in passive agreement, for, if you value intelligence as you should, the former implies a deeper agreement than the latter." When issues of controversy are debated, simply agreeing with me doesn't help me in any way to further my own understanding. And if my aim is to try and grasp the truth(s) of the matter, then only by being a critical friend, willing to challenge me and take my views on, can I hope to develop my own thinking. This is the epitome of 'interthinking,' whereby we combine our intellectual resources to achieve more than we could as individuals on our own. Once Rabbi Yochanan realised he had lost this 'dialogic space,' he could no longer be himself, as his ideas were dependent on Resh Lakish's questioning and criticisms. Culturally, this is borne out in the difference between the enveloping silence of a library in contrast to the incessant hubbub of the yeshivah, the Jewish study hall. Just as I need quiet to grasp the idea I am researching, I also need the to and fro of dialoguing to sharpen that idea with my critical friend. Lessons where we can model both environments as we flow from one technique to the other often lead to quite magical outcomes.

Notes

1. Remember though, in Chapter 2, we saw a fascinating argument on why we should take serious 'disgust' seriously.
2. Herodotus. (1997) *The Histories*. London: Everyman, p. 243.
3. See Donald E. Brown's fascinating 'List of Human Universals' – the things we all do, wherever we are in the world. Retrieved from: http://joelvelasco.net/teaching/2890/brownlisthumanuniversals.pdf.
4. For those of you up for a challenge that is harder than you might think, try this one: give reasons why you think eating your ancestors is wrong. Assume our family members are open to different death rituals after they leave us – whether burying, cremating, or eating – can you give clear reasons as to why one is preferable to the other? (Please don't be tempted to go down the "it's the law" route. After all, debate and discussion are the best ways to change the law or reinforce it.)
5. A brilliant novel that explores this theme is *Never Let Me Go* by Kazuo Ishiguro.
6. J.S. Mill. (1992) *On Liberty*. London: Everyman, p. 52.
7. Adin Steinsaltz. (2010) *The Essential Talmud*. Jerusalem: Maggid Books, p. xi.
8. Jonthan Sacks. (2018) 'God Loves Those Who Argue.' Retrieved from: https://www.rabbisacks.org/covenant-conversation/shemot/god-loves-those-who-argue/.
9. Babylonian Talmud, Eruvin 13b.
10. Midrash Bamidbar Raba 13:16.
11. Cited from Richard Nisbett. (2015) *Tools for Smart Thinking*. London: Penguin, p. 225.
12. Babylonian Talmud, Arachin 5b.
13. Arthur Martine. (1866) *Martine's Hand-Book of Etiquette, and Guide to True Politeness*. Retrieved from: https://www.gutenberg.org/files/36048/36048-h/36048-h.htm.
14. Babylonian Talmud, Eduyot 1:4.
15. J.S. Mill. (1992) *On Liberty*. London: Everyman, p. 19.
16. Ibid.
17. Thomas E. Kelly. (1986) 'Discussing Controversial Issues: Four Perspectives on the Teacher's Role,' *Theory and Research in Social Education*, 14(2): 113-138.
18. Ibid., p. 130.
19. John Hattie. (2009) *Visible Learning*. Oxford: Routledge, p. 25.
20. Guy Claxton. (2021) *The Future of Teaching*. Oxford: Routledge, Chapter 1.
21. Ibid., p. 7.

22. P.A. Kirschner et al. (2006) 'Why Minimal Guidance during Instruction Does Not Work: An Analysis of the Failure of Constructivist Discovery, Problem-based, Experiential, and Inquiry-based Teaching,' *Educational Psychologist*, 46(2): 75–86.
23. Mikhail Bakhtin. (1986) *Speech Genres and Other Late Essays*. Austin: University of Texas, p. 186.
24. Although to be fair, it might also be used to shout down an actual fascist or neo-Nazi.
25. Robin Alexander. (2020) *A Dialogic Teaching Companion*. Oxford: Routledge, p. 36.
26. For an excellent introduction to Dialogic Education, see Rupert Wegerif, 'Defining "Dialogic Education."' Retrieved from: https://www.rupertwegerif.name/blog/defining-dialogic-education.
27. Neil Mercer, cited in Alexander, (2020), p. 108.
28. Babylonian Talmud, Bava Metzia 84a.
29. Paul A. Kirschner and Carl Hendrick. (2020) *How Learning Happen*. Oxford: Routledge, Chapter 1.

4 Mental Toolkit

A Londoner's Dilemma

Figure 4.1 Aerial View of Tower Bridge in London
Source: Shutterstock

I live in London. I was born and grew up here. I married a Londoner and we now raise our kids in this truly global city (Figure 4.1).

And for fellow Londoners I like asking the following question:

How much of the United Kingdom is built on?

To give you an idea of what 'built on' means, let's use the following term called 'continuous urban fabric' (CUF). This refers to an area where 80–100% of the land surface is built on. So, up to a fifth might be parks or gardens, but the vast majority is built on. What figure comes into your mind?

Tick one of the options below:

- 90% and above
- 80–89%
- 70–79%
- 60–69%

DOI: 10.4324/9781003298281-6

- 50-59%
- 40-49%
- 30-39%
- 20-29%
- 10-19%
- 0-9%.

Well, if you're a Londoner (or living in any other large city), I'm thinking that you guessed a lot more than the actual answer of 0.1%!

And even if we are talking about 'discontinuous urban fabric,' which is where 50–80% of the land surface is built on, then such places only account for 5.3% of the whole country.[1]

I like asking my students this question because the answers I get are invariably out of sync with reality. And it reveals how far off we are about something so close to home but in an unthreatening way. The answer really surprises those of us who get the answer very wrong. In the words of Dan Ariely, a leading behavioural scientist, we are "predictably irrational."[2] Whilst we like to think we are rational and think things through in a clear and logical way, this question serves as a healthy reminder that we're influenced by things we're not even aware of. And so the reasons many of us – especially Londoners – get it so wrong should bring a little intellectual humility when discussing issues of controversy about areas of real complexity. As we'll see below, our minds provide numerous heuristics – mental shortcuts – to ease our cognitive load and provide calculated guesses. These are hugely helpful in everyday life. But every so often, we can suffer from biases that throw us way off. Here are three such biases that may affect Londoners thinking about urban Britain:

1. **Availability heuristic:** this is a cognitive bias in which you make a decision based on an example, information, or recent experience that is readily available to you, even though it may not be the best example to inform your decision.[3] With my students all living in London, they were no doubt drawing on their own personal experiences to inform their answers. As we'll see below, rules of thumb such as relying on personal experiences, can be sometimes very helpful but as we saw in this dilemma, the availability heuristic can lead to wildly wrong answers.
2. **Framing effect:** this is a cognitive bias wherein your choice from a set of options is influenced more by the presentation than the substance of the given information.[4] I'll now readily confess that by putting up a picture of central London just above my question, I was sneakily aiming to frame the dilemma in a way that would have you unduly influenced by the context of that London skyline. Whether we like it or not, messages coming at us from all directions in daily life manipulate our decision-making every day.
3. **Anchoring:** this is a heuristic that causes your first judgement to influence your view on all that follows. The order in which we receive information helps determine our perceptions of any subsequent information or viewpoint. Note how I started high in the options I offered: 90% and above, in declining 10% reductions. In class, as I begin with a high anchoring point, I know that just after a few options, the first student will raise her hand very shortly afterwards. This creates a second anchoring point, with the first response in the class influencing the subsequent voices in the classroom, usually leading to all hands up by the time we reach 40%. I once tried the question on a classroom of highly intelligent 15 year olds. One girl, who had put her hand up at 40%, then shouted out that she thought it was probably about 5%. I asked why she said that, and she admitted having learned of this figure recently in a Geography lesson. Remarkably, even though this girl actually knew the answer, peer pressure had led her to give a wildly wrong answer! Even this bright girl proved to be predictably irrational.

Turning Up the Heat

Now I know you're on your guard. So, let's turn our attention to something a little more controversial:

Gay Marriage

If you're a **liberal** (or on the left), read what **Donald Trump** had to say about how he defines a marriage:

> "I believe that marriage is the union between a man and a woman. Now, for me as a Christian - for me - for me as a Christian, it is also a sacred union. God's in the mix."

If you're a **conservative** (or on the right), read what **Barack Obama** had to say about his gay friends getting married:

> "I know both of them, and they get along wonderfully. It's a marriage that's going to work. I'm very happy for them. If two people dig each other, they dig each other."

How do these quotations make you feel?

I can imagine that many liberals get fired up by President Trump's traditional stance just as many conservatives do about President Obama's acceptance of gay marriage. With lines drawn ever more sharply between an Obama-style liberal and a Trump-style conservative, there will probably be little understanding or empathy for the other side: "You see, I told you that their views were awful! What can you expect of such a person?!"

Yet what if I now shock my more unsuspecting readers and told you that it was actually Barack Obama who really said that "marriage is the union between a man and a woman" and that it was really Donald Trump who was quoted wishing congratulations to his friend, Elton John, upon his civil partnership to David Furnish in 2005?[5]

I can now imagine either side being a little more forgiving of 'their man': liberals will no doubt point to Obama's 'evolution' on gay rights just as conservatives will point to Trump's defence of the traditional family as president. They will excuse 'their man' for having 'got it wrong' but ultimately coming to their senses. At the same time, many will no doubt point to the opposition and decry their changing stances as little more than political opportunism and classic examples of sophistry that go to the heart of why we can't trust the other side anymore.

What accounts for our behaviour?

Why are we willing to let personalities and loyalties get in the way of the facts?

On a heated issue that pits supporters of Trump vs fans of Obama, we know that it is all too likely that partisans on both sides of the divide will be guilty of the following biases as they think *and* feel through the issues:

- **In-group bias:** the all-too human tendency to favour those who are part of our group. This leads us to be more forgiving of those on our side and less inclined to recognise the virtues of the other side. Of course, while they're as "thick as thieves," we're simply "birds of a feather flocking together."
- **The halo effect:** and when we like someone - especially someone on our team - we'll make any excuse for them, with impartiality flying out the window. Of course, when we dislike our opponent, it is hard to recognise any good on the other side. If we see them behaving positively, it must be down to bad motives.
- **Belief bias:** with liberals and conservatives alike having very fixed views of leaders like Obama and Trump, they are likely to rationalise anything that supports their belief.

And once our students are far down the rabbit hole, it becomes so much more difficult to educate about the topic of controversy at hand. As we saw in Chapter 1, trying to teach an opposing viewpoint to a student with very fixed views about an issue of controversy can often backfire: it's not that the student doesn't know about the other side but that the very act of challenging their viewpoint only strengthens their attachment to it. If we feel like the other side is preaching to us, telling us what to do and what to think, then we'll dig our heels in. Whether you're a parent or a teacher, you'll know the power of reverse psychology: from Adam and Eve in the Garden of Eden to young people in our care, **reactance bias** is all too human.

It is true that purely rational beings will only consider the epistemic arguments. They will be open to reason and evidence – wherever it comes from. The problem is I have yet to meet such a person! This is especially so when it comes to issues of controversy. When a matter is important to us, it may even become part of our own identity – like a religious or political belief. And so an attack on my worldview becomes an attack on me and on those closest to me. There is a feeling that the 'other side' is trying to restrict me and constrain my thoughts. The issue is thus no longer simply epistemic but becomes existential and social too. Passionate reactions about issues of controversy put into perspective the observation that neuroscientist Antonio Damasio made about human psychology: "We are not thinking machines that feel; rather, we are feeling machines that think." And as we will see, educational pathways that don't get to grips with our students as *thinking* and *feeling* beings will lack the necessary toolkit for successful outcomes.

Bringing the Behavioural Sciences into the Classroom

It was the great Scottish enlightenment philosopher David Hume who overturned thousands of years of thinking on this issue. From Plato to the modern economists, the commonly held belief about human decision-making is that each of us is – or at least should be – a rational agent who pursues our goals through reason, evidence, and intelligence. In one of the most influential calls for enlightenment thinking, Baruch Spinoza, the 17th-century Dutch philosopher, wrote, "Men who are governed by reason… seek nothing for themselves that they would not desire for the rest of mankind; and so are just, faithful, and honourable."[6] Of course, all the great champions of reason, not least Spinoza, recognised that many people "do not abide by the precepts of reason" due to the "human weakness" of "emotion." For such rationalists, which many educational models follow, all would be fine if only we could teach students to be purely rational beings, dismissing those emotions and intuitions that put us on the wrong path.

Yet it was Hume, a century after Spinoza, who recognised that there are no "men who are governed by reason." Turning that idea on its head, he made the pithy observation that, "Reason is, and ought only to be, the slave of the passions, and can never pretend to any other office than to serve and obey them."[7] In other words, intuitions *precede* reasoning. As humans, we often have a feeling deep inside of us that something doesn't feel quite right. This leaves many of us finding ourselves *rationalising* our beliefs rather than arriving at them through *reason* and evidence. In a nod to the power of confirmation bias, Warren Buffett, the legendary investor, said: "What the human being is best at doing is interpreting all new information so that their prior conclusions remain intact." Even Steven Pinker, a leading champion of rationalism, has conceded: "Whatever its ontological status may be, a moral sense is part of the standard equipment of the human mind. It's the only mind we've got, and we have no choice but to take its intuitions seriously."[8]

The impact of Hume's revolution about how we actually operate must frame the way we present ideas and controversies in the classroom. Plato's rationalist model focuses on the evidence and hard facts based on the belief that an epistemic education can ultimately rein in our passions and irrational desires. But as we have seen, our teaching needs to take into account the fact that our students are "predictably irrational" and recognise that intuitions and emotions are part and parcel of who we are– for better or for worse. As the psychologist Jonathan Haidt has warned, "the worship of reason… is a delusion. It is an example of faith in something that does not exist."[9] Any educational approach that maintains such faith is quite simply a "human-incompatible education"[10] and will backfire. For our pedagogy of controversy to be successful, we therefore need to teach according to how students really are rather than how we'd like them to be.

This is why it remains perplexing that although the behavioural sciences have significantly impacted so many areas of our lives, their findings remain sorely lacking in how we teach and learn. Dan Ariely spells out the aims of the behavioural sciences which I think chime well with our goals as educators:

> Behavioural economists want to understand human frailty and to find more compassionate, realistic, and effective ways for people to avoid temptation, exert more self-control, and ultimately reach their long-term goals… As we gain some understanding about what really drives our behaviours and what steers us astray… we can gain control over our money, relationships, resources, safety, and health, both as individuals and as a society.[11]

Now there's a well-rounded education we can all sign up to! So, I want to offer a mental toolkit that takes up the principles of the behavioural sciences. Of course, our focus is on teaching and learning about controversy but based on my own teaching experiences, the principles discussed below will be useful for so many aspects of school life, whether academic, pastoral, or how we collaborate with our colleagues.

Thinking about Thinking (and Feeling)

Shepard tables never cease to amaze me. However, many times I see the brilliant optical illusion, my brain tells me that the long and narrow table on the left is obviously longer than the squarish table to the right (Figure 4.2).

And yes, I'm enough of a geek to have actually measured the length of both tables only to be surprised by the truth (every time). However much I cognitively *know* that they are the same size, it just doesn't *feel* right. This is a very helpful metaphor for how our thinking can be led astray.

Let's raise the stakes a little further. There are a few professionals as well trained as pilots. For obvious reasons, the expertise required can mean the difference between life and death. When all is fine and well, the pilot will follow "visual flight rules" (VFR), operating the aircraft through his expertise.

However, things can go wrong. Perhaps the weather outside is so foggy that relying on human vision simply isn't safe. When this happens, pilots must follow "instrument flight rules" (IFR), where they defer to the plane's sophisticated instruments and allow the aircraft to take over.

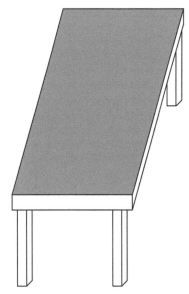

Figure 4.2 Image of Shepard Table
Source: Shutterstock

Reliance on IFR is also necessary when the pilot loses their 'feel' of the plane. The pilot may suffer from an 'optical illusion' through experiencing vertigo. According to the FAA Airplane Flying Handbook:

> Spatial disorientation has been a significant factor in many airplane upset accidents. Accident data from 2008 to 2013 shows nearly 200 accidents associated with spatial disorientation with more than 70% of those being fatal. All pilots are susceptible to false sensory illusions while flying at night or in certain weather conditions. These illusions can lead to a conflict between actual attitude indications and what the pilot senses is the correct attitude. Disoriented pilots may not always be aware of their orientation error. Many airplane upsets occur while the pilot is engaged in some task that takes attention away from the flight instruments or outside references. Others perceive a conflict between bodily senses and the flight instruments, and allow the airplane to divert from the desired flightpath because they cannot resolve the conflict.[12]

The handbook goes on to provide guidance on how to cope with such spatial disorientation. Crucially, there is much a pilot can do *before* the flight begins as well as instructions to follow once the vertigo kicks in. The first piece of advice is: "Understand the causes of these illusions and remain constantly alert for them." In other words, gaining an *awareness* of the potential problems one may face is the first step towards correcting for them. When even the experts need a primer on the pitfalls they face, it is absurd to think that young students can be expected to think about complex issues of controversy without the thinking tools to be on guard against the biases and fallacies that hamper so many debates.

Yet even with all this training, with all the preparation in the world, pilots might still experience vertigo in the heat of the moment. When suffering from such an optical illusion, the FAA guidance is instructive: the "most important" thing to do is to "become proficient in the use of flight instruments and rely upon them. Trust the instruments and disregard your sensory perceptions."

Be prepared! Be aware of the illusions that one may face. By recognising them, one may be able to confront them and ultimately overcome them. But if one doesn't even try to understand them, then there is little hope of beating such illusions. Equally, the moral virtue of humility is paramount to a healthy outcome. For all the cognitive acceptance of the illusion, if one doesn't recognise that they too might be vulnerable, then there is little hope that one will take in and internalise these crucial rules of thumb. Just as the pilot needs to defer to the instruments and recognise his own limitations, good thinkers are critical thinkers, continually on the lookout for those biases and fallacies that cloud our thinking.

Developing *Phronesis*: Teaching Rules of Thumb for the Critical Thinker

From my own experience in the classroom, it has become obvious to me that schools should teach explicitly *how* to think so that our students are aware of those critical thinking tools that they can employ in the heat of the argument. Too many students lack *phronesis*, that ultimate virtue extolled by the likes of Socrates, Plato, and Aristotle, which can be translated as 'prudence' or 'mindfulness' in modern-day English. I'm after a sense of 'practical wisdom' which is helpfully summed up by the Jubilee Centre for Character & Virtues as follows:

> Practical wisdom (*phronesis*) is the integrative virtue, developed through experience and critical reflection, which enables us to perceive, know desire and act with good sense. This includes discerning, deliberative action in situations where virtues collide.[13]

In working towards phronesis, we have to develop the whole character, nurturing intellectual, moral, civic, and performance virtues in what the Jubilee Centre calls 'The Building Blocks of Character'[14] (Figure 4.3):

So before throwing your students into the lion's den, be sure they are well equipped with a mental toolkit that gets them thinking about their thinking. Daniel Kahneman, the father of behavioural economics, provides the tagline to help explain to your students why preparation is elemental to success: "Intelligence is not only the ability to reason; it is also the ability to find relevant material in memory and to deploy attention when needed."

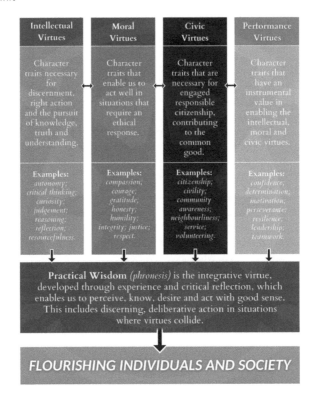

Intellectual Virtues	Moral Virtues	Civic Virtues	Performance Virtues
Character traits necessary for discernment, right action and the pursuit of knowledge, truth and understanding.	Character traits that enable us to act well in situations that require an ethical response.	Character traits that are necessary for engaged responsible citizenship, contributing to the common good.	Character traits that have an instrumental value in enabling the intellectual, moral and civic virtues.
Examples: *autonomy; critical thinking; curiosity; judgement; reasoning; reflection; resourcefulness.*	**Examples:** *compassion; courage; gratitude; honesty; humility; integrity; justice; respect.*	**Examples:** *citizenship; civility; community awareness; neighbourliness; service; volunteering.*	**Examples:** *confidence; determination; motivation; perseverance; resilience; leadership; teamwork.*

Practical Wisdom *(phronesis)* is the integrative virtue, developed through experience and critical reflection, which enables us to perceive, know, desire and act with good sense. This includes discerning, deliberative action in situations where virtues collide.

FLOURISHING INDIVIDUALS AND SOCIETY

Figure 4.3 The Building Blocks of Character (Reprinted with Permission from the Jubilee Centre)

In practical terms, there are two ways teachers can do this: ideally, create a Critical Thinking course – and this chapter aims to provide the outline of such a course. Whether one meets weekly for a term or over a year, the more rules of thumb studied, understood, and applied, will help your students be that bit sharper when listening and speaking. If time in the curriculum doesn't allow for such a standalone course, then prior to each issue of controversy you raise in the classroom, think explicitly about the thinking skills that you want to draw out in that lesson. Content and skills go together: just as you explicitly teach knowledge, be sure to provide those complementary skills to help frame and apply such content so your students can develop greater autonomy going forward. For the rest of this chapter, I will provide the key rules of thumb that I think every high school student should know to help them get the most out of learning about issues of controversy.

Critical Thinking Course for Controversial Topics

Phase 1: Civic Online Skills

In the 21st century, there are fewer thinking skills more important than how to navigate the internet. With the 'democratisation of knowledge,' we're getting our news sources from anywhere and everywhere. Young people in particular rely on social media more than traditional news outlets. With the benefits (and downsides) of artificial intelligence (AI) beginning to make its presence felt, there is no question that AI will be a game-changer in ways we can barely imagine. In the age of fake news and unregulated media, what rules of thumb can we put in place to ensure that our students are not duped by what they are reading?

A few years back, I took a course on Holocaust Education. For a research assignment, I googled the information I was looking for and simply clicked on one of the top links that came up. I thought I hit the jackpot as the website I arrived at was slick, comprehensive, and seemingly scholarly. As I navigated through different articles, I'm embarrassed to admit that it took me quite a while before I realised that I was trawling through an extremist Holocaust revisionist website that aimed to prove that the Holocaust was a hoax.[15] Dressed up in academic language and claiming articles from so-called experts with alleged PhDs, I admit that I was taken in until I started to take in what was actually being written. As someone who has taught courses on the Holocaust and helped lead educational tours to Poland, I had enough expertise on the subject to realise that this website could not be trusted. Yet I'm not sure many students just beginning their journey learning about the Holocaust wouldn't be duped by such a website. And if such websites exist about the Holocaust, we know they exist on just about any and every topic of controversy under the sun. With trusted search engines like Google helping to take us down the rabbit hole just one click away, students are in danger of falling for whatever these websites are spewing at them, especially if they have the veneer of authority and authenticity.

As part of their mental toolkit, students must be able to evaluate sources on the internet. I can't think of a more helpful way to start a critical thinking course than on civic online reasoning.[16] Whatever your subject, choose a topic of research that has an element of controversy and test your students' ability to evaluate the sources they come across on the web:

Controversies within Subjects

Geography: Is climate change real?
History: Explain the causes of the Israeli–Palestinian conflict.
Literature: Was Shakespeare really the author of the plays attributed to him?
Psychology: Nature or nurture?

Whether you choose one of the topics above or your own area of research, Professor Sam Wineburg of Stanford University offers three strategies for your students to try out. I'd recommend your students fill out a template like the one below so they can reflect on how they weighed up the trustworthiness of the sites they found.

Civic Online Reasoning Metacognition Activity

Topic of research:
Name of website:
How did I come across this website?
What markers suggested to me that this website is trustworthy?
What markers suggested to me that I should be sceptical of this website?
Did the website have an agenda? If so, what was it and how do I know?
What could be a better way to search for websites for this research topic?
Did scrutinising the URL and Google blurb help?
Could Wikipedia help? Explain how.
Could an AI platform help? Explain how.
Grade the website's reliability (out of 5):
5/5 is the Gold Standard: everyone can rely on this website
0/5 means stay away: the website is a source for fake news

---

1. **Read laterally:** most of us stay on the website to check if we like what we see. We might get sucked in if the domain name ends in .org or if the website has an important institution-type name. If the website is slick, contains long words and has lovely illustrations, then there's often no turning back. And with AI platforms offering comprehensive answers in seconds, many students are tempted to sit back and let their device do the thinking for them. Now encourage your students to leave the website and do background checks on it – I would recommend at least three such checks. These could range from a simple, "Is Website X reliable?" to checking up on the names associated with the website and seeing who the people might be associated with. Are they recognised authorities in their field? Do they have an agenda? Are they being funded by anyone? Of course, depending on time and sceptic levels, always keep in mind Juvenal's timeless advice: "Quis custodiet ipsos custodes?" In other words, "Who watches the watchers?" Feel free to check up on those commenting on the website you're looking up. Can they themselves be relied upon?

2. **Show click restraint:** for a website to be at the top of a Google search says more about how well the owners are at gaming the system than how reliable their website is. And as we saw above, the anchoring bias means that the first website your students see will have a huge impact on how they view the topic under research. I would be dreadfully worried if my students first saw a Holocaust denial website when researching the genocide. As Wineburg puts it, a key skill for students to learn is click restraint: rather than simply click on the first (few) websites that come up, encourage your students to scrutinise the URL and the little accompanying blurb for clues on the veracity of the website first. Again, use a form like the one above for students to reflect on the differences in quality of the websites they discover. By checking the URLs and blurbs, how many Google search pages did they get through? Did they still only rely on those top two or three links?

3. **Use Wikipedia (and AI)**[17]! It's time to change guidance and dismiss the snobbish school bans on Wikipedia and new AI platforms like ChatGPT. Of course, always be on guard for sneaky copy and paste jobs (from any website) but Wikipedia really is an internet success story and the positive side of democratising knowledge. Many teachers and school librarians reject Wikipedia, pointing out that anyone can edit Wikipedia, not just the experts. On the flipside, this means that Wikipedia pages – especially the most popular ones – are reviewed hundreds if not thousands of times.[18] So instead of banning Wikipedia, teach students how to use the fifth most visited website effectively and responsibly. First, one can check on the reliability of an article – especially those contentious ones – by clicking on the 'Talk' tab, which is on the top left of the page, next to the 'Article' tab. Wikipedia helpfully analyses all aspects of the article under scrutiny, with recommendations for improvements where standards may fall short. Again, the template above can be amended for students to evaluate the relevant Wikipedia pages they have viewed. Second, Wikipedia is particularly useful for references. Simply click on any footnote to view the source(s) used in the article. In teaching your students to read laterally, they will now know that where no source is offered, alarm bells should be ringing. But where references are available, find out about the source used by the author. This is a particularly useful, if nuanced exercise as it shows students how blurry the lines often are: some sources will be more reliable than others. The aim is to nurture a default scepticism and sense of humility when fact-checking: our students should take nothing for granted. With AI in its infancy for the public, students should embrace such platforms in terms of considering how to get the most out of the unparalleled offering of knowledge that AI can bring. Reframing their questions through enhanced disciplinary knowledge of the subject under study can yield educational benefits one could only dream about. And yet, teachers should encourage their students to read laterally on what they find, maintaining that default scepticism on the answer AI offers, to help ensure that young people are making the most of what's on offer.

Phase 2: Rules of Thumb for Good Thinking

Perhaps this chapter started out a little too pessimistically. I shared some activities to show where our thinking often goes wrong. Let's row back a little and understand how we think, appreciating the extraordinary capabilities of our minds. At the same time, we can also capture where the glitches lie and how we can train our students to guard against them.

One of the most revolutionary thinkers in helping us understand our thinking processes is Daniel Kahneman, the brilliant psychologist and Nobel Prize Winner for Economics. Despite his work having a profound effect on finance, politics, medicine, and many other fields, schools have been curiously late to the party. Whilst teachers are (understandably) endlessly discussing how to make the most of the recent developments in the cognitive sciences, very few pay attention to the behavioural sciences. It's time to bring the work of thinkers like Kahneman and his partner Amos Tversky into the classroom.[19]

Kahneman and Tversky's research showed that our thinking operates at two levels: fast and slow[20]:

System 1 is fast, intuitive, and more emotional:

* if a lion roars at you, you're not going to hang around to think the situation through
* 2 + 2 =?
* Better late than …
* a familiar voice says hello on the telephone.

System 2 is slower, effortful, and more logical:

* compare three types of mobile phones
* 17 × 33 =?
* count how many times I use the letter *g* in this chapter.

For your students learning to drive, driving is a helpful metaphor to understand the movement between Systems 1 and 2. When first learning to drive, each of them will rely on System 2 as they need to pay attention to everything: check the mirror, look right and left, indicate, release the break, step on the accelerator. The list is endless and it can all seem a little too much (and they certainly won't have the head space to think about 17 × 33 at the same time). After a few years of driving (hopefully), experienced drivers will shift to System 1; unless faced with an unfamiliar situation, as I drive the same route to work every day, my driving becomes intuitive and automatic.

Of course, during our waking hours, both Systems 1 and 2 are active. Normally, System 1 takes the lead on our automatic setting as System 2 sits in cruise control working at a low-effort level. As Kahneman describes it, "System 1 continuously generates suggestions for System 2: impressions, intuitions and intentions, and feelings. If endorsed by System 2, impressions and intuitions turn into beliefs, and impulses turn into voluntary actions." It is crucial to remember that things go smoothly most of the time. As Kahneman sums it up: "You generally believe your impressions and act on your desires, and that is fine – usually."[21]

However, interesting things begin to happen when Systems 1 and 2 conflict. This may happen in outright dangerous circumstances such as driving. But let's lower the stakes for now and get your students to try the fun exercise below (Figure 4.4):

BLUE	RED	**ORANGE**	PURPLE
YELLOW	BLACK	WHITE	RED
GREEN	**BROWN**	PURPLE	YELLOW
BROWN	ORANGE	BLUE	GREEN

Figure 4.4 The Stroop Test: How Fast Are You?
Source: J. Ridley Stroop, 1935

First, simply ask a student to read out loud to the class the word as it is spelt and hopefully that's a relatively easy System 1 exercise. Next, ask them to read out the colour they see; whilst System 1 will pull them to answer quickly and intuitively, most people begin to hesitate, slow down, and sometimes get the word wrong, confusing the colour with the word spelt.

But the truth of the matter is that such a contrived test that stops us in our tracks is relatively rare. For good reason, with so many things on our plate, we go through life very much relying on System 1. We trust our intuitions on pretty much everything that comes our way and only afterwards consult our System 2 for reassurance. As Haidt put it in homage to Hume: "The emotional tail wags the rational dog." We simplify even the most complicated of issues before us and make a judgement call. Kahneman and Tversky call this *the heuristics and biases approach*. And they define a heuristic as follows: "a simple procedure that helps find adequate, though often imperfect, answers to difficult questions."[22] In other words, a heuristic is a mental shortcut that allows us to make a calculated guess to make judgements and solve problems quickly and efficiently. Such rules of thumb may come about through the evolutionary process, personal past experiences, or social influences.

So, when considering issues of controversy, what are the rules of thumb that we can teach our students to help them build their mental toolkit when thinking about issues of controversy?[23]

Ad hominem

Here are a couple of challenges to make us all squirm a little:

- Name three people that you viscerally disagree with but really enjoy reading or listening to[24]
- Name a key piece of research you wish wasn't true but admit is true.[25]

In other words: can you put your emotions to one side and actually deal with the issue at hand? Sadly, we all too often rate the intelligence and character of people we agree with whilst maligning those on the other side. The ad hominem is the very human but equally ugly habit of attacking your opponent's character in an attempt to undermine their argument. This is done in bad faith, aiming to win the argument rather than actually seek the truth. Sadly, it's very effective in debate and so don't expect any let up just yet. However, at a deeper level, making use of the ad hominem is a sure sign that a person' arguments are failing them. As the musician Winston Marshall put it: "When they can't beat your argument they go for your reputation."

Perhaps the best examples are in politics. More than any other parliament in the world, the British system is set up for adversarial politics and so is not for the faint hearted. Some of the best put-downs in history have been witnessed at the famous dispatch box as British politicians seek to humiliate their opponents. Winston Churchill was merciless about his political rivals, not least Clement Atlee, the then leader of the Labour Party, of whom he said, "he is a modest man with much to be modest about." Not that the Americans aren't without their moments too. Who can forget the put-down in the 1988 Vice-Presidential debate by Democrat Lloyd Bentsen against Republican rival Dan Quayle after the latter compared his years of experience with that of former President John 'Jack' Kennedy? "Senator, I served with Jack Kennedy. I knew Jack Kennedy. Jack Kennedy was a friend of mine. Senator, you're no Jack Kennedy."[26] Bentsen's perfectly delivered insult overshadowed any of the actual issues under debate.

An excellent task for your students: watch Prime Minister's Question Time in the United Kingdom. It's on every Wednesday at noon when the House of Commons is sitting. Simply ask your students to count up each time a politician chooses to "play the man and not the ball" during the course of the session.

- Is such a tactic effective? Which one(s) stood out?
- What would be the correct answer if the politician chose to "play the ball and not the man"?
- How would focusing on the issue rather than the personalities change your view of the political debate and who actually would have 'won' the debate?

Occam's Razor

A particularly useful heuristic in all walks of life (although not infallible), Occam's Razor is a problem-solving principle that tells us that when we are presented with different hypotheses to explain a phenomenon that we should go for the simpler explanation, the one with fewer assumptions. So, if I see a large four-legged animal trotting the streets of London which I can't quite identify from a distance, I should assume a horse rather than a zebra. If I go to the doctor with symptoms that suggest the common cold, the doctor probably shouldn't spend too much time searching for tropical diseases that may present such symptoms as well (unless I've been to a tropical part of the world!). Next time you hear voices in the night, perhaps Occam's Razor will help calm you down: don't opt for ghosts when the rustling of the leaves might be all there is to it.

The law of parsimony is an ancient rule of thumb that can be used in many aspects of life, not least when thinking about controversial issues. When thinking about conspiracy theories, for example, Occam's Razor could be used to help guide us about which explanation is most plausible: did the Americans land those men on the moon or have 415,000 NASA employees managed to keep the hoax secret over 50 years later?[27]

Oh and for those of you wondering: why is *lex parsimoniae* now known as 'Occam's Razor'? Although this thinking tool is a lot older, it is attributed to William of Ockham (even more confusing is the different spelling we use), a 14th-century English Franciscan monk and logician. And as for the 'razor,' in philosophy, 'razors' are rules of thumb that simply 'shave off' unlikely explanations and help focus our thinking.[28]

Occam's Broom

Attributed to the molecular biologist Sydney Brenner, a Nobel Prize Winner of Medicine, Occam's Broom describes how people arguing in bad faith brush inconvenient facts under the carpet. Most obviously, one might think of a politician who conveniently forgets to mention the statistics that undermine his argument.

Perhaps the most famous example of the significance of 'negative facts' comes from Sherlock Holmes' *The Adventure of Silver Blaze*, where Holmes investigates the disappearance of the eponymous horse and apparent murder of its owner. As ever, the astute Holmes is one step ahead:

> Gregory (the Scotland Yard detective): "Is there any other point to which you would wish to draw my attention?"
> Holmes: To the curious incident of the dog in the night-time.
> Gregory: The dog did nothing in the night-time.
> Holmes: That was the curious incident.

The "curious incident of the dog in the night-time" suggests to Holmes that the dog didn't bark because he saw no stranger; rather the intruder was someone the dog new well.

Occam's Broom is a particularly important thinking skill as it induces the virtue of intellectual humility, separating the experts from the rest of us. While we are intuitively thinking about the facts of any debate, we must also be on the lookout for those truths that aren't being presented, that have been hidden away. Their very absence might point to the truth we're seeking to find. An excellent task for students could be to watch propagandists, conspiracists, or even wily politicians being interviewed. Can your students point to what has been overlooked that would undermine the argument being made? If not, how could reading the experts help?

Another fascinating task which could combine both Occam's Razor and Broom is analysing new stories from various new sources:

- Gather together three newspapers of the day: right-wing, left-wing, and centrist
- Put up the headlines from a major news source that claims neutrality, e.g. the BBC or CNN

- Ask your students to name the five leading news stories from each news source, ranking them in order of 'importance' based on the prominence given to their coverage
- What has each source included that is common to all or some of them?
- Occam's Broom: which stories have been left out?
- Occam's Razor: why do you think these stories have been left out? What are the best good faith explanations? Also, might there be an obvious ideological agenda that one could fairly claim?

Caution: when first offering this task, perhaps to students entering high school, don't reveal which news sources are considered right, left, centrist, or neutral. Let them guess and see how well they do.

False Dichotomies

A particularly misleading fallacy is the false dichotomy: claiming that only one of the alternatives is true. "You're either with us or against us," a righteous warrior may cry. "Can't I be neutral?" one might respond. "Isn't there a middle ground?"

The famous joke is told of paramilitaries in Northern Ireland who stop a motorist to ask him: "Are you Catholic or Protestant?" The motorist answers: "I'm an atheist." To which the gunman responds: "Yes, but are you a Catholic atheist or a Protestant atheist?"

In controversial issues, the false dichotomy is often used to simplify the issue before us – and may lead to extreme outcomes. If I speak out against capitalism, my detractors may argue, then that makes me a Communist.

Critical thinkers seeking to get out of such a dilemma need to overcome the limitations of such poor thinking, moving beyond that Manichean worldview. As the case studies in the second of half this book suggest, many issues of controversy are nuanced and require lateral thinking that is prepared to search for alternative answers.

And for those of us prone to a little righteous anger, my favourite example of more sophisticated thinking is from an angel on high. In Chapter 5 of the Book of Joshua, the great leader "lifted up his eyes and saw, behold a 'man' was standing opposite him with his sword drawn in his hand; and Joshua went to him, and said to him, Are you for us, or for our adversaries?" The 'man' turned out to be an angel who had no doubt taken a course in critical thinking and so refused to accept Joshua's false dichotomy, answering: "Neither! I have come as a captain of the army of the Lord." Many a time, the truth rises above the opposing sides.

A particularly interesting and controversial task could be the analysis of any global conflict or major disagreement: stepping into the shoes of different parties to any given crisis may help students recognise that there are often fair and reasonable arguments on either side of the divide. Rarely are human conflicts so black and white as some might like to think. As, Georg Wilhelm Friedrich Hegel, the great German philosopher, put it: "Genuine tragedies in the world are not conflicts between right and wrong. They are conflicts between two rights."

Straw Men and Iron Ladies

With your students growing more sophisticated in their understanding of issues of controversy, they are now ready to think about the strawman fallacy and for a difficult task that would serve as a fitting conclusion for this course. The typical strawman fallacy is when a person misrepresents their opponent's argument in order to make it easier to defeat it.

The strawman fallacy can be achieved in a number of ways:

- Quoting your opponent out of context to misrepresent their argument
- Oversimplifying or exaggerating what your opponent is actually saying
- Pointing to someone who does a particularly poor job of presenting the other side and claiming they represent everyone holding that viewpoint.

A particular shocking example is the fallout from Charles Darwin's theory of evolution. As one of the key revolutionary moments in overturning thousands of years of thinking about humanity, Darwin's theory has faced challenges from all walks of life, with many attacks misrepresenting the idea itself. As the Canadian philosopher, Christopher Tindale notes, look at this passage of a draft bill considered by the Louisiana State Legislature in the United States in 2001:

> Whereas, the writings of Charles Darwin, the father of evolution, promoted the justification of racism, and his books *On the Origin of Species* and *The Descent of Man* postulate a hierarchy of superior and inferior races...
>
> Therefore, be it resolved that the legislature of Louisiana does hereby deplore all instances and all ideologies of racism, does hereby reject the core concepts of Darwinist ideology that certain races and classes of humans are inherently superior to others, and does hereby condemn the extent to which these philosophies have been used to justify and approve racist practices.[29]

Fortunately, the legislature recognised the strawman fallacy and omitted this passage from the final version of the bill. Nevertheless, by misrepresenting Darwin's writings as promoting the justification of racism, the aim is to tarnish the theory of evolution with the stain of racism, leaving opponents in the extremely awkward position of trying to defend 'racism' in their efforts to defend evolution.

Again, note that the aim of the strawman, by creating a caricature of the other side, is to win the argument rather than seek the truth. If we are to become better thinkers, we must rather aim for the 'Iron Lady' or what is sometimes known as 'steelmanning': being asked to articulate and address the strongest form of the opposition's argument. This can also be known as 'the principle of charity,' which the philosopher Simon Blackburn points out, "constrains the interpreter to maximise the truth or rationality in the subject's sayings."[30]

For example, if a guest speaker in a school is arguing a certain cause on a controversial topic, e.g. legalising euthanasia, prepare your students to ask simply: "Please can you present the strongest arguments against your position?" Hopefully, if they are a gifted and well-intentioned speaker, they would have already done so. But if not, certainly don't let them off the hook.

A very useful task that can also help promote your students' debating skills is to ask them to speak on a particular issue of controversy and argue *against* what they believe in. This is a sophisticated task and should come at the end of the course, hopefully signalling how far your students have come.

Coda: And Now to Wikipedia

This chapter has offered a one-term mini-course to help students think critically, especially about controversial issues. As all teachers are aware, making such a course your own will be crucial to its success and so feel free to amend accordingly: you know your students and what will be appropriate for them. It goes without saying that the topics one could potentially cover are endless and so in the interest of consistency, I'll leave you with you these excellent links on Wikipedia. They are my favourite pages on the website and should provide superb material for a comprehensive course for you to put together in your school:

Wikipedia's List of fallacies: https://en.wikipedia.org/wiki/List_of_fallacies

Wikipedia's List of cognitive biases: https://en.wikipedia.org/wiki/List_of_cognitive_biases

As ever, please read laterally!

Notes

1. See, for example, Mark Easton. (2017) 'Five Mind-Blowing Facts about What the UK Looks Like.' Retrieved from: https://www.bbc.co.uk/news/uk-41901297.
2. Dan Ariely. (2009) *Predictably Irrational: The Hidden Forces That Shape Our Decisions*. London: Harper.
3. Amos Tversky and Daniel Kahneman. (1973) 'Availability: A Heuristic for Judging Frequency and Probability,' *Cognitive Psychology*, 5(2): 207–232.

4. Amos Tversky and Daniel Kahneman. (1981) 'The Framing of Decisions and the Psychology of Choice,' *Science*, 211(4481): 453–458.

5. For Obama quotation, please see Tom McCarthy. (2015) 'Obama's Gay Marriage Controversy: 'I Am Just Not Very Good at Bullshitting.'" Retrieved from: https://www.theguardian.com/us-news/2015/feb/10/obama-frustrated-same-sex-marriage-david-axelrod-book. For Trump quotation, please see Maggie Haberman (2016). 'Donald Trump's More Accepting Views on Gay Issues Set Him Apart in G.O.P.' Retrieved from: https://www.nytimes.com/2016/04/23/us/politics/donald-trump-gay-rights.html.

6. Baruch Spinoza. (2002) *Ethics* in *Complete Works*. Indianapolis, IN: Hackett Publishing Company, p. 331.

7. David Hume. (1969) *A Treatise of Human Nature*. London: Penguin, p. 462.

8. Steven Pinker. (2018) *Enlightenment Now*. London: Allen Lane, p. XX.

9. Jonathan Haidt. (2013) *The Righteous Mind*. London: Penguin, p. 107.

10. I have adapted Dan Ariely's "human-incompatible technologies" that describe technologies and processes that don't take into account human fallibility. See Dan Ariely. (2011) *The Upside of Irrationality*. London: Harper.

11. Dan Ariely. (2011) *The Upside of Irrationality*. London: Thorsons, p. 9.

12. U.S. Department of Transportation: Federal Aviation Administration, *Airplane Flying Handbook*: Chapter 5: Maintaining Aircraft Control: Upset Prevention and Recovery Training. Retrieved from: https://www.faa.gov/sites/faa.gov/files/regulations_policies/handbooks_manuals/aviation/airplane_handbook/06_afh_ch5.pdf.

13. 'The Jubilee Centre Framework for Character Education in Schools.' Retrieved from: https://www.jubileecentre.ac.uk/527/character-education/framework.

14. Ibid.

15. For obvious reasons I won't share the name of the website!

16. Professor Sam Wineburg at Stanford University has led the way on this research area. His team has put together an excellent online resource that provides free lessons on developing students' civic online reasoning: https://cor.stanford.edu/.

17. At the time of writing, many schools are feeling even more nervous about AI. Innovative critical thinkers will want to get ahead of the game and think about how to harness AI for educational benefits and not put their resources into stopping the tide.

18. See the helpful research cited in Rachel Cunneen and Mathieu O'Neil. (2021) 'Students Are Told Not to Use Wikipedia for Research. But It's a Trustworthy Source.' Retrieved from: https://theconversation.com/students-are-told-not-to-use-wikipedia-for-research-but-its-a-trustworthy-source-168834.

19. Alice Lucas and I write about our 'Nudge for Learning' ideas in this article: 'How Nudge Theory Can Boost Attainment,' (2022). Retrieved from: https://www.tes.com/magazine/teaching-learning/secondary/how-nudge-theory-can-boost-attainment. Our ideas were recognised by T4's World's Best School Prizes and shortlisted for the Innovation Prize in 2022.

20. Daniel Kahneman. (2011) *Thinking, Fast and Slow*. London: Allen Lane.

21. Ibid., p. 24.

22. Ibid., p. 98. Interestingly, Kahneman adds that *heuristic* cames from the same root as *eureka*.

23. As this book is about teaching and learning about controversy, our mental toolkit will remain focused on this topic. However, there are excellent whole book guides to develop critical thinking. For now, in addition to authors cited in this chapter, I will add Richard Nesbitt's *Mindware* (London: Penguin, 2016), Steven Pinker's *Rationality* (London: Allen Lane, 2021). For students, I'd recommend Tom Chatfield's works, including *Critical Thinking* (London: SAGE, 2018) and *How to Think* (London: SAGE, 2021).

24. It's only fair to put myself on the spot: Thomas Friedman, Christopher Hitchens, and Peter Singer. Please read their works and hear them speak!

25. As a teacher, the obvious one that comes to mind for me is the fascinating research of Professor Robert Plomin on how intelligence is highly heritable and predicts important educational, occupational and health outcomes better than any other trait. See, for example, his *Blueprint: How DNA Makes Us Who We Are* (Allen Lane, 2018).

26. Nothing beats watching the moment and listening to rapturous applause. It's obvious there was no real way back for poor Dan Quayle. You can view the iconic moment here: https://www.youtube.com/watch?v=QYAZkczhdMs.
27. David Robert Grimes. (2016) 'On the Viability of Conspiratorial Beliefs,' *Plos One*, 11(1). Retrieved from: https:// journals.plos.org/plosone/article?id=10.1371/journal.pone.0147905.
28. In line with my advocacy for using Wikipedia, check here for some other interesting 'razors' you might like to offer your students: https://en.wikipedia.org/wiki/Philosophical_razor.
29. Cited in Christopher W. Tindale. (2007) *Fallacies and Argument Appraisal*. Cambridge: Cambridge University Press, p. 21.
30. Simon Blackburn. (2016) *The Oxford Dictionary of Philosophy*. Oxford: Oxford University Press, p. 79.

Bibliography

Archard, D. (1998) 'How Should We Teach Sex?' *Journal of Philosophy of Education*, 32(3): 437–449.

Aristotle, *Politics* BK1 125a20.

Bailey, C. (1971) 'Rationality, Democracy and the Neutral Teacher,' *Cambridge Journal of Education*, 1(2): 68–76.

BBC News. (2018) 'British Asians More Socially Conservative than Rest of UK, Survey Suggests.' Retrieved from: https://www.bbc.co.uk/news/uk-45133717. Last accessed: 17 January 2022.

Beck, J. (2018) 'School Britannia? Rhetorical and Educational Uses of "British values,"' *London Review of Education*, 16(2): 228–238.

Berlin, I. (2003) 'My Intellectual Path.' In Rorty, A.O. (ed.) *The Many Faces of Philosophy*: *Reflections from Plato to Arendt*, pp. 482–497. Oxford: Oxford University Press.

Blair, T. (2008) 'Speech on Multiculturalism and Integration.' Retrieved from: https://webarchive.national-archives.gov.uk/ukgwa/20080909022722/http://www.number10.gov.uk/Page10563#:~:text=The%20values%20that%20nurtured%20it,and%20black%2C%20British%20and%20white. Last accessed: 22 January 2022.

Carver, R. (2009) 'So Much Water So Close to Home.' In *Collected Stories*. New York: Library of America.

Coady, D. (ed.) (2006) 'An Introduction to the Philosophical Debate about Conspiracy Theories.' In *Conspiracy Theories*: *The Philosophical Debate*, pp. 1–11. Farnham: Ashgate.

Dearden, R. (2012) *Theory and Practice in Education*. London: Routledge & Kegan Paul.

Denzel Smith, M. (2018) 'Colin Kaepernick's Protest Might Be Unpatriotic. And that's Just Fine.' Retrieved from: https://www.theguardian.com/commentisfree/2018/sep/12/colin-kaepernicks-protest-unpatriotic-justice. Last accessed: 22 January 2022.

Earl, M. (2016) *Re-Framing Education about Beliefs and Practices in Schools*: *A Lens and Tools (Concept Based) Approach*. Cambridge: Woolf Institute, University of Cambridge.

Economist. (2020) 'Conspiracy Theories in the News.' Retrieved from: https://talk.economistfoundation.org/headlines/conspiracy-theories-in-the-news/resources/. Last accessed: 23 January 2022.

FOX & Friends. (2018) *Twitter*. May 24. Retrieved from: https://twitter.com/foxandfriends/status/999599639996313600?ref_src=twsrc%5Etfw%7Ctwcamp%5Etweetembed%7Ctwterm%5E999599639996313600%7Ctwgr%5E%7Ctwcon%5Es1_&ref_url=https%3A%2F%2Fwww.theguardian.com%2Fsport%2F2018%2Fmay%2F24%2Fdonald-trump-lauds-nfl-anthem-policy. Last accessed: 22 January 2022.

Friedersdorf, C. (2017) 'Kneeling for Life and Liberty Is Patriotic.' *The Atlantic*. Retrieved from: https://www.theatlantic.com/politics/archive/2017/09/kneeling-for-life-and-liberty-is-patriotic/540942/. Last accessed: 22 January 2022.

Grayling, A.C. (2014) *Towards the Light*: *The Story of the Struggles for Liberty and Rights that Made the Modern West*. London: Bloomsbury.

Haidt, J. (2013) *The Righteous Mind*. London: Penguin.

Hand, M. (2007) 'Should We Teach Homosexuality as a Controversial Issue?' *Theory and Research in Education*, 5(1): 69–86.

Hand, M. (2008) 'What Should We Teach as Controversial? A Defense of the Epistemic Criterion,' *Educational Theory*, 58(2): 213–228.

Kashatus, W. (2004) 'A Friend among Quakers.' Retrieved from: https://paheritage.wpengine.com/article/friend-among-quakers/#:~:text=%E2%80%9CI%20have%20found%20amongst%20Negroes,masters%2C%20who%20have%20kept%20their. Last accessed: 15 February 2022.

Kass, L. (1997) 'The Wisdom of Repugnance,' *The New Republic*, 216(22): 17–26.

Mill, J.S. (1992) *On Liberty*. London: Everyman's Library.

Obama, B. (2006) 'Speech on Faith and Politics.' Retrieved from: https://www.nytimes.com/2006/06/28/us/politics/2006obamaspeech.html. Last accessed: 4 August 2019.

Peterson, J. (2018) 'Free Speech & the Right to Offend.' Retrieved from: https://www.youtube.com/watch?v=44pERGAaKHw. Last accessed: 9 January 2022.

Pigden, C. (2007) 'Conspiracy Theories and the Conventional Wisdom,' *Episteme*, 4(2): 219–232.

Pinker, S. (2003) *The Blank Slate*. London: Penguin.

Popper, K. (2002) 'Towards a Rational Theory of Tradition.' In *Conjectures and Refutations*, pp. 161–182. Oxford: Routledge.

Popper, K. (2012) *The Open Society and Its Enemies*. Oxford: Routledge.

Prevent Strategy. (2011) Retrieved from: https://assets.publishing.service.gov.uk/government/uploads/system/uploads/attachment_data/file/97976/prevent-strategy-review.pdf. Last accessed: 16 January 2022.

Russell, B. (1951) 'The Best Answer to Fanaticism - Liberalism: Its Calm Search for Truth, Viewed as Dangerous in Many Places, Remains the Hope of Humanity.' Retrieved from: https://timesmachine.nytimes.com/timesmachine/1951/12/16/Issue.html. Last accessed: 25 August 2019.

Sunstein, C.R. (2014) *Conspiracy Theories & Other Dangerous Ideas*. New York: Simon & Schuster.

Whittington, K.E. (n.d.) 'John Stuart Mill's Big Idea: Harsh Critics Make Good Thinkers.' Retrieved from: https://bigthink.com/neuropsych/john-stuart-mill/. Last accessed: 12 January 2022.

YouGov Survey. (2003) 'The War on Iraq.' Retrieved from: https://cdn.yougov.com/today_uk_import/YG-Archives-Ira-itn-WarIraq-030113.pdf. Last accessed: 22 January 2022.

Part II Controversy in Practice

Your Guide to the Guides

So much for the theory in Part I, now to the practical guidance in Part II. Don't get me wrong, I think my readers will get most out of this book by making their way through Part I first. As a complete handbook for all things controversial, the first half of the book provides the theoretical frameworks for educationalists to think about controversy and understand the underlying issues that shape the practical guidance in Part II.

At the same time, I am well aware that teachers universally complain of lack of time. However much we would like to do our research and continually develop our practice, there are simply too many justified (and unjustified) pulls on our time. And so this handbook is written for time-starved teachers too. Moreover, the school day is full of surprises and sometimes, out of nowhere, a student may ask a question that could leave us stumped. If we can't deal with the issue on the spot, we would do well to respond as soon as possible. This book can be used in that context too: a quick cheat sheet on the major issues young people are grappling with.

While this book can't possibly cover every topic of controversy that may come up, I do provide links at the end of each guide so that you can draw on the guidance and transpose the ideas presented to the similar topic at hand. For example, young children may be wondering about the truth of Santa Claus. As you turn to the guide on how to deal with this tricky topic in the classroom, you may wish to use the ideas within for thinking about how to deal with pupils asking about the tooth fairy. For older students arguing about the Israeli–Palestinian conflict, the guide may be helpful for other international conflicts going on at any time.

The practical aim is for each teacher to flick straight to the guide on the controversy under study as and when an issue of controversy comes up. And they do come up! To help teachers do that successfully, Part II begins with a simple 'Practical Guide to Controversy' explaining how best to use the guides. The layout of the introductory template mirrors those of the guides so you can refer directly to the thinking that underpins each section. Uniformity and consistency have been my own guiding principles in the hope that the more you use this book, the more intuitive the guides become. A simple glance at each guide will give you all you need to know to get your students learning and thinking about the issue of controversy in a deeper and more nuanced fashion.

It is to be hoped that as teachers get more confident teaching controversy, our students not only gain the requisite knowledge and skills to discuss controversy but also appreciate the need for open debate – not so that they can 'win' but so that they can learn from each other in the pursuit of truth and understanding.

Practical Guide to Controversy

Age Group

Each topic of controversy will be appropriate for teaching and learning about at different age groups. Whilst there would be no point in 16–18 year olds discussing whether Santa is real (hopefully), so too would it be inappropriate for 5–8 year olds to discuss the morality of incestuous relationships – albeit for different reasons. This book includes controversies that could apply to pupils from 5 years of age, the start of primary school in many countries, all the way up to the end of high school (and beyond).

How Explosive Is This Topic?

Before dipping into the issues, it is worth considering just how explosive the topic can be. What are the immediate concerns and alarm bells to get you thinking? A key rule of thumb is to think about whether your students or their families have 'skin in the game'. Just how upfront and personal is the issue before you? In the age of social media, what goes on in your classroom could become the topic of conversation online so be sure you feel in control throughout.

How Should I Teach This Topic?

When discussing an issue of controversy, it is vital for the teacher to decide first on whether to teach the issue in a directive or non-directive way

- If the issue is deemed controversial, then the teacher should teach in a non-directive way. For example, on the controversy of whether a country would be better off as a monarchy or republic, there are reasonable arguments for either side. Therefore, a teacher should aim to provide both sides of the argument, allowing her students to decide which arguments they find most convincing.
- If the issue is deemed uncontroversial, then the teacher should teach in a directive way. In turn, just as $1 + 1 = 2$ should be taught as fact so too should the Holocaust be taught as fact. There is simply no place for a teacher to undermine the truth by suggesting that 'alternative facts' could be acceptable for either of these questions.

For those teachers that want a deeper theoretical understanding of the framework for understanding controversy, please see Chapter 2 for the long version and the 'Some theory' section below for a brief summary.

Key Terms and Necessary Knowledge

Building up our students' knowledge before discussing or debating any issue of controversy is crucial: knowledge and skills go together!

In this section, I offer the key terms every student needs to know in order to have an informed discussion on the issue of controversy at hand. Sometimes, the issue may be so explosive that it may be helpful for students to research the term from different perspectives to appreciate the opposing sides, e.g. for the Israeli–Palestinian conflict, it may be worth remembering Jerusalem for Israelis and al-Quds for Palestinians.

DOI: 10.4324/9781003298281-8

For those with more time, perhaps as part of a Critical Thinking course, the creation of 'Knowledge Organisers' is an excellent way to help build up that critical student (and teacher) knowledge and understanding.

For best results, a teacher should create their own knowledge organiser first to help develop their subject knowledge and understanding of the issue. Where the topic is particularly explosive, you may wish to create different knowledge organisers that reflect the differing perspectives. The process of creating knowledge organisers in a specific subject leads the teacher to consider the pedagogical content knowledge, the integration of subject expertise, and an understanding of how that subject should be taught. A knowledge organiser can be a valuable starting point for effective curriculum design and a useful primer for those new to the topic.[1] (I prefer a larger A3 size so it's more substantial – but it's up to you!)

By organising everything, one *must* know about the topic on a single sheet, this task forces us to choose what information is most important and what is secondary. And so, depending on the topic you may wish to include, here are some generic suggestions:

- Key terms
- A timeline
- Maps and illustrations
- Data: quantitative and qualitative
- Main personalities on different sides of the debate
- Flashpoints: what exactly is under debate?
- Best arguments of all sides
- Sources used.

Once you are happy with *your* knowledge organisers, you now have a benchmark to measure your students' knowledge organisers.

Some suggestions when organising this time-intensive task:

- The task is significant and classroom time is important to ensure you can check on their progress throughout so that students don't end up producing extremist or simplistic knowledge organisers (even unwittingly): two one-hour lessons and a homework could be a reasonable time frame
- Students should work in pairs and focus on one narrative
- It may be helpful to match up student experts with those less confident: students teaching their peers is a leadership skill that has great potential here
- Where students hold obviously partisan views, get them to produce a knowledge organiser for 'the other side': this is a great chance to test them for 'steelmanning' (the skill of offering the best arguments for the other side as opposed to providing 'strawman' arguments) and see how intellectually honest they can be for the most contentious of issues
- With pairs completing their knowledge organisers, they should now team up with a pair that has produced a knowledge organiser with the other narrative to help build up a comprehensive understanding of the conflict.

Teachers can now reveal their own knowledge organisers, with the classroom providing a timely opportunity for critiquing each other's work:

- Do our knowledge organisers contain the necessary information?
- Do they get to grips with the different narratives?
- Do they help us understand the crucial aspects of the controversy?

- Teachers should not be afraid to put their own work under the microscope as they model critical thinking to their students.

Skills: **Students' Oracy and Teachers' Socratic Questioning**

Now we have our requisite knowledge, onto the skills!

This section aims to support two corresponding skills:

- For students: developing oracy, in other words, their ability to speak and listen
- For teachers: developing questioning technique, specifically their Socratic questioning.

There is an obvious symbiotic relationship between the two: as teachers improve their questioning skills, they can better promote their students' oracy. Equally, better speech in the classroom means better thinking too. For at the heart of both of these oracy skills is the appreciation that our cognition develops as we translate thought into speech. As Lev Vygotsky put it, "thought and word are not cut from one pattern… thought undergoes many changes as it turns into speech."[2]

I think this is why Genesis Chapter 1 tells us that before creating anything, God puts into words exactly what He wished to create: "And God said, 'Let there be light,' and there was light." For believers in an all-powerful and all-knowing God, it is obvious that God could just have created whatever He wanted without 'speaking.' After all, who exactly was He speaking to before having created anything? As the master pedagogue, God is *modelling* the importance of refining our thought processes through articulating our ideas through speech.

And the research certainly supports God on this. As Robin Alexander, a pioneer in dialogic education, wrote:

> psychological research, increasingly supported by neuroscience, demonstrates the intimate and necessary relationship between language and thought, and the power of spoken language to enable, support and enhance children's cognitive development, especially during the early and primary years.[3]

As a teacher of Religion, Philosophy & Ethics, I unapologetically remind my students of the importance of speaking up and joining in class discussions. This is not because I'm with the extroverts, but because I appreciate how important student talk is for their learning and in helping to build up their confidence. Apart from the benefits of enhancing their cognitive abilities, it is also crucial for their communicative, social, and cultural development. These building blocks of character educate the child holistically, advancing their civic and performance virtues, so vital for becoming flourishing members of society.[4]

Developing Students' Oracy

Depending on the type of controversy being taught and learned about, I offer two broad oracy pathways that you can provide for your students:

1   Classroom discussions: collaborative
2   Classroom debates: adversarial.

In each guide, I will recommend the pathway that I think works best based on the literature as well as my own classroom experience. Of course, each teacher knows their classroom best and so I offer the guidance here for you to decide which method is most suitable for your context.

My rule of thumb is the more explosive the issue, the more collaborative the pathway should be – especially at the early stages of teaching and learning about controversy. If the issue is divisive – such as whether transwomen are women – then an adversarial pathway like a debate is liable to raise animosity and lower student learning. Moreover, to single out a student to present their perspective on such an issue is a fine recipe for bullying and ensuring they never speak up again. However, on less divisive issues, such as monarchy vs republic, debates can develop important oracy skills that can build confidence and aid cognitive development. Of course, as levels of teacher and student confidence grow, and the better your rapport with your students, exposing them to more competitive and adversarial talk is so important for your students' confidence, with research suggesting girls especially benefitting from such opportunities.[5]

Ultimately though, school leaders and classroom teachers have a responsibility to curate a healthy learning classroom culture that embeds the collaborative yet divergent thinking we want to see in our students as they explore new ideas. Organisational psychologist Adam Grant summed it up so well:

> In consensus cultures, arguments are attacks on sacred beliefs. People take offence at dissent and dismiss those who dare to disagree.
> In learning cultures, arguments are tools to sharpen ideas. People invite dissent to enrich their thinking and agree to keep disagreeing.[6]

For school leaders and teachers to develop healthy 'learning cultures,' research suggests that there are three barriers to overcome:

i. lack of a supportive environment in the classroom
   • the teacher must build pupil confidence through allowing and even encouraging risk-taking and disagreement
ii. lack of a strong conceptual understanding of the topic under discussion
   • the teacher must give pupils appropriate time and support to gain strong knowledge and understanding of the topic being discussed or debated
iii. lack of personal enjoyment of the subject
   • the teacher must provide a range of oracy activities – discussions, debates, role plays, and presentations – to stimulate enjoyment, which boosts confidence, which in turn is a prerequisite for student participation.[7]

The pathways below are designed to promote such a learning culture, where we are happy to explore ideas with those we disagree with, in pursuit of truth and understanding rather than cheap and easy wins.

Classroom Discussions

Rather than looking for fault or seeking to side with one side over the other, the class collaborates like a 'hive mind,' through reasoning and critical engagement, in a joint endeavour to understand the controversy at hand. Classroom discussions are excellent examples of 'dialogic education' in aiming to elevate classroom talking and listening. Yet the literature shows many different formats for dialogue in the classroom, with some focusing on peer-on-peer talk and others on teacher–student interactions. Drawing on Robin Alexander's work, I think teaching and learning about controversy should attend to both for:

> although student talk must be our ultimate preoccupation because of its role in the shaping of thinking, learning and understanding, it is largely through the teacher's talk that the student's talk is facilitated, mediated, probed and extended – or not, as the case may be.[8]

Whilst there is some healthy debate on the issue, increased opportunities for student talk but with minimal teacher intervention, "did not necessarily result in concomitant increases in student comprehension, critical thinking and reasoning," with group work often leading to *groupthink* as the talk becomes "cooperative, collaborative and consensual."[9] Rather, as Clare Wagner concludes, when pupil talk is planned and structured carefully by a teacher, pupils enjoy their learning, develop confidence, and feel motivated.

To help generate such a learning culture where students feel they are in a safe environment, ground rules are crucial to success. James Mannion and Kate McAllister helpfully provide ideal features of exploratory talk which could serve as your ground rules for classroom discussion. I have slightly adapted them as follows:

- Everyone is encouraged to contribute
- Everyone listens actively
- Students seek to ask questions
- Students seek to share relevant information
- Ideas and opinions are treated with respect
- There is an atmosphere of trust
- There is a sense of shared purpose
- Contributions build on what has gone before
- Everyone gives reasons for their thinking
- Ideas may be challenged (with the aim of reaching the truth, not to 'win')
- The group seeks agreement for joint decision/the group accepts that individuals may think differently about the issues in the end.

If anyone breaks the ground rules, the teacher or another student can refer back to these rules of engagement. The more such rules are embedded, the more you can ensure a safe and welcoming learning culture.

Classroom Debates

Structured debates help develop four key skill sets that are vital for life:

i. Reasoning and Evidence
ii. Listening and Response
iii. Expression and Delivery
iv. Organisation and Prioritisation.[10]

Debates are designed to be adversarial and encourage argument. As the section on Socratic Questioning below highlights, debates and discussions require open-ended questions that can't be answered with a simple 'yes' or 'no' but require participants to offer reasons as they elaborate on their viewpoints. By definition, controversial questions should generate open-ended questions. For example, note the contrast between the following two questions:

- Who is the president of the United States? [A closed, uncontroversial question with a factually correct answer]
- Who do you think should be the president of the United States? [An open-ended, controversial question with different legitimate viewpoints].

There are many different forms of debate you can take up in the classroom, including:

- 'Parliamentary' debate: can be based on the U.K. House of Commons debating style, (in)famous for its adversarial approach and rules of procedure:
  - The class can be split into 'parties' based on where they stand on the issue
  - A host to chair the debate as Speaker of the House of Commons – initially, could be the teacher to help model hosting the debate
  - Party 'leaders' or 'ministers' and their 'shadows' could make opening speeches, with all participants standing when they speak
  - The rest of the class act as backbenchers, contributing by raising their hand and the Speaker calling on them
  - Depending on class decorum, you may wish to model the layout of the classroom on the House of Commons, with your students using the appropriate terms and following the formal procedures; they can even cheer and jeer to add to the atmosphere[11]
  - Of course, you can amend the format for a model United Nations style debate,[12] or for any other democratic legislature.
- 'Hot seating':[13] a favourite for drama teachers
  - Student roleplays a character who takes a stance on an issue of controversy, e.g. a priest who opposes legalising euthanasia or a feminist activist in favour of abortion rights
  - The class questions the student in the hotseat on their viewpoint, probing their reasoning, assumption, and implications of their ideas.
- 'Question Time' debate:[14] based on the long-standing BBC TV topical debate programme:
  - Five students make up a panel representing different sides of a debate
  - A host to chair the debate – initially, could be the teacher to help model hosting the debate
  - The rest of the class act as the audience asking questions, probing the panel, and offering their own viewpoints on the issue under discussion.
- 'Moral Maze' debate:[15] based on the long-standing BBC radio debate programme:
  - Four students make up a panel representing two different sides of a debate
  - A host to chair the debate – initially, could be the teacher to help model hosting the debate
  - Four 'witnesses' who provide expert evidence and ideas under cross-examination from the panel
  - The rest of the class can vote on which side they found most convincing and also have the chance to ask questions (to prevent lower proportion of participants).

And here are some rules of thumb to get the most out of debates:

- Clarity on ground rules before the debate begins (see Mannion and McAllister's ideas for exploratory talk above or Sources and Resources section for more ideas)
- Knowledge and skills go together: time allocated to gain knowledge and understanding of the issues will lead to higher-quality debates
- Encourage your students to move away from over-reliance on notes to thinking on their feet, e.g. only be allowed to write bullet points in preparation
- View an exemplar debate, e.g. Prime Minister's Questions (PMQs) in the Commons Chamber, in preparation, with students discussing the merits and failings of what they see
- During the debate, the designated host should ensure:
  - all pupils are involved to increase thinking ratio of class
  - no pupils dominate the discussion, e.g. you could limit time for speaking to encourage pithy and focused contributions too.

- After the debate, offer feedback on both content and skills to help students improve over time
- Seek a variety of settings for the debates to develop your students' confidence in speaking in unfamiliar and even intimidating settings
- Offer a variety of debating-styles to hone your students' technique
- Remind your students that practice really does make perfect: many will be nervous, shy and intimidated at first; yet there are no shortcuts to becoming a proficient and engaging speaker and debater.

Socratic Questions

Good questioning in the classroom not only promotes student thinking, but is also an excellent pedagogical method to assess it.[16] The problem is that much questioning falls short as many of us go into auto-pilot mode, following the all too predictable 'IRE' exchange:

 i.   Initiation question by the teacher
 ii. Response by a student
 iii. Evaluation from the teacher.

All too often the teacher asks a closed question, receives an answer, and offers minimal feedback. If I call on one student, expecting an answer within seconds, and then offer a (metaphorical) thumbs up or down in response, the ratio of students thinking hard is minimal. Yet this remains the pedagogical default in many classrooms throughout the world, leaving far too many of us guilty of using an exchange structure that "wastes much of talk's discursive, cognitive and educational potential."[17]

And so, in advocating dialogic education that recognises the teacher's role in developing student talking, listening, and cognition, I am particularly sensitive to Alexander's call

> to move beyond the monologic dominance of recitation/IRE and develop patterns of classroom interaction that open up students' speaking and listening, and hence their thinking, and which strive to distribute the ownership of talk more equitably.[18]

Fran Spalter, a teacher of History, puts it beautifully, "Teaching is like conducting an orchestra." Just as the skilful conductor knows how to draw in his musicians and get the best out of them, allowing them to shine as a unit, so too will the best teacher gauge how to bring her students into the conversation, ensuring each can play their part. Just as the musicians perform in harmony for the complete musical experience, so too should all members of a class engage in the flow of the open dialogue for a full and enriching conversation.[19]

For issues of controversy, Socratic questions are a classic method to help you achieve this worthy aim. The higher-order questioning immediately lifts the level of discussion. As Rob Coe put it so brilliantly and succinctly: "Learning happens when people have to think hard."[20] Let this be the guiding principle of every question you put to your students going forward. As I tell my students, if their heads are hurting by the end of the lesson, I know I've succeeded.

Some 2,500 years ago in Athens, Socrates was the model teacher who was unrivalled in making his students think hard. He understood that thinking is driven by questions. Socratic questioning is thus a form of dialogic education which, as Richard Nisbett explains, sees its participants:

> trying to reach the truth by stimulating critical thinking, clarifying ideas, and discovering contradictions that may prompt the discussants to develop views that are more coherent and more likely to be correct or useful.[21]

Let's explain how this Socratic Method might work through a classroom dialogue that took place in one of my lessons on the ethics of relationships and families. For 16-year-old students studying this topic, examination boards typically include a question on the morality of different kinds of sexual relationships, with an evaluative question like this one to answer: 'It is wrong to disapprove of homosexual relationships.'[22]

At the very least, this is a behaviourally controversial issue as in many classrooms around the world, students will think very differently on this issue. Interestingly, my own students are typically liberal-minded young people who year after year don't voice the view that there is anything to disapprove of when it comes to homosexual relationships. Nevertheless, the AQA examination board requires students to provide:

- reasoned arguments in support of this statement
- reasoned arguments to support a different point of view
- reference to religious arguments
- optional reference to non-religious arguments
- a justified conclusion.

And so to discuss and evaluate the issue, we must. Here is how we went about doing just that:

Socratic questioning	Classroom dialogue
Question to probe viewpoint	Mr Bezalel: "Who supports the statement: 'It is wrong to disapprove of homosexual relationships'?"
	Lily: "I do, Sir. Love is love. It doesn't matter if it's heterosexual or homosexual."
Question to probe assumption	Mr Bezalel: "Thank you, Lily. Can you explain why you think this way?"
	Lily: "Ultimately, if people voluntarily enter into a relationship and they love each other, it's up to them."
Question to probe reasoning/evidence	Mr Bezalel: "Can anyone else give me a religious source or example that Lily might use to support her argument?"
	Ellie: "Perhaps a good source would be from the Gospel John, the idea that 'God is Love'."
Question to probe assumption	Mr Bezalel: "Good. What assumption are you making in connecting that idea to the acceptability of homosexual relations for Christians?"
	Ellie: "It's based on the concept of 'imitatio Dei'. If God is all-loving and accepting, so too should we be."
Question of clarification	Mr Bezalel: "Thank you, Ellie. And Lily, is that your reasoning for concluding as you do?"
	Lily: "No, Sir. I believe that we should have autonomy over our lives. As long as we don't harm other people it's up to us to decide what makes us happy. If we fall in love with someone then I don't think it's for other people to interfere or stop us from have a relationship with whoever we want to be with."

Question to probe viewpoint	Mr Bezalel: "Excellent. Lily has articulated really well the important liberal concepts of autonomy and consensual relationships. [After checking for understanding of these concepts...] Can anyone else tell me why someone might disagree with Lily? Why might someone disapprove of homosexual relationships?"
	Amelia: "Because they're a bigot!"
Question to probe reasoning/evidence	Mr Bezalel: "Come on, Amelia. We must resist the *ad hominem* however strongly we feel about the issue. Turn to Lily and offer reasons for why some might oppose her."
	Amelia: "Fair enough. Well, Christians might disapprove of homosexual relationships because of the Natural Moral Law. St Thomas Aquinas saw nature as a moral guide to what is right and wrong. So as two men or two women can't have children through homosexual sex that clearly shows it's wrong."
Question to probe viewpoint	Mr Bezalel: "Who likes this argument? Is it a strong argument?"
	Hannah: "I think it's a silly argument. After all, lots of sexual relationships might not allow for children. An elderly married couple, for example. Would it be wrong for them to have sex even though they're heterosexual?"
Follow-up question to probe viewpoint	Mr Bezalel: "Good. [We then explored other arguments pro and against but for our purposes, let's pick up on Lily's initial point.] So, let's explore together Lily's claim that 'love is love': as long as people voluntarily enter into a relationship and they love each other, it's up to them. Who agrees with that?" [All hands go up.] "What about a brother and sister (let's say they're 23 and 21 years old) who want to enter into a sexual relationship. That would be fine, right?" [Pause to increase ratio in thinking.] [This time no hands go up. One or two girls hesitant, looking around the room with only hands half-raised.] "What do you think, Kayla?" [One girl who had an expression of disgust on her face.]
	Kayla: "Ew, that's gross!"
Question to probe viewpoint	Mr Bezalel: "Explain why you think 'that's gross'."
	Kayla: "It just is. There's clearly something wrong with them."
Question to probe implications and consequences	Mr Bezalel: "But something tells me that if we were living a hundred years ago or so and we were having the same discussion, many of you would have had the same reaction about homosexual relationships. Can anyone explain why none of you are willing to apply 'love is love' to this scenario?"

	Kayla: "Well, it's illegal for a start."
Question to probe implications and consequences	Mr Bezalel: "But again, so was homosexual sex in the UK until 1967. Believe it or not, sibling incest is legal in a number of countries. In France, for example, sibling incest between adults has been legal since just after the 1789 French Revolution. That timing is important for what we're discussing in terms of Christian morality."
	Hannah: "But what if they [the incestuous couple] have children? The chances are the children will have several genetic disorders."
Question of clarification	Mr Bezalel: "That sounds like a Natural Moral Law argument to me [by basing the morality of the issue on the natural consequences]. You said you didn't like that argument before when it came to homosexual couples unable to have children."
	Hannah: "But this is different…"
Follow-up question of clarification	Mr Bezalel: "Explain why." [No response] "Anyone else? For our discussion, let's assume they're using contraception throughout. What then?"
	Lily [brave but a little uncertain this time round]: "I know this sounds gross but yes, I think it's morally fine. I mean I don't like it but maybe that's because it's something we're not used to. The French changed the law when they were secularising and getting rid of Christian influences. Maybe we feel the way we do because of that religious influence in our society. So yes, I'm willing to stand by the idea that 'love is love' and as long as they're not harming anyone else, then I think it's fine."
Question to probe viewpoint	Mr Bezalel: "Thank you, Lily. Anyone else agree with her?" [One other hand half goes up. The rest of the class looks incredulously on but no one can offer a reason for their view beyond, "That's disgusting. It just is!"]

As you can see, classroom learning is driven by the different styles of Socratic questioning. Throughout, I had three key aims in mind, which I believe this pedagogical method achieves well:

- explore and monitor my students' level of knowledge and understanding
- encourage higher-order thinking
- probe the viewpoints raised.

I know this style of questioning got my students thinking hard, especially when having to argue for the other side and having their own assumptions questioned. And so I hope such a dialogue lives up to Socrates' reflections on this rigorous educational method:

> Can it be, Ischomachus, that asking questions is teaching? I am just beginning to see what is behind all your questions. You lead me on by means of things I know, point to things that resemble them, and persuade me that I know things that I thought I had no knowledge of.[23]

In this case, my style of teaching was clearly non-directive. With the context of the lesson aiming for a comprehensive answer that my students may expect to be examined on, I was not interested in reaching consensus. Indeed, on such an issue I had detected a sense of 'groupthink' among my students and so I wanted to spoil this through poking holes in their arguments. In the tradition of J.S. Mill, I wanted to expose their ideas to contrarian viewpoints to help them refine their viewpoints and sharpen their reasoning.

By the end of the lesson, only one brave soul, "Lily" as I called her, was willing to take the 'love is love' idea to its logical conclusion and support the legitimacy of sibling incest. Nevertheless, what seemed so obvious before the lesson, that 'love is love' was now being questioned. The students left the room still discussing the issue – as they often do when learning issues of controversy – surely a healthy mark for a successful lesson! As the lesson concluded, it was clear that their heads were hurting as they were continuing to think hard.

Parenthetically, I don't believe from the dialogue above that it is possible to detect my own viewpoint on the issue. In the classroom, my questioning took on a decidedly neutral and impartial approach. I was playing devil's advocate, but my students knew that whatever perspective they would have advocated, my Socratic questioning would have set out to probe their thinking and compel them to realise the implications and consequences of their viewpoints. In such a behaviourally controversial issue such as this – from potentially having students who oppose homosexual relationships on religious grounds to having students who themselves are in a homosexual relationship – I believe that revealing my own viewpoint would have undermined the process, with those opposing my view perhaps feeling I was biased and that they were being judged. Questioning is therefore a very helpful technique to move the focus away from the teacher's perspective towards concentrating on what the students think.

Each guide offers specific Socratic questions that pertain to the controversy at hand. As you probably noticed, the more knowledge shared by the class (including you the teacher), the healthier the discussion. In turn, I also include a 'cheat sheet' with the best arguments I can muster for any side of the debate at hand. This will allow you the teacher to:

- build up your own knowledge and understanding of the key arguments
- ensure your students are offering the best arguments on all sides of the debate and not getting away with 'straw man' arguments or *ad hominem* attacks
- play devil's advocate and challenge the arguments offered by your students
- model the importance of offering the other side, no matter what the issue of controversy.

Some Theory

This section is for those teachers who want that bit more theoretical discussion behind the controversy of the issue at hand. So, when it came to the 'How should I teach this topic?' you'll find straightforward practical advice on whether to take a directive or non-directive approach. It is in this section that I'll provide links to thinkers and commentators on the issue, giving you deeper insight into understanding the nature of controversy as it relates to the issue at hand. Thus in Part I, we saw that there are three major ways to define controversy:

- Behavioural controversy: a topic is deemed controversial as long as two or more people disagree about the issue at hand (which is pretty much anything including whether Earth is flat!)

- Political controversy: a topic is deemed controversial when more than one approach is compatible with a commitment to basic rights and liberties (such as conservative vs liberal arguments)
- Epistemic controversy: a topic is deemed controversial if contrary views can be held without those views being contrary to reason (such as debates on moral issues like abortion or euthanasia).

We saw positives and negatives for each criterion, depending on the issue under discussion. For many of the topics, the epistemic criterion is the one many of us would opt for to help nurture reason and critical thinking.

At the same time, this book does include issues of behavioural controversy even if they are not epistemically controversial – such as teaching and learning about the Holocaust and other such unwarranted conspiracy theories – because they can be explosive. Teachers need guidance on how to deal with such issues if students raise them in class. Shying away from them or simply dismissing them outright is rarely if ever the best way to handle them.

And so, where relevant, this section will also include a recommendation on which teacher stance to take, depending on the issue:

- Exclusive neutrality: avoid teaching the issue of controversy altogether, e.g. "great topic but now is not the time to explore the boundaries of free speech."
- Exclusive partiality: teach the issue of controversy with the aim of winning over students to your views, e.g. "with the election coming up, it is obvious to me that everyone of sound mind should support ..."
- Neutral impartiality: teach the issue of controversy by ensuring competing perspectives receive a fair hearing without disclosing your own view on the matter, e.g. "this is why some people support legalising euthanasia and this is why some people believe it should be illegal."
- Committed impartiality: teach the issue of controversy by ensuring competing perspectives receive a fair hearing and offer your own view on the matter, e.g. "there are excellent reasons to have a monarchy such as ..." and "I'm a republican because ..."

Again, as explained in Part I, neutral impartiality is the approach generally favoured for issues of controversy, whilst there may be times where other approaches may be more suitable.

Beware!

Every issue of controversy has its pitfalls and traps that a teacher should consider before beginning. Once the debate is underway, classrooms have their own dynamic and the discussion could go anywhere! The best teachers are those who think on their feet and this is often down to experience: the more you deal with issues of controversy, the greater your awareness – especially when you're armed with the requisite knowledge and arguments. As a teacher who welcomes debate and has experience of all the issues discussed, I include the danger signs we should be aware of as we go down the rabbit hole...

Yet as I argue in Part I, the epistemic arguments aren't our only consideration. Beyond the best arguments we can offer, teachers also need to be alert to classroom sensitivities. Whilst this book argues that our students should be exposed to opinions that they disagree with and even find offensive, classroom etiquette remains important. We need to model healthy and positive discussions and so be on the lookout for *ad hominem* attacks, gratuitously offensive sloganeering, and extremist language that promotes violence or goes against school policies and even our legal duties as teachers.

It has often been remarked that swearing suggests a limited vocabulary. So too, simplistic and sweeping generalisations suggest poor thinking. Sadly, there is simply too much of this going about. And so, in our efforts to counter poor thinking and bad behaviour, we would do well to regularly remind our students that the aim is to learn and understand, not to win!

Sources and Resources

No book can cover everything! 'Teaching to the top' includes introducing your students to the experts so that they can explore the issue in further depth. Whether you or your students want to know where to go next to build up your expertise on the subject, I provide links for further research, always including those sources and resources I have looked to as well. Of course, a crucial critical thinking skill we need to teach our students is the importance of studying a range of perspectives, including those we disagree with. In this spirit, just because I recommend a source doesn't at all mean that I endorse the views expressed!

For this section, I have made use of the following sources:

Alan Howe (2022), '"Disturbingly Different": 5 Great Dialogic Talk Moves.' Retrieved from: https://oracycambridge.org/5-great-dialogic-talk-moves/.

AQA GCSE Religious Studies A, Paper 2A Thematic Studies, Monday 20 May 2019. Retrieved from: https://filestore.aqa.org.uk/sample-papers-and-mark-schemes/2019/june/AQA-80622A-QP-JUN19.PDF.

BBC, 'Moral Maze: Eight Ways to Win an Argument.' Retrieved from: https://www.bbc.co.uk/programmes/articles/251N2YBLLwmPJnVvDn94GQR/moral-maze-eight-ways-to-win-an-argument.

BBC Question Time, 'Frequently Asked Questions.' Retrieved from: https://www.bbc.co.uk/programmes/articles/5HrMm77Yz7vwzCZZ57OnTdp/frequently-asked-questions.

C.J. Rauch (2022), 'The Art of Questioning.' Retrieved from: https://evidencebased.education/the-art-of-questioning/.

Clare Wagner (2015), 'An Investigation into Pupil Oracy with Year 10 Pupils Studying GCSE History in an All Girls' School.' University of Oxford: MSc Learning and Teaching Dissertation, Unpublished.

David Farmer, '"Hot Seating" Drama Resource.' Retrieved from: https://dramaresource.com/hot-seating/#:~:text=What%20is%20Hot%20Seating%3F,of%20fleshing%20out%20a%20character.

English Speaking Union (2022), 'Resources.' Retrieved from: https://www.esu.org/resources/.

Intel Teach Programme (2007), 'Designing Effective Projects: Questioning - The Socratic Questioning Technique.' Retrieved from: https://www.academia.edu/29586688/Intel_Teach_Program_Designing_Effective_Projects.

James Mannion and Kate McAllister (2020), *Fear Is the Mind Killer*. Woodbridge: John Catt Educational Ltd.

Jubilee Centre (2022), 'The Jubilee Centre Framework for Character Education in Schools.' Retrieved from: https://www.jubileecentre.ac.uk/527/character-education/framework.

L.S. Vygotsky (1962), *Toward a Theory of Instruction*. Cambridge, MA: Belknap.

Mark Miller (2018), 'Organising Knowledge: The Purpose and Pedagogy of Knowledge Organisers,' *Impact*. Retrieved from: https://my.chartered.college/impact_article/organising-knowledge-the-purpose-and-pedagogy-of-knowledge-organisers/.

Neil Mercer and Lyn Dawes (2018), 'The Development of Oracy Skills in School-Aged Learners.' Retrieved from: https://languageresearch.cambridge.org/images/CambridgePapersInELT_Oracy_2018_ONLINE.pdf.

Robert Coe, 'Improving Education: A Triumph of Hope over Experience.' Retrieved from: http://eachandeverydog.net/wp-content/uploads/2015/05/ImprovingEducation2013.pdf.

Richard Nisbett (2015), *Mindware: Tools for Smart Thinking*. London: Penguin.

Robin Alexander (2020), *A Dialogic Teaching Companion*. Oxford: Routledge.

Xenophon, *Economics*. Retrieved from: https://www.perseus.tufts.edu/hopper/text?doc=Perseus%3Atext%3A1999.01.0212%3Atext%3DEc.%3Achapter%3D19.

Links to Other Controversies

Where the principles in a Guide could be used for another issue of controversy that young people are grappling with, I offer related topics to think about – whether they are in the book or not.

Notes

1. Mark Miller. (2018) 'Organising Knowledge: The Purpose and Pedagogy of Knowledge Organisers,' Impact. Retrieved from: https://my.chartered.college/impact_article/organising-knowledge-the-purpose-and-pedagogy-of-knowledge-organisers/.
2. L.S. Vygotsky. (1962) *Toward a Theory of Instruction*. Cambridge, MA: Belknap, p. 219.
3. Robin Alexander. (2018) 'Developing Dialogic Teaching: Genesis, Process, Trial,' *Research Papers in Education*, p. 2. Retrieved from: http://robinalexander.org.uk/wp-content/uploads/2019/12/RP-IE-2018-Alexander-dialogic-teaching.pdf.
4. Jubilee Centre. (2022) 'The Jubilee Centre Framework for Character Education in Schools.' Retrieved from: https://www.jubileecentre.ac.uk/527/character-education/framework.
5. Clare Wagner. (2015) 'An Investigation into Pupil Oracy with Year 10 Pupils Studying GCSE History in an All Girls' School' (MSc Learning and Teaching Dissertation, University of Oxford, Unpublished), p. 9.
6. Adam Grant. (2021) 'In Consensus Cultures, Arguments Are Attacks on Sacred Beliefs...' [Twitter]. Retrieved from: https://twitter.com/adammgrant/status/1470106386398912514?s=11.
7. Wagner, ad loc., pp. 62–63.
8. Alexander (2018) ad loc., p. 3.
9. Wagner (2015) ad loc., p. 9.
10. English Speaking Union. 'Key Skills.' Retrieved from: https://www.esu.org/resources/.
11. UK Parliament. 'Debates.' Retrieved from: https://www.parliament.uk/about/how/business/debates/.
12. Model United Nations. 'Model UN Portal.' Retrieved from: https://una.org.uk/get-involved/learn-and-teach/model-un-portal
13. David Farmer. 'Hot Seating,' *Drama Resource*. Retrieved from: https://dramaresource.com/hot-seating/#:~:text=What%20is%20Hot%20Seating%3F,of%20fleshing%20out%20a%20character.
14. BBC Question Time. 'Frequently Asked Questions.' Retrieved from: https://www.bbc.co.uk/programmes/articles/5HrMm77Yz7vwzCZZ57OnTdp/frequently-asked-questions.
15. BBC. 'Moral Maze: Eight Ways to Win an Argument.' Retrieved from: https://www.bbc.co.uk/programmes/articles/251N2YBLLwmPJnVvDn94GQR/moral-maze-eight-ways-to-win-an-argument.
16. C.J. Rauch. (2022) 'The Art of Questioning.' Retrieved from: https://evidencebased.education/the-art-of-questioning/.
17. Alexander (2018) ad loc., p. 2.
18. Alexander (2018) ad loc., p. 3.
19. There are brilliant guides out there on developing dialogic education in the classroom, with links provided in the 'Sources and Resources' section. Yet our concern is for developing the oracy skills for teaching and learning about issues of controversy. In this vein, I provide guidance on Socratic Questioning in this section.

20. Robert Coe. 'Improving Education: A Triumph of Hope over Experience,' p. xiii. Retrieved from: http://eachandeverydog.net/wp-content/uploads/2015/05/ImprovingEducation2013.pdf.
21. Richard Nisbett. (2015) *Mindware: Tools for Smart Thinking*. London: Penguin, p. 206.
22. See, for example, AQA GCSE Religious Studies A, Paper 2A Thematic Studies, Monday 20 May 2019. Retrieved from: https://filestore.aqa.org.uk/sample-papers-and-mark-schemes/2019/june/AQA-80622A-QP-JUN19.PDF.
23. Xenophon, *Economics*. Retrieved from: http://www.perseus.tufts.edu/hopper/text?doc=Perseus%3Atext%3A1999.01.0212%3Atext%3DEc.%3Achapter%3D19.

Practical Guide to Controversy

Is Santa Claus real?

Age group: 5-11

How explosive is this topic?

This is a fun topic, but if it does goes wrong, the parents' WhatsApp group will blow up.

How should I teach this topic?

Yes, to either:

Directive positive teaching: "Yes, of course Santa Claus is real! Merry Christmas to us all!"
Or

Non-directive teaching: "I like to think Santa Claus is real. What do you think? What does the class think?"

But no to:

Directive negative teaching: "Bah humbug! Obviously Santa Claus isn't real and it's time we all stopped this nonsense!"

Key Terms and Necessary Knowledge:

Coca-Cola: Thinking of Santa Claus often invites an image of an elderly, rosy-cheeked gentleman, with a long white beard and larger than usual belly. He is also often clad in a red and white outfit. This image actually only originated in 1931, thanks to probably the most successful advertisement of all time. That's why our Santa is wearing the Coca-Cola colours. What did Santa look like pre-Coca-Cola? Get your pupils to find out.

Myths: According to the dictionary, there are two major meanings for the word 'myth':

1. a traditional story, especially one concerning the early history of a people or explaining a natural or social phenomenon, and typically involving supernatural beings or events.
2. a widely held but false belief or idea.

So it's really important to be clear on what we mean by the Santa Claus myth. Just because we might believe in the myth of Santa, does that mean it is a 'false' idea? Might some of the legends or folklore be true? For example, there really was a Saint Nicholas (see below). At what point does history end and the myth begin? Also, for high-level students to consider: just because something isn't *literally* true, does that mean it isn't true in other ways? It seems that myths are often foundational stories that go to the heart of what it means to be human. Can we think of other myths that help us think more deeply about who we really are and what we want to be?

Reindeer: Tradition and modern culture collide again. Purists usually name eight reindeer: Dasher, Dancer, Prancer, Vixen, Comet, Cupid, Donner, and Blitzen (from Clement Clarke Moore's popular 1823 poem 'A Visit from St. Nicholas'). Yet Rudolf the Red-Nosed Reindeer is the one most of us name, coming from a story of the same name by Robert L. May in 1939 and then popularised further in Gene Autry's song ten years later. Probably fair to call Rudolf the ninth reindeer by now. L. Frank Baum's story, 'The Life and Adventures of Santa Claus' (1902) named ten different reindeer. Can you name any of them?

Saint Nicholas of Myra: In Dutch, Saint Nicholas is pronounced Sinterklaas – hence our nickname for him, Santa Claus! But the original Saint Nicholas (270-343 CE) was an early Christian bishop known in the Church for his many miracles. He was also known for secret gift-giving and ultimately became the patron saint for children. Sounds like the topic for a great research project. Other names for Santa Claus:

DOI: 10.4324/9781003298281-9

- France: Père Noël
- Germany: Weihnachtsmann
- Italy: Babbo Natale
- Spain: Papa Noel
- United States: Kris Kringle

Socratic Questions and Critical Thinking:

Why might some people believe in Santa Claus? Why might other people not believe in Santa Claus?

These are excellent questions to help develop your students' abilities to present and develop arguments for opposing sides. Whatever their own view, get your students to brainstorm possible reasons for each side of the debate. The more the merrier!

After your pupils identify the arguments and respond to the counterarguments, they can move on to the important thinking skill of trying to evaluate the credibility of the different reasons offered. 'Five finger feedback' is always useful for quick responses: five fingers mean the reason is most reliable; one finger suggests the evidence or source lacks credibility. Ultimately, we might conclude with the following question: can we set up an 'experiment' to test out whether Santa Claus is real or not?

Reasons to believe in Santa Claus	Reasons to not believe in Santa Claus
Testimony: My parents told me about Santa and so do many other people that I trust.	**Testimony:** Other people that I trust have said that Santa doesn't exist.
Evidence: Lots of milk and cookies get devoured each year in homes across the world just as presents are being delivered! No evidence can ever be brought to prove Santa doesn't exist (it is 'unfalsifiable' and so unscientific): perhaps there are things we just believe in even if we don't have scientific evidence?	**Lack of evidence:** No one has ever seen the 'real' Santa – just lots of people claiming to be him. There was a historical figure called St Nicholas – but surely no one lives for nearly 2,000 years? No evidence can ever be brought to prove Santa does exist (it is 'unfalsifiable' and so unscientific): why believe in things with no scientific evidence?
Intuition: I just feel he exists. I know it I tell you!	**Reasoning:** Occam's Razor: is it more likely that a magical figure exists or that lots of people are determined to keep the Santa Claus fantasy alive?

Other questions you may wish to explore:

- *We know that Saint Nicholas did exist. Is this who we mean when we say 'Santa Claus?'*
- *How do we know what is real?*
- *Can myths be 'true?'*
- *Why is this question important?*

Some Theory:

Many educationalists believe that the primary purpose of education is to nurture rational thought and action. If this is true, then Santa Claus seems to be an open and shut case: however much we might like to believe in him (spoiler alert), there is no Santa Claus! This means that there is nothing epistemically controversial here and so we should simply teach the truth in a directive manner. Yet something tells me many of us will wince at being asked to spoil some of our pupils' Christmas.

Jeff Standley, a philosopher of education, offers a helpful way out that allows teachers to lie reluctantly in order to let students reap the intellectual benefits of experiencing such low-level deception, "before then actively helping them to learn important epistemic lessons and foster key intellectual virtues as a result of their experiences."

Yet this approach has a "bah humbug" feel to it that I can't shake off. The dilemma of Santa points to a weakness of the epistemic criterion, where Standley frames this controversy in terms of reason and evidence. Standley believes that Santa provides an apt opportunity for teachers to help develop intellectual virtues such as intellectual thoroughness, intellectual humility, open-mindedness, intellectual courage, and intellectual autonomy. For example, as students grow older, they will come to possess and further develop those abilities and skills required to disabuse themselves of false beliefs, like Santa, and so nurture their intellectual autonomy. For sure, this is a good argument but is it the whole story?

As Jacqueline Woolley, a professor of psychology, counters, "even if there are no cognitive benefits of believing, or disbelieving, in Santa Claus, just the fact that it's fun might be good enough." Fun for children and fun for adults!

Indeed, returning to the idea of virtues, we must remember that the ultimate virtue is what is known as *practical wisdom* or what the Greeks called *phronesis*, "developed through experience and critical reflection, which enables us to perceive, know, desire and act with good sense. This includes discerning, deliberative action in situations where virtues collide." We sometimes call this 'common sense' (yet not always so common...).

So yes, of course *intellectual* virtues such as the pursuit of knowledge and truth are crucial. But so are *moral* virtues such as compassion, respect, and humility; and so are *civic* virtues such as civility, community, and awareness. To take these fully into account, we need to move beyond the 'ethic of autonomy,' which focuses on a harm-rights-and-justice code, which cannot deal effectively with cases such as these. Rather, in considering the teacher's role when it comes to Santa, our 'moral language' must extend to an 'ethic of community,' which relies on concepts such as duty, respect, and loyalty, that aims to preserve institutions such as the family, religious, and cultural values.

In turn, the virtue of *phronesis* tells us that it really isn't the teacher's place to spoil this special family and cultural tradition. The huge benefits of being transported to those fictional and fantastical worlds are all too rare and yet collectively so precious. Going along with some parents' 'white lie' or omitting to tell the truth is surely a right of passage our pupils deserve and ultimately enjoy (despite the momentary shock when inevitably finding out the truth at some point).

As we have shown above, there are ways to teach and learn about Santa that not only enhance our students' festive joy but that can also help develop their epistemic tools too.

Beware!

Honesty may not always be the best policy: This is trickier than we might first think! Asking teachers to lie doesn't seem the healthiest way forward. Yet if a five year old asked you the teacher how babies come about, I'm not sure you'd rush to tell them the truth either. In other words, there are topics that are 'age appropriate' and telling children before their time is sometimes unbecoming (like the sex chat) and other times a killjoy (most obviously, Santa Claus). 'White lies' for the sake of the child is something many of us may do whether for our pupils or for our own children. Of course, it would be unacceptable to lie for our own advantage, and so don't be tempted to use Santa as a method of class control: "One more word out of you and I'll be on the phone to Santa to tell him not to bother with your presents!"

Teachers cannot be forced to lie: No teacher should be forced to say something that goes against their conscience. And so as Santa Claus isn't real, some teachers might find it difficult to lie and pretend otherwise. In such a scenario, I would recommend answering in a non-directive manner: even the staunchest of Immanuel Kant's followers – who forbid outright lying under all circumstances – would allow one to offer an answer that may lead the pupil to infer a false answer, such as: "I like to think Santa Claus is real." You may also be more comfortable with omitting the answer and change the focus to: "What do you think? What does the class think?"

Sources and Resources:

Alberto Giubilini (2018), 'Should we Believe in Santa Claus?' *Practical Ethics*. Retrieved from: http://blog.practicalethics.ox.ac.uk/2018/12/should-we-believe-in-santa-claus/.
Jacqueline Woolley (2020), 'Is Believing in Santa Bad or Good for Kids?' *Texas Perspectives*. Retrieved from: https://news.utexas.edu/2020/01/06/is-believing-in-santa-bad-or-good-for-kids/.
Jeff Standley (2020), 'The Santa Claus Deception: The Ethics of Educator Involvement,' *Theory and Research in Education* 18(2): 174-190.
Judith Ketteler (2019), 'Should You Be Lying to Your Kids About Santa?' *Time*. Retrieved from: https://time.com/5752951/lying-kids-santa/.
Sophie Heizer (2018), 'We Asked Five Experts: Should I Lie to My Children about Santa?' *The Conversation*. Retrieved from: https://theconversation.com/we-asked-five-experts-should-i-lie-to-my-children-about-santa-106930?fbclid=IwAR0U7daZBCCaUIbuPTX-HzdG0MwrF7_mDin0B4sfOG6vvlRx5Pw3JFJbSucw.

Links to Other Controversies:

Tooth Fairy

Do I have a 'normal' family?

Age group: 5-11

How explosive is this topic?

Sensitivities are especially high when schools may potentially clash with home life. With children coming from differing backgrounds but most, if not all, wanting to fit in, this topic of controversy is important to get right.

How should I teach this topic?

Yes to:

   Non-directive teaching: "It's not for me to discuss your own family but let's explore two important words you mentioned and see what they mean: 'normal' and 'family'."

   But no to:

   Directive positive teaching: "Yes, your family would be considered normal" (and so implying some other pupil's family might not be, and vice versa).

Key Terms and Necessary Knowledge:

Cohabiting: Long-term partners living together without marrying or in a civil partnership. In the United Kingdom, this form of living arrangement has increased from 20.6% in 2011 to 24.3% in 2021.

   Diversity: the practice of including and celebrating people from different types of backgrounds.

   Family: at the very basic level, a family can be defined as "a group of one or more parents and their children living together as a unit" (Oxford Languages Dictionary). In the Knowledge Organiser task below, perhaps your students can research into different kinds of families based on culture or religion.

   Love: I love my wife! I love football! I love Bob Dylan! I love cake!

   Whilst I do love all of the above, I am obviously using 'love' in very different ways (at least my wife would like to think so). The Ancient Greeks had four famous words for love and they are really useful to draw on for a high-level discussion about family and relationships:

- **Storge** (pronounced: 'store-gay'): familial, natural love of family members.
- **Philia**: the love between close friends.
- **Eros**: romantic love.
- **Agape** (pronounced: 'aga-pay'): universal, unconditional love. With roots in Christianity, this selfless love is seen by many as the highest form of love to achieve precisely because it is selfless.

(Remember, young children can learn the Greek terms too! Don't shy away from referring to such classical sources. The use of such terms will enrich the classroom conversations you'll have on this topic.)

   Marriage: a cultural or religious union between people, often recognised legally, establishing the rights and obligations between them and their children. Whilst the institution of marriage is pretty universal, it may well vary according to different cultures and beliefs. For example, in the West, the predominant type of marriage is monogamy between one man and one woman. In some Eastern cultures, polygamy might be practised.

Normal/Typical/Predominant: Words matter!

Cambridge Dictionary defines these terms as follows:

- **Normal:** ordinary or usual; the same as would be expected.
- **Typical:** showing all the characteristics that you would usually expect from a particular group of things.
- **Predominant:** more noticeable or important, or larger in number, than others.

If our students from a young age are told their families aren't 'normal,' i.e. abnormal, it takes a particularly strong type of personality to cope with that idea. However, if they understand that their families are simply not typical or predominant, then that may well be an idea they can live with and even celebrate, recognising diversity as a value in itself. Moving away from the normal/abnormal frame of thinking will be crucial when discussing families and other areas of personal sensitivities.

This doesn't mean that "anything goes" and that we need to be relativist and non-judgemental. As the Socratic questions below suggest, there are key ingredients for healthy, happy families, which can be explored and learned about in a classroom context.

Socratic Questions and Critical Thinking:

What are the ingredients for a happy family?

Leo Tolstoy (1828-1910), one of the greatest Russian authors of all time, began his great novel called Anna Karenina (written in 1878) as follows: "Happy families are all alike; every unhappy family is unhappy in its own way." Was he right? What makes your family happy? What might make your family unhappy? Can you compare and contrast your answers with peers on your table?

If you had to order the four forms of love in levels of importance, what would you put at the top and why?

These three questions will help develop your students' abilities to think critically about issues that impact on their lives. The four forms of love celebrate diverse kinds of relationships which each student will experience in different ways.

With your students exploring concepts like love, obligations, duties, and respect, here is an interesting dilemma to get a great discussion going:

If there is a fire and you can save only your mum (assuming you love her) and a scientist with the cure to cancer – who would you save and why?

Of course, you might wish to set this question up as a balloon-style debate. Your pupils will have to think carefully about their reasoning and what arguments will win over their classmates.

Knowledge Organiser on 'Families':

To celebrate different types of families, your students could research and provide a Knowledge Organiser on families, which could focus on a range of issues, depending on how specific or broad their research might be:

- The family across different cultures or religions
- Modern families
- Different types of wedding ceremonies
- Families in cultures different from our own
- The Four Types of Love.

Some Theory:

Families are a hugely important and sensitive topic for all students, especially younger children. They go to the heart of who we are. Yet the discussion of families is also a foundational topic for character education. Research has long shown that at the heart of effective character education is a strong partnership between parents and schools.

The focus on families is an opportunity to think about the virtues they can nurture within each of us. Mark Pike and Thomas Lickona of the 'Narnian Virtues: A Character Education English Curriculum' Project at the University of Leeds write:

> The family is the first school of virtue. It is where we learn to receive and give love. It is where we learn about commitment, sacrifice, and faith in something larger than ourselves. The emotional bond between parent and child deepens the impact of a parent's values and example. Parents are positioned to surround a child with a spiritual heritage that provides a vision of life's meaning and ultimate reasons to lead a good life. The family lays down the foundation on which all other formative institutions build.

The virtues they write about, such as love, commitment, and sacrifice, are very much the ingredients that go into healthy and happy families. Focusing on these virtues – rather than the structure of the family – is much healthier for students to think about and explore.

Indeed, the research of Marvin W. Berkowitz and John H. Grych identified five 'core parenting practices' that contribute to children's social and moral development:

* demandingness: high expectations and support for meeting them
* reasoning: helping children understand how their actions affect others
* nurturance: warmth and responsiveness
* modelling: setting a good example in the treatment of others
* empowerment: practices that give children a voice in, and responsibility for, helping to create a happy family.

Beware!

Get the focus right: Whatever your own ideological leanings, especially about matters of family, there are certain educational principles to abide by in order to get things rights – because they can easily go wrong.

Respect and tolerance are key values in any educational system and so showing disrespect for different family lifestyles isn't acceptable. Nevertheless, this doesn't mean we can't promote core virtues that unite healthy and happy families – no matter how they might be structured. In any event, your young students have no real control over their family structures and dynamic and so potentially making them feel bad can only be damaging for them.

Cultural understanding: This topic is also ideal for exploring different cultures and lifestyles. Depending on age-appropriate subject matter, students might be somewhat surprised to learn about polyandry in some cultures as well as the fact the marriage only became a sacrament in the Church in the 12th century, over 1,000 years after the birth of Christianity. As they build up their knowledge and understanding, perhaps through Knowledge Organisers or class presentations, they can then evaluate different approaches to the family and which structures support the virtues central to good family life.

Sources and Resources:

C.S. Lewis (2013), *The Four Loves*. London: Collins.

Humanists UK (2021), 'A History of Humanist Ceremonies.' Retrieved from: https://understandinghumanism.org.uk/wp-content/uploads/2021/12/History-of-humanist-ceremonies.pdf.

Mark Pike and Thomas Lickona (2023), 'Narnian Virtues: A Character Education English Curriculum.' Retrieved from: https://narnianvirtues.leeds.ac.uk/.

Marvin W. Berkowitz and John H. Grych (1998), 'Fostering Goodness: Teaching Parents to Facilitate Children's Moral Development.' Retrieved from: https://www.researchgate.net/profile/John-Grych/publication/248960311_Fostering_Goodness_teaching_parents_to_facilitate_children%27s_moral_development/links/53ef7f4d0cf26b9b7dcdeffd/Fostering-Goodness-teaching-parents-to-facilitate-childrens-moral-development.pdf.

University of Birmingham, 'The Jubilee Centre.' Retrieved from: https://www.jubileecentre.ac.uk/.

Links to Other Controversies:

'Surely no one can disagree with the idea that 'love is love?''

Surely no one can disagree with the idea that 'love is love'?

Age group: 13-18

How explosive is this topic?

Potential for a fascinating discussion but be wary of things getting personal.

How should I teach this topic?

Yes to:
   Non-directive teaching: "Views on human relationships have changed over time. Are there relationships we consider immoral today that may be accepted by many in the future?"
   And yes to:
   Directive teaching: "Even if we disagree with human relationships on moral or religious grounds, we may not be rude and insulting about others, just as we would not them to be rude about the human relationships or deeply held beliefs that are important to us."
   Whilst many students will be fascinated by this topic and contribute well, there are some who may be insulting about lifestyles that could well be very up close and personal for you and other students in the classroom. Conversely, other students may be rude about religions that may prohibit certain sexual relationships or acts. Irrespective, intellectual virtues such as critical thinking and curiosity can and should stand alongside the moral virtues of compassion and respect, together with the civic virtues of civility and neighbourliness. There is simply no room in the classroom for insulting and intimidating behaviour – which has no bearing on the rights of students to freely express their genuinely held views in a polite and sensitive manner.
   Furthermore, you may teach in a country where schools have a legal duty to foster tolerance and safeguard the rights of people with 'protected characteristics,' which may include sexual orientation and religious beliefs. And so, in the broad range of different sexual relationships, there will be much to debate, which may be done in a non-directive manner. At the same time, the teacher should be clear on their responsibility to maintain an inclusive and tolerant classroom, directing students when they cross the line.

Key Terms and Necessary Knowledge:

Bigamy: a crime in many countries of having more than one spouse.
'Deepity': a thinking tool described by the philosopher Daniel Dennett as a "proposition that *seems* both important and true – and profound – but that achieves this effect by being ambiguous." We all love one-liners and easy slogans. For the purposes of critical thinking though, we should steer our students away from glib expressions that may well belie the complexity of the issues before us. Perhaps 'love is love' is guilty of being a 'deepity?'
Hermeneutics: the branch of knowledge that deals with interpretation, especially of the Bible or literary texts. Scholars often differentiate between:

*   **Exegesis:** seeking to understand what the text means on its own terms
*   **Eisegesis:** bringing your own meaning to Scripture, regardless of what it meant to its original author and audience.

Incest: sexual relations between close family members. Most types of incest are illegal in many countries but sibling incest is legal in countries such as Argentina, Brazil, China, France, Russia, and Spain.

- **Genetic sexual attraction (GSA):** a contentious theory that suggests a phenomenon of intense sexual attraction between biological family members can occur after close relatives are reunited are a long period of separation, such as adoption.

Pederasty: sexual activity involving a man and a boy or youth, which was quite common in ancient Greece and ancient Rome.

Polyamory: having open intimate or romantic relationships with more than one person at a time.

Polyandry: one woman with more than one male intimate partner or husbands (rarer type of polygamy, practised in Himalayan mountain societies).

Polygamy: the practice of marrying more than one spouse; could involve a number of "husbands and wives" in one group or conjoint marriage.

Polygyny: one man with more than one female intimate partner or wives.

Socratic Questions and Critical Thinking:

What are the ingredients for a healthy romantic relationship?

Which types of sexual relationships were frowned upon 100 years ago but are now considered fine in our own society?

Which types of sexual relationships do we disapprove of in our own society that might be considered fine in 100 years from now?

Why might people oppose/support homosexual relationships?

This question is often discussed in A Level Religious Studies specifications in the United Kingdom as well as among teenagers throughout the world. Students deal with the issues well but there must be sensitivities surrounding participants' own sexual preferences as well differing religious or philosophical beliefs that may arise. Here are some key arguments a teacher can draw on to develop a healthy classroom discussion:

Opposing Homosexual Relationships
Religious Authority:
Many great religious texts have been interpreted to prohibit homosexual relations leading to restrictions on homosexual relationships in some of the world's great religions.
In Judaism, for example:
• Leviticus 18:22: "You shall not lie with a male as with a woman; it is an abomination."
In Christianity, for example:
• 1 Corinthians 6:9-10: "Or do you not know that wrongdoers will not inherit the kingdom of God? Do not be deceived: Neither the sexually immoral nor idolaters nor adulterers nor men who have sex with men, nor thieves nor the greedy nor drunkards nor slanderers nor swindlers will inherit the kingdom of God."
In Islam, for example:
Quran 27:55: "Do you indeed approach men with desire instead of women? Rather, you are a people behaving ignorantly."

Natural Law:
The human body doesn't seem 'designed' for homosexual relations, with reproduction not possible. As St Thomas Aquinas reasoned, sex between people of the same gender misuses the body parts and so disregards their functions, such as wasting semen. (For this reason, Aquinas would oppose masturbation too.) Rather, the purpose of sex is to have children and where procreation isn't possible, this is nature's way of telling us that this is morally wrong.
As the Catechism of the Catholic Church (2357) puts it: "They [homosexual acts] are contrary to the natural law. They close the sexual act to the gift of life. They do not proceed from a genuine affective and sexual complementarity. Under no circumstances can they be approved."

Supporting Homosexual Relationships
Religious Authority:
The sources cited above are debated in terms of how we interpret texts (known as 'hermeneutics').
Some modern scholars, for example, might argue that the verse in Leviticus is really opposing promiscuity: choose your lover and stick with them!
Other modern scholars interpret the verse in Corinthians as referring to the sexual exploitation of young men by older men, a practice called pederasty, which was commonly practised in parts of the ancient world.
Rather, other biblical texts can be interpreted as acceptance of homosexual relationships:
Many Jews and Christians point to the fundamental belief that all of humanity is created in God's image (Genesis 1:27), seeing this as a celebration of diversity, including gender diversity, as well as the importance of treating everyone with dignity and respect.
In Christianity, the foundational principle of agape. Jesus' command in John 13:34-35 expresses the universal love of agape: "A new command I give you: Love one another. As I have loved you, so you must love one another. By this everyone will know that you are my disciples, if you love one another."
Some Christian scholars see this in action is the story of 'The Faith of the Centurion' (Matthew 8:5-13 and Luke 7:1-10), modelling an accepting and welcoming attitude towards homosexuals. Rather than criticise the implied homosexual relationship between the centurion and his servant, Jesus not only praises the faith of the centurion but also heals his servant boy who had been unwell.
Indeed, in 2013, when asked about gay priests, Pope Francis responded: "If they [gay priests] accept the Lord and have goodwill, who am I to judge them? They shouldn't be marginalised. The tendency [same-sex attraction] is not the problem... they're our brothers."
Within Islam, some point to the basic principle of celebrating diversity: "We created you different tribes and nations so that you may come to know one another and acknowledge that the most honourable among you are those that stay the most conscious of Allah" (Surat al-Hujarat 49:13). As Scott Siraj al-Haqq Kugle, a scholar on Islam, reasons, with the Qur'an celebrating diversity at so many levels in both the natural and human world, it would be logical that this value of diversity applies to sexuality as well.
Natural Law:
Who is to say what the 'purpose' of sex is? For example, many heterosexual married couples have sex with no intention to have children, e.g. if the wife is already pregnant or postmenopausal. Sex may be for the couple to enjoy each other or have a 'unitive' purpose and bring them closer together. Such relationships are promoted by the great religions and so should homosexual relations too as they bring the same levels of unity, comfort, and enjoyment.
Moreover, philosophers like David Hume (1711-1776) reject natural moral law. Hume points to a 'logical fallacy' in trying to base a moral value on a scientific fact. Just because nature doesn't allow homosexual couples to procreate doesn't necessarily mean it's wrong.

Consent and Autonomy:
For many students in the West, the liberal concepts of consent and autonomy are paramount in any discussion of sexual relations. 'Love is love' is so powerful because as long as the individuals in the relationship consent – whatever kind of relationship: heterosexual or homosexual, monogamous or polyamorous, etc. – then it's no one else's business what they get up to! Teaching experience shows this reason to be the most popular among young people and it goes to the heart of values such as individual liberty, respect, and tolerance, which underpin liberal democratic societies.
Jeremy Bentham, the radical utilitarian thinker, summed up this notion powerfully when he wrote:
If there be one idea more ridiculous than another it is that of a legislator who, when a man and a woman are agreed about a business of this sort, thrusts himself in between them, examining situations, regulating times, and prescribing modes and postures.

My experience in a London classroom is that the issue of homosexuality is behaviourally uncontroversial for nearly all teenagers today. Outside of faith schools, I haven't come across students who think there is a real moral dilemma over the legitimacy of homosexual relationships. Indeed, the discussion is often 'academic' in trying to explore why different cultures and religions may raise objections.

Nevertheless, with nearly all students relying on the principles of 'consent' and 'personal autonomy,' it is interesting and revealing to explore how far they're willing to push these arguments. There is no better thought experiment to try in the classroom than Jonathan Haidt's brilliant 'Julie and Mark' scenario, which will leave most of your students 'morally confounded':

> Julie and Mark are brother and sister. They are traveling together in France on summer vacation from college. One night, they are staying alone in a cabin near the beach. They decide that it would be interesting and fun if they tried making love. At the very least, it would be a new experience for each of them. Julie was already taking birth control pills, but Mark uses a condom, too, just to be safe. They both enjoy making love, but they decide never to do it again. They keep that night as a special secret, which makes them feel even closer to each other. What do you think about that? Was it okay for them to make love?

Classic student responses (*and helpful teacher responses*) are:

- Yuck! That's just wrong!
  Can you explain why it's wrong? Is 'yuck' good enough? For them it clearly wasn't 'yuck.'

- It's illegal!
  In France it isn't! Sibling incest is legal in many countries around the world. So what's wrong?

- But if they have a child, there will be genetic defects because of inbreeding.
  Yes, but they used two forms of birth control and Julie could get an abortion if they didn't work. So with little to no chance of having children, is it still wrong?

- It will ruin the relationship and cause emotional problems.
  The scenario is clear that it brought them closer together, they never do it again, and they look back happily on that special occasion. They both consented and are happy. So what's wrong?

- It's bad for society. Younger people may learn from them.
  But they kept the night as a special secret. No one else ever found out. So what's wrong?

It is worth noting that many of the typical objections to Mark and Julie's night of passion will be similar to many people's arguments against homosexual sex:

- Not long ago, many in society thought homosexual sex was 'yuck'
- Homosexual sex was illegal even in many Western countries. Laws change
- The problem of genetic defects due to inbreeding is a Natural Moral Law argument similar in logic to homosexual sex being wrong because it doesn't allow for procreation at all
- Many traditionalists have opposed homosexual relationships on similar grounds that they are corrupting, immoral, and point to emotional and psychological problems. Yet these claims are not taken seriously by many in liberal society today.

In turn, these Socratic questions force students to reconsider their reasoning. Are they being consistent in their thinking?

There will be a few who are willing to accept that as long as the incestuous relationship is consensual between two adults, then it is morally acceptable. But Socratic questioning like this will certainly test how far your students are willing to go.

Some Theory:

Applying epistemic reasoning to matters of love hardly seems the most romantic of ideas. Well, true but remember you're in the classroom!

For Professor Michael Hand, an influential philosopher of moral education, homosexuality should be taught in a directive manner as legitimate as there are no reasonable arguments against it. Along the lines of the arguments that we gave above in support of homosexual relationships, Hand concludes that "the established arguments for the moral illegitimacy of homosexual acts quickly buckle under the pressure of rational examination, we may say with some confidence that homosexuality does not satisfy the epistemic criterion of controversiality."

However, as I think the Julie and Mark scenario suggests, Hand's arguments could equally apply to sibling incest. Does this mean that as teachers we should be directive in our teaching that sibling incest is uncontroversially acceptable? I'm not convinced many teachers (let alone parents, pupils, and policy makers) could accept this.

It would therefore seem that the epistemic criteria falls short in capturing the complexity of moral dilemmas. Rather, some teachers might prefer to look to Jonathan Haidt's influential Moral Foundations Theory (MFT) for a pluralist moral framework to help guide their handling of such dilemmas in the classroom.

Firstly, MFT recognises the values of our moral intuitions. We are 'morally confounded' because we have an immediate disgust but as we look for reasons to justify our disgust, this scenario cleverly closes them off. Rationally, it seems we're forced to say Mark and Julie behaved morally.

Yet MFT not only considers the liberal ethic of autonomy, which is hugely popular with Western students, but it also extends consideration to the ethics of community and divinity, which is crucial for meeting the broader aims of moral and religious education, such as developing reason, identity, and cultural understanding.

On the one hand, the 'ethic of community' relies on concepts such as duty, respect, and loyalty, that aims to preserve institutions and social order. On the other, the 'ethic of divinity' relies on concepts such as purity, sanctity, and sin, that protects the divinity inherent in each person against the degradation of hedonistic selfishness. These ethical spheres offer us a moral language to help us appreciate the dynamics of family and sanctity of those relationships which this incestuous relationship would seem to cut against. Concepts like sanctity and degradation may not be entirely rational, but they play a major role in moral communities and so help articulate our disgust. Teachers may therefore want to bring them into play to see if they speak to their students and help broaden their own considerations when thinking about issues of moral controversy.

In this vein, perhaps the most articulate defence in recent years of the notion that 'love is love' in the context of gay marriage, was Justice Anthony Kennedy's judgement that he wrote for the U.S. Supreme court's landmark decision to legalise gay marriage in America:

> No union is more profound than marriage, for it embodies the highest ideals of love, fidelity, devotion, sacrifice, and family. In forming a marital union, two people become something greater than once they were. As some of the petitioners in these cases demonstrate, marriage embodies a love that may endure even past death. It would misunderstand these men and women to say they disrespect the idea of marriage. Their plea is that they do respect it, respect it so deeply that they seek to find its fulfilment for themselves. Their hope is not to be condemned to live in loneliness, excluded from one of civilization's oldest institutions. They ask for equal dignity in the eyes of the law. The Constitution grants them that right.
>
> (Supreme Court of the United States, 2014)

Kennedy grounded the institution of marriage within the ethics of autonomy, community, and even divinity, through terms such as devotion, sacrifice, and family. His celebrated judgement not only focused on the Western values of liberty and equality but also showcased the wider virtues of marriage, recognising its central and sacred feature across all civilisations. Referring to the 'the transcendent importance of marriage' which 'promised nobility and dignity' (Supreme Court of the United States, 2014), Justice Kennedy wrote that:

> through its enduring bond, two persons together can find other freedoms, such as expression, intimacy, and spirituality. This is true for all persons, whatever their sexual orientation. There is dignity in the bond between two men or two women who seek to marry and in their autonomy to make such profound choices.
>
> (Supreme Court of the United States, 2014)

By presenting Kennedy's judgement to your students, the discussion may be elevated beyond the purely epistemic to recognise other values that so enrich our lives and relationships.

Beware!

Up close and personal: this topic is as personal as it gets and so beware of personal sensitivities. Students are inherently interested in the topic and so it raises an excellent opportunity to develop their thinking about complex issues. In turn, it would be helpful to keep the conversation at a distance, moving away from personal anecdotes or experiences.

Teacher stance: This is the kind of topic that tempts students to pry into their teacher's private life, which could be deeply inappropriate. To help mitigate against this, think carefully about the stance you'll be taking in such a discussion. 'Neutral impartiality,' where the teacher will lead the debate without disclosing her own view, seems most appropriate here to help defend against accusations of intolerance or bias. This may be especially apt where it is obvious that the teacher subscribes to a religious belief and lifestyle. In turn, playing 'devil's advocate' and offering those Socratic questions to elicit deeper student thinking – no matter their perspective – will keep the focus on the issues rather than the personalities involved.

Sources and Resources:

C.S. Lewis (2013), *The Four Loves*. London: Collins.

Cumbria County Council (n.d.), 'Genetic Sexual Attraction: Adoption Support.' Retrieved from: https://www.cumbria.gov.uk/eLibrary/Content/Internet/327/857/6802/42109163456.pdf.

Daniel C. Dennett (2014), *Intuition Pumps and Other Tools for Thinking*. London: Penguin.

Glenn Y. Bezalel (2020), '"Moral Dumbfounding": Moral Foundations Theory for the Classroom,' *Theory and Research in Education*, 18(2). Retrieved from: https://journals.sagepub.com/doi/full/10.1177/1477878520934014.

Jonathan Haidt (2012), *The Righteous Mind: Why Good People Are Divided by Politics and Religion*. London: Penguin.

Justice Kennedy's Opinion, 'Obergefell vs Hodges.' Retrieved from: https://www.law.cornell.edu/supct/pdf/14-556.pdf.

Scott Kugle (2010), *Homosexuality in Islam*. London: Oneworld Academic.

The Human Rights Campaign, '"Religion and Faith" Resources.' Retrieved from: https://www.hrc.org/resources/religion-faith.

Links to Other Controversies:

Do I have a 'normal' family?

Are transwomen women?

Are transwomen, women?

Age group: 13-18

How explosive is this topic?

This is such an explosive topic that there are people who even refuse to debate it:
"Transwomen are women. Full stop!"
"A man can't become a woman. Simple!"
This has arguably become the most controversial of issues, splitting parts of society, with opponents decrying the other side as bigoted. There have even been news reports of students, teachers, and academics hounded out for their views. Proceed with caution.

How should I teach this topic?

From the outset, a teacher must recognise how sensitive the topic will be for some, especially if personal for them or for a loved one. In turn, it may be worthwhile introducing any discussion of the issue with a 'directive' teaching stance that explicitly opposes any discrimination because of a person's "protected characteristics." In the United Kingdom, under the Equality Act 2010, this means it is against the law to discriminate against anyone because of:

- age
- gender reassignment
- being married or in a civil partnership
- being pregnant or on maternity leave
- disability
- race including colour, nationality, ethnic, or national origin
- religion or belief
- sex
- sexual orientation.

Quite simply, teachers have a legal duty to uphold the law and ensure no discrimination takes place in the classroom based on these protected characteristics. This includes gender reassignment as well as sex.
Remember though, it also includes religion or belief, and a protected belief extends to deeply held views on either side of this debate, even if offensive and distressing to others. It is important therefore to engender a classroom culture that tolerates (and, I believe, celebrates) opposing views whilst having no truck with gratuitously discourteous behaviour. Such a balance would be supported not just in terms of the law but also within a responsible school ethos.
Now that you have set the scene, I would recommend one of two teaching approaches, depending on how confident you are in hosting such a debate:

1. 'Neutral impartiality': where a teacher is less confident, she may wish to lead a debate on the matter without disclosing her own view. Under the principle of charity, she will present the best versions of competing viewpoints so that her students are empowered to decide for themselves. Understandably, she may feel that by offering her own perspective, she

may alienate students with differing viewpoints, distracting from the educational aims of the discussion.

2. 'Committed impartiality': where a teacher is more confident, she should express her own view on the issue whilst ensuring that competing perspectives receive a fair hearing too. The teacher thus highlights the importance of "owning" her viewpoint and having to justify her perspective in light of other reasonable approaches. This allows her to model intellectual, moral, and civic virtues like reflection, humility, and civility. If done well, this will empower students to offer their own perspectives and be open to hearing competing approaches too. It goes without saying, that for a matter of controversy, the teacher cannot present her view with the aim of winning over her students to her side of the debate.

Key Terms and Necessary Knowledge:

As you'll see below in our debate on Jaffa Cakes, words matter! How we define these terms can in itself be controversial. For example, take the word, "woman." Of late, quite a few people are tying themselves up in knots trying to define what this word means. In 2022, the online Cambridge Dictionary expanded its definition of a woman. A long-time definition is simply, "an adult female human being," providing a biological understanding of the term. Yet the dictionary now offers the following definition too: "an adult who lives and identifies as female though they may have been said to have a different sex at birth." It sounds like the Cambridge Dictionary is giving a nod in answer to our student's question, as the examples of usage suggest:

*   She was the first trans woman elected to a national office.
*   Mary is a woman who was assigned male at birth.

Will your students agree with these definitions of woman?
What about the following terms related to the debate:

*   Ageism
*   Binary/Non-binary
*   Cisgender
*   Culture appreciation
*   Cultural appropriation
*   Intersectionality
*   Intersex
*   Sex
*   Sexism
*   Gender
*   Man
*   Transgender
*   Transgracial
*   Transracial
*   Woman.

On these most explosive of issues, I am happy to leave your students with a helpful introductory task of finding out what these terms mean, being prepared to offer more than one definition where controversy abounds.

Socratic Questions and Critical Thinking:

Classroom Discussion:

•   *Are Jaffa cakes biscuits or cakes?*

I have found that tackling the issue of transgenderism head on rarely works. Emotions are running high, students are worried about offending their peers, and there is a rush to stand loyal with one's side. 'In-group' bias is very likely to be on display here. All these emotive realities undermine any chance for a rational debate.

And so I would suggest tackling the issue sideways through – I kid you not – Jaffa Cakes![1]

McVities, the manufacturer, have always classified their Jaffa Cakes as cakes. This became of legal interest in 1991 because the U.K. tax authorities wanted to challenge this, arguing that Jaffa Cakes are in fact biscuits. This was important because while there is no tax on cakes, there is tax charged on chocolate-covered biscuits. And so the case went to court.

In a celebrated judgement, Mr Charles Potter QC sought to answer the following questions: what makes a cake a cake and what makes a biscuit a biscuit. He did so by analysing all the properties of these different types of foods. Before reading his ideas, perhaps you'd like to have a go (and students love having a go too):

Man	Woman
Student's judgement:	

After filling in your thoughts on the issue, it is now time to reveal the judge's analysis[2]:

Cakes	Biscuits
My view: Jaffa Cakes are .... because...	

If your brain is already beginning to hurt, how about considering whether the question of "cake" or "biscuit" might be a classic false dichotomy? In other words, could there be other options? Could Jaffa Cakes be something in between? How about a "biscake?!"

As the philosopher David Edmonds suggests, just as we think about what makes a cake a cake (or not), so too can such classifications help us think about other concepts proving controversial. For example, how might we attempt to classify a "man" or a "woman?" Just as Judge

Potter sought to identify the salient features of cakes and biscuits in order to define those very terms, can we do so for men and women? This may not be as simple as some might think...

Evidence for cakes	Evidence for biscuits
Name: Jaffa 'Cake' This is a very minor consideration indeed. **Ingredients** Cakes differ widely, from at one end sponge cakes, at the other Christmas cakes, which may appear to have little in common. However, the ingredients of the sponge part of the Jaffa Cake are virtually the same as the ingredients of a traditional sponge cake. Egg, flour, and sugar are kneaded together, and the result is aerated. The sponge-cake part of a Jaffa Cake is in itself "cake." **Texture.** Reference was made by the witness Mr Wood to texture, but he regarded visible texture as important; what I have in mind is the physical texture. Generally, I would expect a cake to be entirely or mainly soft and friable, not able to be snapped and not crisp. The Jaffa Cake has the texture of a sponge cake, which the brittleness of the chocolate does not displace. **Other considerations:** • The sponge part of a Jaffa Cake is made from a thin batter containing egg, flour, and sugar, whereas most biscuits may be expected to be made from a rather thicker mixture that may be cut. Generally cakes may be moulded from a thin batter whereas biscuits may not be moulded but cut. However, I do not regard this as an important factor. • A Jaffa Cake is moist to start with and in that resembles a cake and not a biscuit; with time it becomes stale, and last becomes hard and crisp; again like a cake and not like a biscuit. Generally I would expect a stale biscuit to have become soft. • The sponge-cake part is not simply a base for the jam and chocolate; it is a substantial part of the product, not in flavour, but in bulk and texture when eaten.	**Size.** The Jaffa Cake is small, being a couple of inches across, substantially smaller than the average cake. Generally I would expect a biscuit to be smaller than a cake, and the size of a Jaffa Cake is typical of a biscuit and not typical of a cake. **Packaging.** Jaffa Cakes are packaged in a way that I regard as "uncakelike." They are sold in packets of 3 or 6 or 12 or 24; in any event in cylindrical packets, much like Digestive biscuits, which packets are then contained in cardboard boxes. This factor clearly points against Jaffa Cakes being cakes. **Marketing.** Generally, in supermarkets, where cakes and biscuits are found in separate places, Jaffa Cakes are found with biscuits and are not found with cakes. The buyer will be unlikely to find Jaffa Cakes on a cake counter. **Other considerations:** • Jaffa Cakes are presented, and accepted by the public, as being snacks, normally eaten with the fingers; whereas a cake, although sometimes eaten with the fingers, is normally to be found eaten from a plate, perhaps with a knife or pastry fork. • Jaffa Cakes may be expected to appeal particularly to children, who may consume one of them in one, possibly two, mouthfuls. In this respect, it resembles a biscuit or a sweet.

Mr Potter QC's judgement:
"Generally, I come to the conclusion that Jaffa Cakes have characteristics of cakes, and also characteristics of biscuits or non-cakes. I conclude that they have sufficient characteristics of cakes to qualify as cakes... If it be relevant, I also determine that the Jaffa Cakes are not biscuits. I therefore allow the appeal..."
(In other words, McVities won the case and Jaffa Cakes were deemed to be cakes, not biscuits.)

Indeed, this is a particularly difficult controversy as the issue will divide opinion on what the salient characteristics are. For example:

- Is the self-identifying name important here?
- Is it all about the "ingredients" or biology?

Such considerations mean the transgender controversy is a classroom topic that may be taught as a cross-disciplinary endeavour. I can imagine biologists wanting a say; philosophers and sociologists will want input too. Whatever angles are taken up, it is crucial that, as the judge demonstrated, students provide reasons for why they consider a factor important or otherwise.

And remember, students don't have to go down the man *or* woman route to answer the question. We may argue that just as there really is a third option of a "biscake" for Jaffa Cakes, so too might there be a third (or more) option for gender classification. Perhaps the world isn't so binary after all...

Yet we could nuance this even further. Even if there are many gradations between a cake and biscuit – or man and woman – is this better seen as a sliding scale or as clusters of differing but distinct identities? If the former, one can see why definitions can begin to feel more blurred than we might have imagined as we extend our definitions along the scale. If the latter, with the vast majority of confectionary (or people) really belonging in one category or the other, then we might well argue that our definitions cannot be reimagined to include a small minority and so undermine the identity of the vast majority.

The real-world implication of cake vs biscuit was tax. However, the real-world applications of our discussion have very real and sensitive outcomes for those involved. The debate is primarily about the very existential identity of people (which cakes and biscuits presumably don't have to grapple with). Yet it is also about the ramifications for how we think about highly contentious issues such as transgenderism in sport, use of public bathrooms, and the preservation of single-sex spaces to protect vulnerable women and girls. These issues do entail a clash of rights and so it is important to understand why people on both sides of the divide feel so passionately about the issues under discussion.[3]

Further Socratic questions to get your students thinking:

- *Can a white woman identify as a black woman?*

In 2015, a scandal broke out when Rachel Dolezal, an anti-racist campaigner in the United States, was "outed" by her parents as biologically white and that she was pretending to be black. Dolezal acknowledged that she was indeed born to white parents but that she self-identified as black as a transracial person, sincerely dedicating her adult life to black causes. Critics slammed her for cultural appropriation and for lying about her identity.

In 2016, Ronnie Gladden, an American academic, wrote about their identifications as follows: "In spite of presenting as outwardly black and male – by in large I view myself as white and female." In describing their "transgracial" journey – from black to white, from male to female – Gladden spoke of feeling "an urgency to be forthcoming about my true identity in an era where transparency is not just encouraged; it is demanded." Gladden's testimony continues:

> Due to my internalised transgender and transracial collisions, I am slowly expressing elements of my transgracial tensions. My "inner white woman" is at the centre of my identity constitution, which most often harmonises with my core instincts and deepest authentic sense of self; I have been aware of this truth since the age of four. It is my internal standard.

You may wish to share this testimony with your students, asking the following questions for your students to clarify their thinking:

- Do you respect Gladden's self-identification as a woman?
- Do you respect Gladden's self-identification as white?
- If you have answered differently for these questions, explain why they are different.

Interestingly, although the controversy of transgenderism is all over the media, students will be less aware of "transracialism," even though it is hardly new. As the scholar Lewis Gordon notes, there is a long line of people whose racial identities come apart from their recent ancestries. Meanwhile, Rogers Brubaker points out that even though many might find transracialism offensive, it is psychologically real: just as one may assume 'good faith' among transgender people, this is no less the case for the transracial people either.

Yet it is worthwhile to note that how we feel about these issues may depend on how we are politically and socially aligned. Brubaker traces two possible dividing lines:

First, "essentialists" assume that gender and race are grounded in "nature" and "history," things that just are and can't be changed. In contrast, "voluntarists" argue that race and gender are identities that can be "chosen." So while essentialists would lean towards not recognising the chosen identities of transgender or transracial people, voluntarists would accept the possibilities of such changes in identity.

Second, and more complicated, is that our view towards transgenderism and/or transracialism may well depend on whether we are aligned to the 'right' or to the 'left.' Brubaker observes that many so-called social justice warriors fighting for transgender rights are precisely those who oppose transracialism, "policing" race more than gender. Yet for many on the right, it is sex and gender that are "more closely policed" than race. Could the debate be more about which camp we belong to rather than sound reasoning? What social and existential considerations are impacting our differing stances?

I suspect you're going to have an interesting debate on your hands – and your students are going to have to think hard!

- *Can a 25-year-old man identify as a 15-year-old boy?*

In 2018, Emile Ratelband, a Dutchman biologically aged 69 years at the time, went to court to change his birth date by 20 years, as he identified as a 49 year old. In his own words: "We live in a time when you can change your name and change your gender. Why can't I decide my own age?" For Ratelband, this was important as he felt like a 49 year old (with his doctors telling him that he had the body of someone in their 40s), and that he was discriminated against because of his age. "If I'm 49, then I can buy a new house, drive a different car. I can take up more work. When I'm on Tinder and it says I'm 69, I don't get an answer. When I'm 49, with the face I have, I will be in a luxurious position." Ageism – discrimination against someone because of their age – is felt acutely by many elderly people, with some commentators noticing similarities with sexism and racism.

The court agreed that age – like a person's gender or name – is part of a person's identity. Nevertheless, they dismissed the case as they felt the complications of allowing people to change their age "would cause all kinds of legal problems." The court said: "Rights and obligations are also attached to age... for example, the right to vote, the right to marry, the opportunity to drink alcohol and to drive a car." Interestingly, the novelty of the case also worked against Mr Ratelband: for though there has been a worldwide campaign for transgender rights, his was a lone voice in the fight to change his age.

Once our students get over the initial temptation to laugh off Mr Ratelband's case, assuming good faith, as we have for transgender and transracial causes, should we view "trans-ageism" in the same manner? If so, are there limits? My question purposely chooses provocative ages, with potentially catastrophic ramifications for a "trans-15-year-old" having a romantic relationship with a biological 15 year old.

• *Is a lesbian transphobic if she refuses to date a transgender woman?*

The philosopher, Amia Srinivasan, has noted that transwomen "often face sexual exclusion from lesbian cis women who at the same time claim to take them seriously as women." This is sometimes known as the 'cotton ceiling' (based on the phrase, 'glass ceiling') and refers to the (underwear) barrier some transwomen feel they face when seeking relationships or sex with women. For Nancy Kelley, the CEO of Stonewall, a lesbian, gay, bisexual, and transgender rights charity in the United Kingdom, outright refusal of women to date transgender women is analogous to "sexual racism." Cathryn McGahey KC, a leading barrister, concurs, likening transgender women overcoming lesbians' sexual boundaries "to South Africa attempting to racially integrate society." In other words, just as we might claim that a white person refusing to date a non-white person per se is racism, so too is it discriminatory to sexually exclude a transgender woman whilst dating ciswomen. Is this argument correct?

Moreover, have your students been consistent in their reasoning about whether one can draw analogies between race and gender? Have they applied the same logic for the transracial vs transgender question above and for the "sexual racism" claim here?

Of course, the question can be flipped, especially for those teaching boys. For example:

• *Is a heterosexual man transphobic if he refuses to date a transgender woman?*

Some Theory:

There are claims on both sides of the divide that this is not a 'controversial' issue. In other words, the question, "are transwomen, women?" is a closed one and deserves a one-word answer.

On one side, you might hear the claim: "A man can't become a woman. Simple." For this side, the answer is no. Germain Greer, for example, believes that transgender male-to-female people are not women, that they don't "look like, sound like or behave like women."

Yet for the other side: "Trans women are women." As Rachel Stein put it: "Whether you are trans or not, your identity is yours alone. I do not question your identity... and in return, I wouldn't expect you to question mine – or anyone else's. What right would you have to do so?" For this side, the answer is simply yes.

That this issue is *behaviourally* controversial is unquestionable – opinion really is sharply divided. In the United Kingdom, for example, a YouGov report showed whilst 55% of the public support the right of people to identify as being of a different gender to the one they had recorded at birth, only 40% say the law should allow people to change their legal gender. YouGov shows a partisan split with "Conservative voters hold less permissive views on transgender rights than Labour voters across the board." Indeed, while 71% of Labour voters say someone should be able to change their social gender, just 41% of Conservative voters agree.

Meanwhile, according to the Pew Research Center in the United States, 60% of people say a person's gender is determined by their sex at birth. Opinion is highly partisan on the issue, with 59% of Democrats saying that society hasn't gone far enough in accepting people who are transgender; in contrast, 66% of Republicans say society has gone too far in accepting people who are transgender.

It is also *politically* controversial as liberal democracies generally protect philosophical beliefs from discrimination, including opposing beliefs with regard to gender. Just as some feminists don't accept the view that transgender women are women in defence of women's rights, so too many other human rights activists argue that they are simply fighting for trans identity rights. Yet as scholars like Germaine Greer readily admit, these differing approaches are simply "opinions" which societies and their political representatives alike are grappling with.

Despite the wishes of those with entrenched positions, the issues involved are *epistemically* controversial and highly complex. Move away from the heat of passionate activists towards the light of serious thinkers, and a teacher can expose her students to the fascinating debates raging between supporters of gender self-identification and those who advocate the primacy of biological sex; between "voluntarists" and "essentialists"; between different historically oppressed groups; and between different schools of feminism.

As students are trying to make sense of these issues, it would be an educational own goal to not teach and learn about these debates in the classroom, a relatively controlled environment that can allow students to seek the truth in a safe and inclusive manner.

Beware!

Perhaps best to avoid altogether? Studies suggest this is the preferred approach of many teachers for issues such as this. Transgenderism is seen as too controversial. Who wants to be "cancelled" or be labelled a bigot? However, here are four reasons why 'exclusive neutrality' – the stance of avoiding the subject altogether – is counterproductive:

- Cultural capital: it is a key public debate in wider society and so our students should be more aware and literate about the world around them.
- Promote cultural understanding: a greater appreciation for the complexities of the debate can help counter divisions raging in society. The classroom is a healthy environment to appreciate the sensitivities and complexities surrounding such issues.
- Students bring it up: yet avoiding any education about transgenderism only helps breed ignorance on a matter of real personal and social importance. For those interested, they'll find out about it elsewhere and so surely the classroom is the preferable place for studying such issues of controversy.
- Curriculum: this conflict may well feature in biology, history, politics, civics or religious studies.

Polarity management:[4] This concept is going to be crucial for the success of any discussion on this most sensitive of topics. Teachers will be aiming for two separate and seemingly competing goals:

- reaching the truth through considering the arguments (the epistemic aim)
- maintaining an environment where all feel safe and included (the virtue aim).

Yet skilful classroom management can ensure that both are pursued. Remember, school students aren't adults! Whilst there may well be good arguments for only pursuing the epistemic aim in public discourse, including at university level, school pupils are your responsibility in the classroom. Disagreement needn't mean disrespect.

Sources and Resources:

Amia Srinivasan (2021), *The Right to Sex*. London: Bloomsbury.
BBC News (2018), 'Emile Ratelband, 69, Told He Cannot Legally Change His Age.' Retrieved from: https://www.bbc.co.uk/news/world-europe-46425774.

Cambridge Dictionary (2022), 'woman.' Retrieved from: https://dictionary.cambridge.org/dictionary/english/woman.

Caroline Lowbridge (2021), 'The Lesbians Who Feel Pressured to Have Sex and Relationships with Trans Women.' Retrieved from: https://www.bbc.co.uk/news/uk-england-57853385.

David Edmonds (2017), 'Cake or Biscuit? Why Jaffa Cakes Excite Philosophers.' Retrieved from: https://www.bbc.co.uk/news/magazine-38985820.

Germain Greer (2016), 'Germaine Greer: Transgender Women Are "Not Women" - BBC NEWSNIGHT.' Retrieved from: https://www.youtube.com/watch?v=7B8Q6D4a6TM.

ITV News (2023), 'Nicola Sturgeon Flounders on Trans Policy for Female Prisons.' Retrieved from: https://www.youtube.com/watch?v=5fSEVUMGIKY.

Julie Bindell (2022), 'QC Compares Lesbians Refusing Sex with Transwomen to Apartheid.' Retrieved from: https://unherd.com/thepost/qc-compares-lesbians-refusing-sex-with-transwomen-to-apartheid/.

Kim Parker et al. (2022), 'Americans' Complex Views on Gender Identity and Transgender Issues.' Retrieved from: https://www.pewresearch.org/social-trends/2022/06/28/americans-complex-views-on-gender-identity-and-transgender-issues/.

Matthew Smith (2022), 'Where Does the British Public Stand on Transgender Rights in 2022?' Retrieved from: https://yougov.co.uk/topics/society/articles-reports/2022/07/20/where-does-british-public-stand-transgender-rights.

Nancy Kelly (2022), 'Stonewall Statement on Women's and Equalities Minister's New Approach to Equality.' Retrieved from: https://www.stonewall.org.uk/about-us/news/stonewall-state-ment-women%E2%80%99s-and-equalities-minister%E2%80%99s-new-approach-equality.

Rebecca Tuvel (2017), 'In Defense of Transracialism,' *Hypatia* 32(2): 263–278.

Rogers Brubaker (2016), *Trans: Gender and Race in an Age of Unsettled Identities*. Oxford: Princeton University Press.

The Economist (2018), 'Transgender Identities: A Series of Invited Essays.' Retrieved from: https://www.economist.com/open-future/2018/06/29/transgender-identities-a-series-of-invited-essays.

Tim Crane (n.d.), 'Jaffa Cakes.' Retrieved from: http://www.timcrane.com/jaffa-cakes.html.

Links to Other Controversies:

Surely no one can disagree with the idea that 'love is love?'

Should there be any limits on free speech?

Being 'Woke' just means being kind to others, especially vulnerable people. How can anyone disagree with that?

Who's to blame for the Israeli-Palestinian conflict?

Age group: 11–18

How explosive is this topic?

Everything about the Israeli-Palestinian Conflict is controversial! I'm even mindful that putting 'Israeli' before 'Palestinian' in the title might lead some to claim bias. On the flipside, perhaps 'The Israeli-Arab Conflict' might better describe the ruptures in the Middle East for the last 100 years or so. Of course, fans of Occam's Broom will point out that other conflicts in the Middle East have caused far more deaths and so that this book lacks guides on those wars and focuses on this one, shows bias too!

How should I teach this topic?

This topic is so fraught; it will be near impossible to reach consensus. It is also highly complex, with many experts pointing out that there are actually a number of conflicts going on all at once. In turn, students should learn about the conflict through different narratives: one 'mainstream' Israeli, another 'mainstream' Palestinian. Remember, teachers have a responsibility to challenge extremism and prevent radicalisation; in many countries, this responsibility may well be a legal duty. The conflict sadly invites extremism and so teachers should aim to provide a blend of non-directive and directive teaching as follows:

Yes to 'just causes':

1. Mainstream Palestinian cause: 'A Palestinian struggle – within international law – to create an independent state alongside Israel.'
2. Mainstream Israeli cause: 'An Israeli fight – within international law – for the security of Israel within negotiated and agreed borders.'

In presenting these approaches, the teacher should take the approach that is known as 'neutral impartiality,' that is, teaching these major perspectives while remaining neutral on their own view. With some students potentially identifying with a side of the conflict, some may feel excluded if they feel the teacher is 'against' them. Moreover, on epistemic grounds, the conflict is genuinely complex with rights and wrongs on both sides and so it would be wrong for a teacher to direct pupils to their perspective. Indeed, modelling neutrality will help students gain a more nuanced and sophisticated understanding.

However, this does not mean that people can have their own facts: history can still be taught even as one offers different interpretations and narratives of the events in question, making clear where views are contested.

But no to 'unjust causes':

1. Radical Palestinian cause: 'A Palestinian war to destroy the state of Israel'
2. Radical Israeli cause: 'An Israeli war for Greater Israel, with no room for a Palestinian state'
3. Extremist unlawful conduct: 'The use of terrorism or any actions that go against international law.'

Directive teaching here means teachers have a duty to 'direct' their students away from such 'unjust causes' that promote extremism and radicalisation. However, this doesn't mean a teacher should shut down such views without providing just arguments in the classroom. This would hardly model good critical thinking! Indeed, high-quality education means providing reasons and evidence for the position taken. Simply dismissing extremist perspectives may likely lead to growing grievances among students; some might go on to voice their views elsewhere. (Of course, student safety comes first: if a student is expressing violent and threatening attitudes, then this needs to be dealt with according to the school's disciplinary procedures.)

Key Terms and Necessary Knowledge:

Israeli and Palestinian narratives will often differ about key aspects of the conflict. Many of these issues are still being debated impacting how the key terms below will be defined. It is obvious to me that however I define these key terms, I'll be accused of bias and so I'll happily suggest that your students begin their research into the conflict by seeking out the meanings of these key terms. Such work, including creating a timeline on the conflict, will provide an excellent opportunity to develop their research skills, including civic online reasoning and the ability to gauge websites through sophisticated lateral thinking. It will therefore be important to encourage your students to seek out Israeli and Palestinian narratives as well as reliable third-party commentaries on the issue under study. Of course, as ever, I offer some websites to get your students started.

For our purposes, where narratives are strongly contested, I have offered mainstream Israeli and Palestinian terms to help your students think about the differing narratives:

Mainstream Israeli Narrative	Mainstream Palestinian Narrative
Zionism	Palestinian nationalism
Israeli independence 1948	Nakba 1948
Jewish exodus from Muslim countries	Palestinian refugee crisis
Six Day War 1967	
Judea and Samaria (Jewish Settlements)	West Bank and Gaza (Hamas)
Jerusalem	Al-Quds
Yom Kippur War 1973	
Camp David Accords 1978	
Lebanon War 1982	
First Intifada 1987–1991	
Oslo Accords 1993 and Israeli–Palestinian Peace Talks	
Israel–Jordan Peace Treaty 1994	
Abraham Accords 2020	

However the issue is raised, teachers should have the following starter questions up their sleeve to ensure the requisite level of knowledge is shared by the class before moving on to the Socratic questions below:

• Where do the names 'Israel' and 'Palestine' come from?
• Where are Israel and Palestine on the map?
• What are the populations of Israel and Palestine?
• What are the main languages spoken in Israel and Palestine?

- What are the main religions practised in Israel and Palestine?
- Name five prominent Israelis and five prominent Palestinians.

These questions not only help gauge student starter knowledge about the conflict; they will also provide a sense of intellectual humility. For example, I have never been in a classroom where one child can name five Israelis *and* five Palestinians. Those interested in the conflict – often students who identify with either side – can name five Israelis *or* five Palestinians at best. I remind my students that if one can't even name the ten most famous people party to this conflict, then perhaps one needs a bit of intellectual humility before claiming one side is right and the other wrong.

The answers to the above questions could be the start of student 'Knowledge Organisers' to help build up their basic understanding of the facts before attempting to evaluate the causes of the conflict. For those wishing to be more ambitious, here would be other key aspects to include:

- **Key terms**: Israelis and Palestinians will have different terms for the same event/concept/place, e.g. Jerusalem/Al-Quds: be sure that the Knowledge Organisers reflect this
- **Timeline of major events**: not just regarding the conflict but anything crucial to understand development of Israel or Palestine
- **Maps**: historical and current
- **Main characters**, e.g. pictures, positions held, and major achievements
- **Flashpoints of the conflict**: positive as well as negative developments
- **Causes of the conflict**: most controversial aspect – look out for those 'straw man' claims
- **Sources used for the information above**: are they reliable?

Note that the Israeli narrative will lead to very different information being presented from the Palestinian one. For example, when thinking about the timeline:

- Israelis look to ancient Israel, with the year 70 CE being crucial to understanding that this marked the end of Jewish rule over what was then called Judea, with Jews returning in significant numbers at the beginning in the 19th century.
- For Palestinians though, your students may wish to begin their timeline in the 2nd century CE when the Romans renamed Judaea (ancient Israel) as 'Syria Palaestina.' In the modern period, 1918 is when the first major Palestinian Arab nationalist organisations emerged.

Socratic Questions and Critical Thinking:

Classroom Discussion:

Debates about Israel–Palestine are usually woefully sad and self-defeating events. Too often on display are the worst logical fallacies and cognitive biases as each side is intent on knocking the other down and winning the propaganda war rather than seeking the truth, reconciliation, and peaceful coexistence. By pursuing 'disputational talk,' the outcomes are inevitably divergent rather than convergent in character: the environment is oppressively competitive rather than collegiate and collaborative. Schools can and must do better.

Through 'exploratory talk,' which should see the class 'interthinking' as they collaborate and critically engage with each other, students can delve into these Socratic questions that get to the heart of the conflict and possible ways out:

• What are the causes of the Israeli-Palestinian conflict?

Mainstream Israeli Narrative	Mainstream Palestinian Narrative
Palestinian rejectionism: *throughout the conflict, Palestinians have ultimately rejected Israel's right to exist. Until the Palestinians overwhelmingly accept Israel is here to stay and that the use of terrorism is wrong, the conflict will continue as Israel must act in self-defence.*	**Israeli rejectionism:** *while Israel was established in 1948, it has ultimately rejected the Palestinian right to a homeland, illegally occupying the territory marked out as a Palestinian state, namely the West Bank and Gaza Strip. The continuing building of illegal Jewish settlements proves Israel isn't interested in peace.*
1948 and Jewish return: *While Jewish leaders accepted the 1947 United Nations plan to partition the land into separate Jewish and Arab states, the Arab world rejected this and invaded the fledgling Jewish state instead. While Israel absorbed 900,000 Jews from Arab countries and Iran, it is time for the Arab world to absorb the Palestinian refugees as they should take responsibility for invading Israel. The demand for the return of Palestinian refugees would overwhelm Israel with a largely hostile population and mean the end of the Jewish state.*	**Nakba and Palestinian refugees:** *Israel has always refused to allow the Palestinian refugees from the 1948 war of Israel's independence to return to their homes. Some 85% of Palestinians who lived in historic Palestine – approximately 700,000 people – fled or were expelled from their homes. They and their descendants have since lived as refugees in the West Bank and Gaza, as well as surrounding countries such as Lebanon, Jordan, and Syria. Any just peace must ensure that those displaced and their descendants can return to their homes and receive compensation to help correct the injustices of the 'Nakba.'*
Palestinian leadership: *The Palestinians have been failed by their leaders. With a lack of democratic accountability (the last Palestinian presidential elections were in 2005 and the last parliamentary elections in 2006), the Palestinians are led by de facto dictators. Liberal democracies ultimately lower the chances of war. Israel is a thriving democracy and the sooner the Palestinians turn towards democracy, the better the chance for peace.*	**Israeli occupation:** *With Israel having ultimate control of Palestinian lives and territory, they are to blame for the breakdown in Palestinian society, including the economy, political system, and social structures. Now more than 600,000 Jews live in some 150 settlements since Israel's occupation of the West Bank and East Jerusalem in 1967. These settlements are considered illegal under international law and damage any prospects for a two-state solution.*
Religion: *What others call 'the West Bank,' Israelis call 'Judea and Samaria,' the birthplace of the Jewish people, where many of the Bible stories take place. It is unfair to suggest that Jews can't live in settlements in their historic homeland. Furthermore, Jerusalem has only ever been the capital of the Jewish people – dating back nearly 3,000 years since King David – and is Judaism's holiest site with the Western Wall, the last remnant of the ancient Jewish Temple.*	**Religion:** *Al-Quds is the third holiest city in Islam. The al-Haram al-Sharif is over 1,000 years old with the Dome of the Rock, the world's oldest surviving work of Islamic architecture. It is the place where Muslims believe the Night Journey of Muhammad began. East Jerusalem, where these holy sites are, should be the future capital of Palestine, with continuing Jewish control of the city, including the expansion of illegal Jewish settlements in the area, undermining Palestinian sovereignty.*
International community: *Israel now has peace deals with the following Arab countries: Egypt (1979), Jordan (1994), the United Arab Emirates (2020), Bahrain (2020), Morocco, (2020) and Sudan (2020). This shows that many in the Arab world are recognising that Israel is not blocking peace efforts with the Palestinians.*	**International community:** *the vast majority of countries recognise that Palestine should be an independent country. Arab countries that have normalised relations with Israel have done so out of economic and diplomatic advantages, especially due to Israel's special relationship with the United States, the world's only superpower.*

- *What are the possible solutions of the Israeli–Palestinian conflict?*

Two-state solution: since the 1990s, two states for two peoples has been the solution overwhelmingly supported by the international community if begrudgingly accepted by Israeli and Palestinian leaders. Essentially this would mean:

- An independent Jewish state and an independent Palestinian state living side by side in peace and security along the 1967 borders, perhaps with some equivalent land swaps to ensure contiguity for a Palestinian state and a secure border for Israel

- Both parties accept the other party's right to land and legitimate national aspirations

- The vast majority of Palestinian refugees will resettle into the future Palestinian Arab state – not into pre-1967 Israel

- Jerusalem will be shared: one city as two capitals without physical barriers, with both governments sharing the peaceful running of the city

Advantages:

- Only plan that has near unanimous support of the international community

- Seems the fairest way to deal with two peoples that have legitimate claims to one land

Disadvantages:

- This plan has been on the cards for decades now with no realistic move towards a resolution

- Recent polls of both Israelis and Palestinians show decreasing support for the two-state solution

- Some Israelis fear that a Palestinian state will leave Israel vulnerable to attack: its border would be just 10 kilometres wide at its narrowest point

- Some Palestinians fear that with Israel being the far stronger party, it will leave a future Palestinian state vulnerable and unable to defend itself

- Both sides fear that their ultimate demands will remain unmet as negotiations will mean giving up on the ideal. This includes control of Jerusalem, a Jewish presence in Judea and Samaria, and the Palestinian refugee right to return in pre-1967 Israel

Other Solutions:

One-State Solution:

With the two-state solution seemingly going nowhere, how about a one-state solution? This would mean a bi-national state of Israel–Palestine, with the whole land being shared by both populations in a democratic country

Advantages:

- Offers a possible idealistic pathway for both peoples to get everything: sharing Jerusalem, Israelis and Palestinians get to live anywhere they like, with joint sovereignty leading to dignity and equal rights

- There is support for this solution among some Israelis and Palestinians (often left-wing intellectuals on both sides of the divide)

Disadvantages:

- The one-state solution is seen by many as 'utopian': when populations are hostile, it is a bad idea to put them closer together! Think of what happened to Lebanon from 1975 to 1990 and what took place in Yugoslavia from 1991 to 2001. Rather than a brotherhood of peoples, it will more likely lead to civil war between different populations

- Officially, neither the Israelis nor the Palestinians want this solution: even though the two-state solution is less popular of late, it is still the overall preferred option for both Israelis and Palestinians

Conflict Management
There is a growing viewpoint that a solution to end the conflict is sadly unrealistic at the moment. Many see that 'conflict management' should be the current guiding principle rather than 'conflict resolution.' This means trying to better the everyday lives of Palestinians on the one hand, whilst ensuring security for Israelis on the other
Advantages:
• Despite the current situation hardly being ideal for both sides, the unpredictability of the conflict perhaps means that it is more realistic to take small steps to build trust and cooperation between both sides

• There are too many balls up in the air. Both sides need greater calm and stability before moving towards a comprehensive settlement:
   • For the Palestinians, Gaza is led by Hamas, an extremist Islamist group that rejects Israel's right to exist; meanwhile, at 87 years old, Palestinian President Mahmoud Abbas is elderly and in a weakened position
   • For Israelis, there have been five parliamentary elections between 2019 and 2022, with leaders finding it very difficult to maintain a stable coalition

Disadvantages:
• Many people will continue to suffer until a comprehensive peace plan is agreed
• Rather than advance peace, it is just as likely that as things stand, both sides will carry out actions that both undermine peace and cause more suffering
Extremist and Unlawful 'solutions':
The 'one-state' solution can also be a euphemism for expelling the opposing side. Rather than one state for two peoples (as above), extremists mean one state for one people. They therefore call for the forced removal of the entire population of the other side. Such a move would not only be obviously unlawful, but would lead to huge numbers of deaths and suffering, and is clearly based on racist ideology. Sadly, there are people who hold such views, including Hamas on the Palestinian side and far-right Kahanists on the Israeli side. If raised in the classroom, such racist views must be countered by the teacher

Other forums for learning about the Israeli–Palestinian conflict:
   Assembly/Lecture/Conference/Co-curricular discussion group:

• Whether you lead on these activities or invite guest speakers into school, it is vital to include both mainstream narratives on the issue.
• Students should come 'armed' with knowledge and understanding to any such planned event. They will be left at the mercy of the speaker if they aren't equipped appropriately to ask probing questions and hold the speaker to account. This may leave them feeling frustrated rather than informed.

Some Theory:

The Israeli–Palestinian conflict elicits every possible reaction: from outright apathy and utter confusion to either side certain that God is on their side. After 100 years of attempting to resolve the conflict, the world's finest minds still haven't managed it. This most controversial of issues therefore invites opportunities for fascinating debate and discussion – just as it provokes rancour and animosity. It is crucial for teachers to get this right. The aim is to curate a learning experience aiming for understanding and making sense of other worldviews, whilst minimising the chance for anyone to use it opportunistically for point-scoring or propaganda.

We can therefore reject the 'behavioural' criterion for teaching this controversy outright. Just because people – however many – hold certain views, doesn't make it right. Schools have an obligation to challenge extremist rhetoric, such as support for terrorism or advocating the illegal expulsion of an entire people. Sadly, people on all sides of the debate may support radical outcomes, using extremist language. Such views can't be allowed to go unchallenged in the classroom.

At the same time, the 'epistemic' criterion for controversy has its weaknesses too. In global affairs, there may be very good utilitarian reasons to support terrorism and other radical behaviours, especially if they can be shown to advance one's cause. Whether terrorism works is hardly a settled question in terms of evidence or reason. Many analysts and commentators have sought to justify the use of terrorism as a means for their perceived legitimate struggle. Yet for a teacher to remain neutral on such a question and so teach it in a non-directive manner seems unconscionable – and no doubt illegal in some countries.

Rather, the 'political' criterion may provide a helpful rule of thumb for teachers grappling with this subject in the classroom. According to this framework, teachers need to check whether the view expressed is compatible with a commitment to basic rights and liberties. Where the view expressed opposes basic human rights, e.g. support for terrorism or the oppression of innocent civilians, then the teacher needs to intervene in a directive manner. Such an approach will propel students to delve into the complexities of the conflict and move away from making sweeping claims or opting for simplistic sloganeering. There are many facets to the conflict where it may be reasonably argued that both sides are right: two peoples with legitimate claims to one land, based on deep historical, religious, and political ties. Yet there are many aspects of the conflict where it may reasonably be argued that different sides have behaved in an illegitimate and immoral fashion: the Israelis, the Palestinians, and different parts of the international community. The political criterion – through a benchmark of basic rights and liberties – helps provide the values by which students can evaluate the rights and wrongs of the conflict. For example, students may wish to explore whether different parties to the conflict have upheld values, such as democracy, the rule of law, individual liberty, and mutual respect and tolerance of different faiths and beliefs – or not.

Beware!

Perhaps best to avoid altogether? Studies suggest this is the preferred approach of many teachers for issues such as this. The Israeli–Palestinian conflict is seen as too controversial. However, here are four reasons why 'exclusive neutrality' – the stance of avoiding the subject altogether – is counterproductive:

- Cultural capital: it is a key conflict in global politics and so our students should be more aware and literate about the world around them.
- Promote cultural understanding: sadly, anti-Semites and Islamophobes will use the conflict to promote their own hatred. A greater understanding of the complexities of the conflict can help counter such divisiveness.
- Students bring it up: this is especially so during flare ups and teachers are often very reticent to deal with it. Yet avoiding any education about the conflict only helps breed ignorance on a matter of real global importance, leading to misconceptions especially during those inevitable flashpoints in the conflict. For those interested, they'll find out about it elsewhere and so surely the classroom is the preferable place for studying such issues of controversy.
- Curriculum: this conflict may well feature on the History, Politics or Civics curriculum; it can also relate to Religious Studies in the study of Judaism and Islam.

Identity: A minority of students, especially those who identify with one side or the other in the conflict, may know huge amounts about the issue both in terms of history and ongoing concerns. Teachers might find themselves knowing less than certain participants and so this puts them in a difficult position. In such situations, pedagogy becomes even more important!

The situation is too complex: Well, that's what this guide is for! Just as you might have students with skin in the game and so sensitivity is required throughout, it is even more likely that you will have students that find this topic absurdly complicated and too involved. They can get lost as the geography, history, and main characters are unfamiliar. These students may fear voicing their opinion due to their own ignorance or for not wishing to offend a classmate. Such an impassioned topic can create a chilling effect and lead to apathy for many. As for so many issues of controversy, the teacher must build up her students' knowledge and understanding before aiming to debate and evaluate the issues at hand.

Sloganeering: When we recognise just how complex these issues are, we will do well to insist on intellectual rigour and specificity in our analysis. Debates and discussions invariably tempt some to sloganeering. Not only is that to be discouraged in favour of sharper thinking, it may also lead to outright extremism, even unwittingly. So as we seek to learn rather than to win, be on the lookout for sweeping claims such as:

"All Palestinians think… / All Israelis think… / All Muslims think… / All Jews think…"

People are complicated and the idea that *all* people of a particular domination or group have identical views is belittling, often racist, and simply wrong. Just as there are Muslim Zionists, so too are there Jews who campaign for the rights of Palestinians. As ever, beware of the *ad hominem*! Insist your pupils stick to the facts and remain specific in their claims.

"From the River to the Sea, Palestine will be free."

Support and understanding for one side of the conflict should not include calling for the destruction of the other side. Classrooms must be inclusive, promote respect, and aim to model tolerance. Once we realise that the 'River' refers to the River Jordan and that the 'Sea' means the Mediterranean, a glance at the map shows that these borders negate Israel's very existence. Calling for the destruction of a country is hardly in keeping with a commitment to basic rights and liberties.

"Islam is a religion of hate and promotes terrorism."

This is Islamophobia plain and simple. Claims such as these are wrong because they are hateful, sweeping, and examples of shallow thinking or outright non-thinking. However, religions are complex and multifaceted and no religion is above fair criticism in a democratic society. Classrooms must not be bound by laws of blasphemy that hinder intellectual debate and critique. Texts and clerics in Islam have promoted hatred and terrorism, as they have done in Christianity, Judaism and many other religions. Classrooms must be the place where such texts can be considered and understood in their full context without recourse to simplistic and hateful claims.

"'Palestinian' is just a made-up term."

Part of the importance of learning about this conflict is to appreciate where both sides are coming from and gain a greater awareness of their wider histories and cultures. Palestinians and Israelis alike should be considered as peoples in themselves, without only referring to them in the context of conflict. There is so much more to people's identities and the more we learn about each other, the more we can break down those barriers and come to appreciate what is common to us all – and what makes us different.

"I'm anti-Zionist, not anti-Semitic."

This would be like claiming, "I am not anti-French, I just don't believe France has the right to exist." This is as disingenuous as it gets. Unless one is opposed to all nation-states – which is a reasonable argument to make – singling out the world's only Jewish state for destruction is clearly anti-Semitic. At the same time, it is obviously not anti-Zionist or anti-Semitic to criticise Israeli government actions (Israelis do this every day!), just as one might criticise the actions of any other government around the world.

Sources and Resources:

Third-party Sources on the Israeli-Palestinian Conflict:

Is Peace Still Possible? (2022), Retrieved from: https://www.ispeacestillpossible.com/.

Comprehensive resource that examines the conflict from both perspectives, suggesting possible routes to peace.

BBC News (2020), 'Israel's Borders Explained in Maps.' Retrieved from: https://www.bbc.co.uk/news/world-middle-east-54116567.

BBC News (2021), 'How Children in Both Israel and Gaza Experienced the Conflict - BBC News.' Retrieved from: https://www.youtube.com/watch?v=-cOxmVxOYXA.

BBC Newsround (2015), 'Guide: Why Are Israel and the Palestinians Fighting over Gaza?' Retrieved from: https://www.bbc.co.uk/newsround/20436092.

Michael Walzer (2002), 'The Four Wars of Israel / Palestine.' Retrieved from: https://www.ias.edu/sites/default/files/sss/pdfs/Walzer/FourWarsIsrael.pdf.

For more advanced students, Professor Walzer provides really helpful frameworks for understanding the conflict.

Vox, 'Everything You Need to Know about Israel-Palestine.' Retrieved from: https://www.vox.com/2018/11/20/18079996/israel-palestine-conflict-guide-explainer.

Wikipedia, 'Timeline of the Israeli-Palestinian Conflict.' Retrieved from: https://en.wikipedia.org/wiki/Timeline_of_the_Israeli%E2%80%93Palestinian_conflict.

Sources from different sides of the divide:

American University of Beirut (2022), 'Al-Nakba: 1948 Palestinian Exodus.' Retrieved from: https://aub.edu.lb.libguides.com/Al-Nakba.

Anti-Defamation League (2022), 'Questions, Complexities and Context: Insights into Israel and the Israeli-Palestinian Conflict.' Retrieved from: https://www.adl.org/resources/glossary-term/questions-complexities-and-context-insights-israel-and-israeli-palestinian.

Council for Arab-British Understanding (2022), 'Education.' Retrieved from: https://www.caabu.org/education.

Jewish Virtual Library (2022). Retrieved from: https://www.jewishvirtuallibrary.org/.

Palestine Advocacy Project (2022), 'Our Campaigns.' Retrieved from: https://www.palestineadvocacyproject.org/.

Stand With Us (2022), 'Arab-Israeli Conflict Factsheets.' Retrieved from: https://www.standwithus.com/.

Links to Other Controversies:

Who's to blame for any international conflict?

Should there be any limits to free speech?

Being 'Woke' just means being kind to others, especially vulnerable people. How can anyone disagree with that?

You really don't believe what the government/media is telling us?

Is the Holocaust a hoax?

Should there be any limits on free speech?

Age group: 11-18

How explosive is this topic?

The topic of free speech should yield fascinating perspectives and challenging ideas. Nevertheless, there are related issues that could well lead to ferocious debates, and so the teacher must be wary of keeping the discussion focused and productive.

How should I teach this topic?

From the outset, it is important to get the parameters right.

First, there are two major types of 'limits' that have – despite what many claim – been controversial for thousands of years:

- Censorship: this refers to a top-down prohibition on certain forms of expression, whether ruled on by political leaders, judges, or others in authority
- Cancel culture or call-out culture: this refers to a bottom-up phenomenon where members of society or a profession may shun, ostracise, or boycott someone based on their beliefs or actions.

While there is some overlap, it may be helpful to be clear on which type of 'limit' the class wishes to discuss as they raise different arguments. Of course, you may wish to throw both into the mix but, as ever, insist on the correct use of terminology for clear thinking and expression. Second, aim to get out of the way the more uncontroversial limits on free speech that are pretty standard in most liberal democracies. In general, these would be limits on free speech when they clash with other people's rights. Prominent instances include:

- Blackmailing someone for your gain or for their loss through unwarranted demands with menacing behaviour. For example, someone threatening to share a compromising photo of you unless you hand over money.
- Defaming someone, i.e. saying something unfair or untrue about them, which is likely to negatively impact their reputation. For example, someone claims you cheated on your exams (when you didn't, obviously).
- Inciting violence or hatred to create "a clear and present danger" for others. Perhaps most famously, "shouting 'fire' in a crowded theatre" is the analogy used for speech designed to create panic and harm. In the United Kingdom, inciting hatred would apply where it is based on people's protected characteristics, e.g. whipping up racial hatred.

Check for classroom agreement on the above scenarios first so that students become focused on the more contentious areas for debate, which we will focus on below.

Now that you have set the scene, I would recommend one of two teaching stances, depending on how confident the teacher is in hosting such a debate:

1. 'Neutral impartiality': where a teacher is less confident, she may wish to lead a debate on the matter without disclosing her own view. Under the principle of charity, she will present the best versions of competing viewpoints so that her students are empowered to decide for themselves. Understandably, she may feel that by offering her own perspective, she may alienate students with differing viewpoints, distracting from the educational aims of the discussion.

2. 'Committed impartiality': where a teacher is more confident, she should express her own view on the issue whilst ensuring that competing perspectives receive a fair hearing too. The teacher thus highlights the importance of "owning" her viewpoint and having to justify her perspective in light of other reasonable approaches. On an issue like 'free speech,' this might be a welcome opportunity to model intellectual, moral, and civic virtues like reflection, humility, and civility. If done well, this will empower students to offer their own perspectives and be open to hearing competing approaches too. It goes without saying that for a matter of controversy, the teacher cannot present her view with the aim of winning over her students to her side of the debate.

Key Terms and Necessary Knowledge:

Blasphemy: the online Oxford Languages dictionary defines this word as follows: "the action or offence of speaking sacrilegiously about God or sacred things." Considered the most serious of offences in religious societies, being found guilty of such a charge could lead to ostracism, imprisonment, and even death penalty in certain parts of the world today. It is interesting to note that in the West, defenders of free speech argue bitterly against any notion of 'blasphemy,' observing that the notion of 'sacred things' has now seemingly expanded into many parts of life, disturbingly leaving them off limits for open discussion, lest people be accused of 'secular blasphemy.' As this chapter will discuss, are there and should there be issues that are so 'sacred,' that it would be wrong, offensive even, to challenge them?

'Calling out': In the marketplace of ideas, just as you have the right to express your thoughts, you must also recognise that bigotry and mockery have consequences. Critics of the term 'cancel culture,' prefer using the term 'calling out'; as the academic Arionne Nettles put it: "In truth, Black, brown, and LGBTQ+ people – particularly Black and trans people – can now critique elites publicly and hold them accountable socially…"

'Cancel culture'/'Social censure': described by the author, Chimamanda Ngozi Adichie, as punishing people who commit "secular blasphemy" by "virtual vigilante action whose aim is not just to silence the person who has spoken but to create a vengeful atmosphere that deters others from speaking." This is often known as a 'chilling effect.'

Censorship: a top-down prohibition on certain forms of expression, whether ruled on by political leaders, judges, or others in authority.

Chilling effect/Self-censorship: public shaming is often said to have a 'chilling effect' or serve as a deterrence for others who may have wished to voice the same opinion in public. Out of fear of personal or professional reprisals, people may practise 'self-censorship' and 'choose' to not voice their views.

Deplatform/no-platform: the attempt to boycott someone by removing the 'platform' for them to voice their opinions, e.g. banning a person from speaking at a venue or blocking them online.

Public shaming: punishing a person by dishonouring or humiliating them in public. Critics of 'cancel culture' claim it has come back in recent years in the form of 'mob justice' as 'offenders' are shamed on social media.

Sensitivity readers: hired by publishers to make editorial suggestions about content that may be regarded as offensive.

Socratic Questions and Critical Thinking:

Classroom Discussion:

To help frame a broad debate on free speech, you may wish to begin by placing these famous ideas before your students and exploring how they think about the arguments raised.
First, let's begin with two classic arguments that pit John Stuart Mill against Karl Popper:

In Favour of Freedom of Speech
John Stuart Mill, passage from Chapter II in *On Liberty* (1859):
...the peculiar evil of silencing the expression of an opinion is that it is robbing the human race; posterity as well as the existing generation; those who dissent from the opinion, still more than those who hold it. If the opinion is right, they are deprived of the opportunity of exchanging error for truth; if wrong, they lose, what is almost as great a benefit, the clearer perception and livelier impression of truth produced by its collision with error
Mill argues that the surest way to reach the truth - which we should all value - is through freedom of expression. This is a founding principle of a liberal democratic society.

In Favour of Limiting Freedom of Speech
Karl Popper, passage from *The Open Society and Its Enemies* (1945):
Less well known is the paradox of tolerance: Unlimited tolerance must lead to the disappearance of tolerance. If we extend unlimited tolerance even to those who are intolerant... then the tolerant will be destroyed, and tolerance with them. In this for-mulation, I do not imply, for instance, that we should always suppress the utterance of intolerant philosophies; as long as we can counter them by rational argument and keep them in check by public opinion, suppression would certainly be most unwise. But we should claim the right to suppress them if necessary even by force; for it may easily turn out that they are not prepared to meet us on the level of rational argument, but begin by denouncing all argument; they may forbid their followers to listen to rational argument... and teach them to answer arguments by the use of their fists or pistols. We should therefore claim, in the name of tolerance, the right not to tolerate the intolerant
Popper argues that it is self-defeating for the tolerant to extend freedom of speech to intolerant extremists who, if they could, wouldn't hesitate to limit the freedom of expression with whom they disagree with.

Questions for your students:

- *Explain Mill and Popper's arguments.*
- *Which arguments do you find most convincing? Explain why.*
- *How might the problem of people having different levels of power and influence in society impact Mill's argument?*
- *If you are sympathetic with Popper, who gets to decide what is intolerant? In turn, what problems might this raise?*
- *What about the following scenarios? Should there be limits on what people can say?*

- *"I don't accept that transwomen are women."*
- *"I love the film, 'The Life of Brian,' and who cares if some people think it mocks Christianity." (Would you feel differently about another religion being 'mocked?')*
- *"I don't believe the Holocaust really happened."*
- *"All lives matter. Not just Black lives."*
- *"I support Russia's invasion of Ukraine."*
- *"We all know that women make better leaders than men."*
- *"According to my religion, gay relationships are forbidden."*

Let's move on and examine updated arguments on 'calling-out culture' vs 'cancel culture':

Yes to 'call-out culture':	No to 'cancel culture':
There was never a fair playing field but a myth of free speech. Rather, well-established figures, often white, wealthy, and dominant men, with easy access to the media, are trying to protect their hold on power, by playing the victim, and not allowing traditionally marginalised voices challenge the status quo.	A free society means hearing viewpoints that will infuriate and offend. Rather than limit free speech, we need more free speech to offer different perspectives that can be argued freely and productively. Quite simply, shutting down others – whoever they are – is not the way to get one's own voice heard.
'Cancel culture' is a made-up term to silence new voices who are 'calling out' bigotry, including racism and sexism. Far from limiting free speech, calling people out holds them accountable for what they say, recognising that free speech carries responsibilities.	Creativity and progress means making mistakes. People are fallible and so social censure and cancel culture are new modes of blasphemy that create a chilling effect for many who become afraid to speak out and say what they really think.
True free speech means opening up the marketplace of ideas to include alternative voices. The reality is that the mainstream media and seats of power have restricted perspectives that challenge them – often for commercial and protective reasons. Social media platforms now offer a chance for all to speak up and have their voices heard in the spirit of democracy.	Ultimately, who decides which voices need to be shut down? Who decides what is offensive? Cancelling our opponents turns them into martyrs. It leads many to seek out their ideas underground as they wonder why society is banning them. Ideas should be countered with argument and reason, not censure. Cancel culture always backfires. You'll be next!

Questions for your students:

- *Offer arguments in favour of 'call-out culture.'*
- *Offer arguments opposing 'cancel culture.'*
- *Which arguments do you find most convincing? Explain why.*

We can now move on to narrower, more specific arguments about free speech that come up in modern society. Let's look at three highly debated issues which seem to be of particular importance and interest for young people:

i.   **Is it right to 'cancel'/'call out' people for offending others?**

George Orwell wrote the following passage in an unused preface to *Animal Farm*; it is now inscribed at BBC Headquarters:
    "If liberty means anything at all, it means the right to tell people what they do not want to hear."

This proposition by Orwell would make an excellent motion for a formal debate. As discussed in the Introduction to the Guides, different debating formats may be considered.

To assist students researching this debate, a number of (in)famous case studies of 'cancelling' / 'calling out' may be researched:

- Many claim that Thomas Hardy stopped writing novels after the public outcry over *Jude the Obscure* in 1895, leading him to dedicate the last 30 years of his life to poetry.
- In the 1930s, the German Student Union conducted a book burning campaign targeting works that were seen "Un-German" under Nazism.
- Sir Salman Rushdie was threatened by Islamist extremists, including a *fatwa* calling for his death issued by the supreme leader of Iran, after the publication of his novel, *The Satanic Verses*, in 1988. Living under threat of assassination after it was claimed that the novel was offensive to Muslims, Rushdie was stabbed repeatedly by an Islamist as he was about to give a public lecture in New York in 2022. It was reported that Rushdie lost sight in one eye and the use of one hand as a result of the attack.
- Sir Tim Hunt, a Nobel Prize winning scientist, resigned from several research posts after outrage was expressed for his "trouble with girls" comments in 2015.
- J.K. Rowling has come under intense criticism for her views on transgenderism, including by stars of the Harry Potter films.
- Kanye West, also known as Ye, had a number of lucrative contracts cancelled in 2022 after making a number of anti-Semitic comments.
- In 2022, comedian Dave Chapelle had a show cancelled by First Avenue nightclub in Minnesota due to controversy over transgender jokes.
- Since 2022, documentary filmmaker Meg Smaker's *The UnRedacted*, originally released as *Jihad Rehab*, is unavailable to the general public after being cancelled for alleged Islamophobia.
- Law students at Stanford University derailed Federal judge Stuart Duncan's address to the Federalist Society on campus in 2023, claiming that his views harmed the rights of marginalised groups. Stanford president Marc Tessier-Lavigne and law dean Jenny Martinez apologised to Duncan afterwards, writing: "What happened was inconsistent with our policies on free speech, and we are very sorry about the experience you had while visiting our campus."
- In 2023, a Florida school principal resigned after parents complained about a lesson that included a picture of Michelangelo's statue of David. The nude statue was seen as "pornographic" and therefore inappropriate to show 11–12-year-old students.

To help your students with further research, here are two opinion pieces offering various arguments for both sides of the debate:

Thomas Chatterton Williams et al. (2020), 'A Letter on Justice and Open Debate,' *Harper's Magazine*. Retrieved from: https://harpers.org/a-letter-on-justice-and-open-debate/.

Amaka Dominic-Udeagbaja (2021), 'On the Myth of Cancel Culture,' *Varsity*. Retrieved from: https://www.varsity.co.uk/opinion/21749.

Questions for your students:

- Explain the concepts of 'punching up' and 'punching down.' How might one's attitude towards these ideas impact your thinking on the above scenarios?
- Explain the 'chilling effect' phenomenon. How might it impact 'freedom of speech?'
- In all the scenarios above, people reacted the way they did – 'called out' or 'cancelled another' – because they were 'offended.' Explain your own view on each scenario. Is your reasoning consistent?

i.   **Should books, films, or music considered offensive be banned or edited?**

Heinrich Heine, a 19th-century German poet, wrote:
"Where they burn books, they will, in the end, burn human beings too."
This proposition made by Heine – particularly potent as his books were burnt by Nazi students in the first stages of the Holocaust – would make an excellent motion for a formal debate. As discussed in the Guide to the Guides, different debating formats may be considered.
As a class, three case studies are offered for discussion:

In September 2020, Newsweek reported that copies of Harry Potter books are being burnt as part of a new TikTok trend. *As one protestor argued: "The positive impact that J.K. Rowling's work had on millions of readers does not negate how her hateful lobbying has affected the trans community. This doesn't even touch on the harmful fatphobia, racism and valorization of supramacists [sic] and child abusers in her most famous work."*	*In February 2022, The Guardian reported that a Christian pastor in Tennessee led a livestreamed Facebook book burning to fight "demonic influences."* *Harry Potter books were burnt in protest of their depictions of witchcraft and other "accursed things."* *The event in a Nashville suburb "drew large crowds as participants threw in copies of the Harry Potter and Twilight series, among other books."*

a.   ***Harry Potter book burnings***
  • What are your views on the Harry Potter book burnings? Is your reasoning consistent?
  • Is it ever acceptable to burn books, however much we might be offended by them or their author?

b.   ***Roald Dahl and Agatha Christie books edited by 'sensitivity readers':***

In February 2023, the BBC reported that 'sensitivity readers' had checked Roald Dahl's children's books and made "small and carefully considered" changes where language was considered potentially offensive. *Changes include:* • *Augustus Gloop, from Charlie and the Chocolate Factory, is now described as "enormous" instead of "fat."* • *Mrs Twit, from The Twits, is now described as "beastly" rather than "ugly and beastly."* • *The Twits has removed the word "weird" from the sentence "a weird African language."* • *"Crazy" and "mad" have also been taken out of the books.*	*In March 2023, The Telegraph reported that Agatha Christie books were being "rewritten for modern sensitivities."* *'Sensitivity readers' had reworked or removed passages considered offensive, often due to claims of racism.* *Changes include:* • *Words like "Oriental" and "native" have been removed.* • *Where a young woman was referred as "of gypsy type," that description has been removed.* • *Where the detective Hercule Poirot refers to another character as "a Jew, of course," that has now been removed.* • *The word, "n-----" has been taken out.*

- What are your views on editing classic works of fiction to remove offensive passages? Why might others disagree with you?
- Many religious texts that are holy for billions of people around the world are considered by many others to contain racist, homophobic, transphobic, and misogynistic passages. Would it be acceptable to edit, ban, or even burn such holy scriptures because of their allegedly offensive content?
- If a text contains a word that many might find offensive, e.g. racial slurs like the 'n' word or the 'p' word or the 'y' word, or misogynistic words like the 'c' word or 'p' word or 'b' word, should the teacher or reader voice these words aloud? Why might others disagree with you?[5]
- How can a class of students 'measure' offence? For example, if the word 'fat' might offend a student, can that word no longer be voiced?
- Does it matter who is saying the word? For example, is there a difference if a Pakistani says the 'p' word rather than a white person?
- Does context matter? For example, whilst some might complain of the 'n' word in literature, it is often used in rap music, as are misogynistic words. Is there a difference?

c. ***Life of Brian and The Lady of Heaven banned from cinemas after being accused of blasphemy.***

When Monty Python's The Life of Brian was released in 1979, many religious Christian groups protested against the film, claiming the religious satire was blasphemous. *While it was banned in some countries and in 39 local authorities in the United Kingdom, it went on to become a huge commercial and critical success.* *Religious protests in America were said to have given the film publicity, leading it to be screened in many more cinemas than originally planned.* *The Monty Python team were characteristically defiant. Terry Gilliam noted: "I thought at least getting the Catholics, Protestants and Jews all protesting against our movie was fairly ecumenical on our part... We had achieved something useful."*	*In June 2022, Cineworld, a U.K.-based cinema chain, cancelled all screenings of The Lady of Heaven, a film about the daughter of the Muslim Prophet Muhammad, after protests outside some of its cinemas.* *BBC News reported that Cineworld made the decision "to ensure the safety of our staff and customers."* *More than 120,000 people signed a petition for the film to be pulled from U.K. cinemas, with the Bolton Council of Mosques calling the film "blasphemous" as it "disrespects the most esteemed individuals of Islamic history."* *The film's producer, Malik Shlibak, said "no one should dictate for the British public what they can and cannot watch or discuss," describing the protestors as "fringe groups."*

- What are your views on films being pulled from viewing because they may cause offence? Why might others disagree with you?
- Should any topics be 'off-limits' for films or literature?
- In 2018, a number of American radio stations banned the classic Christmas song, 'It's Cold Outside,' after some listeners complained that the lyrics were inappropriate, especially in the age of #metoo. Critics said the song's lyrics are about a man pressuring a woman to stay at his home, despite her protests that she should leave. Others countered that the lyrics are nowhere near as offensive as many songs in today's charts that are played on the radio, often with highly explicit sexual lyrics. Who, if anyone, should decide what gets played?

Some Theory:

The word 'ostracism' comes from the ancient Greek and describes the democratic procedure in Athens during the 5th century BCE whereby any citizen could be expelled for ten years. It was democratic because each year Athenians gathered together in an assembly to vote on whether anyone should be ostracised. If they agreed on such a vote, whoever got the most votes would be banished and go into exile. The ostracised person could only return after ten years. As the Greek historian Plutarch wrote of the practice, "[ostracism] was not a penalty, but a way of pacifying and alleviating that jealousy which delights to humble the eminent, breathing out its malice into this disfranchisement." People were 'cancelled' or 'called out' to instil in them a sense of humility and warn them of overstepping the mark, especially people in positions of power. Throughout history, such forms of 'public shaming' have been practised in many different societies to not only humiliate the offender but also to create a 'chilling effect' on others tempted to follow in the same path.

Some 100 years later in 399 BCE, Plato expressed his distaste for such excesses of democracy. His teacher, Socrates, was tried by fellow citizens and sentenced to death for the twin crimes of impiety and corrupting the youth of Athens. While the jurors no doubt felt that they were 'calling out' Socrates for his offensive behaviour, Plato condemned the 'cancelling' of Socrates as the hysteria of a mob culture that shuts down the free speech of experts.

And so on the one hand, dictatorships – religious or secular – have been known for their top-down censorship of ideas that challenge their ideology or power structures: think of Galileo in 17th-century Catholic Italy and Alexandr Solzhenitsyn in 20th-century Communist Russia.

On the other hand, democracies have been criticised by liberals for what they see as a bottom-up 'cancelling' of viewpoints not in vogue with the zeitgeist of the day. In the prudish Victorian era, John Stuart Mill was said to be more fearful of public opinion stifling free speech than potential government bans. As he wrote in Chapter 1 of *On Liberty* on the threat from 'the tyranny of the majority':

> Protection, therefore, against the tyranny of the magistrate is not enough; there needs protection also against the tyranny of the prevailing opinion and feeling; against the tendency of society to impose, by other means than civil penalties, its own ideas and practices as rules of conduct on those who dissent from them; to fetter the development, and, if possible, prevent the formation, of any individuality not in harmony with its ways, and compel all characters to fashion themselves upon the model of its own. There is a limit to the legitimate interference of collective opinion with individual independence; and to find that limit, and maintain it against encroachment, is as indispensable to a good condition of human affairs, as protection against political despotism.

So too, many of the world's leading thinkers – from Noam Chomsky to Salman Rushdie – wrote an open letter in Harper's Magazine in 2020 warning of "a new set of moral attitudes and political commitments that tend to weaken our norms of open debate and toleration of differences in favour of ideological conformity." For them:

> The free exchange of information and ideas, the lifeblood of a liberal society, is daily becoming more constricted. While we have come to expect this on the radical right, censoriousness is also spreading more widely in our culture: an intolerance of opposing views, a vogue for public shaming and ostracism, and the tendency to dissolve complex policy issues in a blinding moral certainty. We uphold the value of robust and even caustic counter-speech from all quarters.

In response, many other thinkers countered that: "Under the guise of free speech and free exchange of ideas, the letter appears to be asking for unrestricted freedom to espouse their points of view free from consequence or criticism." They criticise the open letter in Harper's for being guilty of restricting free speech as the signatories refuse to "acknowledge... their role in perpetuating a culture of fear and silence among writers who, for the most part, do not look like the majority of the signatories. When they demand debates, it is on their terms, on their turf." Rather, they conclude:

> Their letter seeks to uphold a "stifling atmosphere" and prioritizes signal-blasting their discomfort in the face of valid criticism. The intellectual freedom of cis white intellectuals has never been under threat en masse, especially when compared to how writers from marginalized groups have been treated for generations. In fact, they have never faced serious consequences – only momentary discomfort.

Indeed, it is interesting to note that people on both sides of the debate often claim that it is their approach that ultimately protects free speech. Those fearful of 'cancel culture' claim that its device of public shaming ostracises people with allegedly 'offending' views and creates a chilling effect that leads to self-censorship as people are too afraid to speak up lest they be a target of the next witch hunt. Society faces complex issues and so people need to take risks and explore new ideas, including those seemingly unpalatable. Remember Bertrand Russell's seventh commandment of learning: "Do not fear to be eccentric in opinion, for every opinion now accepted was once eccentric."

In contrast, those supporting a 'calling-out' culture argue that just as those – often in privileged positions – get to speak out on the issues of the day, it would be hypocritical of them not to extend such 'free speech' to others who disagree and wish to challenge their perspectives. Just as you have the right to speak up, you also have a responsibility to speak responsibly and with sensitivity. And if you don't, then others have an equal right to speak up against you.

In the best traditions of free speech, this is a debate that will continue to rage for some time.

Beware!

Getting the balance right.

All schools aim to provide two vital services for their students: academic study and pastoral care. The free speech debate highlights a potential tension between these two endeavours: on the one hand, teachers want to provide their students with the knowledge and skills to help reach the truth; on the other hand, schools want their students to feel safe and happy. But what if the truth hurts?

In his book, *Antifragile*, Nassim Nicholas Taleb opens with an astute metaphor helpful for pastoral school leaders and parents alike: although wind extinguishes a candle, it energises a fire. Overprotecting our children turns them into candles, unable to withstand the softest of breezes. As Taleb puts it: "You want to be the fire and wish for the wind."

School is precisely the place to expose our students to hard truths about life. Teachers can explore topics like free speech in the safest and happiest of environments. If schools avoid such topics, which will inevitably involve risk and difficulty, then they are failing in their pastoral care as students will get knocked over by the slightest of challenges as they are coddled by overprotective systems.

As Greg Lukianoff and Jonathan Haidt starkly warn:

> If we protect children from various classes of potentially upsetting experiences, we make it far more likely that those children will be unable to cope with such events when they leave our protective umbrella. The modern obsession with protecting young people from "feeling unsafe" is, we believe, one of the (several) causes of the rapid rise in rates of adolescent depression, anxiety, and suicide.

Teachers are well aware of the Pygmalion effect on academic performance: high expectations lead to improved performance and low expectations lead to worse performance. Perhaps schools can apply this thinking in pastoral terms too: coddle our students too much and who can blame them from running away from adversity when it inevitably comes calling?

Plenty of examples to choose from without needing to offend your students gratuitously: This book has consistently argued for polarity: for teachers to recognise the primacy of adhering to the truth whilst nurturing the moral virtues in our students. Remember, even high school students are still children, and this context means legal and moral responsibilities upon the teacher that may well be irrelevant for the university, workplace, or public arena.

For example, blasphemy laws were formally abolished in England and Wales in 2021, whilst in the United States, the idea of legislating for blasphemy has long been seen as anathema to the Constitution (despite some states wishing to pass laws at the local level). As the First Amendment to the U.S. Constitution famously states: "Congress shall make no law respecting an establishment of religion, or prohibiting the free exercise thereof; or abridging the freedom of speech, or of the press..."

Nevertheless, every so often there are stories in the news of teachers being attacked for allegedly mocking a religion. For example, a teacher in West Yorkshire is still said to be in hiding some two years after showing pupils a cartoon of the Muslim Prophet Muhammad. Samuel Paty, a secondary school teacher in France, was killed and beheaded by an Islamist terrorist after a social media campaign against him for allegedly showing his students *Charlie Hebdo*'s 2012 cartoons depicting Muhammad. French president Emmanuel Macron was reported to have said that "our compatriot was killed for teaching children freedom of speech." Whilst Macron was obviously correct and such barbaric attacks have no place in a civilised society, one can still teach children the critical value of freedom of speech without needing to show such pictures that may well leave some of one's own students feeling alienated and upset. Indeed, one can even debate healthily the rights and wrongs of mocking religion – without needing to mock the religion oneself. This distinction is important and may be extended to any belief system, whether religious, political, or social.

Sources and Resources:

Afua Hirsch (2018), 'The Fantasy of "Free Speech."' Retrieved from: https://www.prospectmagazine.co.uk/magazine/the-fantasy-of-free-speech.

Arionne Nettles et al. (2020), 'A More Specific Letter on Justice and Open Debate.' Retrieved from: https://objectivejournalism.org/2020/07/a-more-specific-letter-on-justice-and-open-debate/.

BBC News (2022), 'Cineworld Cancels the Lady of Heaven Film Screenings after Protests.' Retrieved from: https://www.bbc.co.uk/news/business-61729392.

BBC Newsround (2023), 'Roald Dahl: Why Are They Rewriting Roald Dahl?' Retrieved from: https://www.bbc.co.uk/newsround/64715287.

Chimamanda Ngozi Adichie (2022), 'Freedom of Speech.' Retrieved from: https://downloads.bbc.co.uk/radio4/reith2022/Reith_2022_Lecture1.pdf.

Craig Simpson (2023), 'Agatha Christie Classics Latest to be Rewritten for Modern Sensitivities,' *The Telegraph*. Retrieved from: https://www.telegraph.co.uk/news/2023/03/25/agatha-christie-classics-latest-rewritten-modern-sensitivities/.

Emma Nolan (2020), 'J.K. Rowling Book Burning Videos Are Spreading Like Wildfire Across TikTok,' *Newsweek*. Retrieved from: https://www.newsweek.com/jk-rowling-books-burned-tiktok-transgender-issues-1532330.

John Stuart Mill (1859), 'Chapter I: Introductory,' *On Liberty*. Retrieved from: https://www.utilitarianism.com/ol/one.html.

John Stuart Mill (1859), 'Chapter II: Of the Liberty of Thought and Discussion,' *On Liberty*. Retrieved from: https://www.utilitarianism.com/ol/two.html.

Karl Popper (2011), *The Open Society and Its Enemies*. Oxford: Routledge.

Maya Yang (2022), 'Tennessee Pastor Leads Burning of Harry Potter and Twilight Novels,' *The Guardian*. Retrieved from: https://www.theguardian.com/us-news/2022/feb/04/book-burning-harry-potter-twilight-us-pastor-tennessee.

Nassim Nicholas Taleb (2013), *Antifragile: Things that Gain from Disorder*. London: Penguin.

Nicholas Barber (2019), 'Life of Brian: The Most Blasphemous Film Ever?' *BBC Culture*. Retrieved from: https://www.bbc.com/culture/article/20190822-life-of-brian-the-most-blasphemous-film-ever.

Rowan Atkinson (2012), 'On Free Speech.' Retrieved from: https://www.youtube.com/watch?v=BiqDZlAZygU.

Sam Harris (2022), '#300 - A Tale of Cancellation: A Conversation with Meg Smaker.' Retrieved from: https://www.samharris.org/podcasts/making-sense-episodes/300-a-tale-of-cancellation.

Sky History (n.d.), 'Ostracism: "Cancel Culture" Ancient Greek-Style.' Retrieved from: https://www.history.co.uk/articles/ostracism-cancel-culture-ancient-greek-style.

Thomas Chatterton Williams et al. (2020), 'A Letter on Justice and Open Debate,' *Harper's Magazine*. Retrieved from: https://harpers.org/a-letter-on-justice-and-open-debate/.

Links to Other Controversies:

Are transwomen, women?

Being 'Woke' just means being kind to others, especially vulnerable people. How can anyone disagree with that?

Being 'Woke' just means being kind to others, especially vulnerable people. How can anyone disagree with that?

Age group: 15-18

How explosive is this topic?

Just turn on the TV, log in to social media, and read any newspaper, and it will be clear that the 'Woke' controversies have become *the* explosive issue in many Western countries in our time. It is not unusual for either side on a whole range of debates, often known as 'the culture wars,' to resort to *ad hominem* attacks on their enemies: fascists, communists, racists, misogynists – and the list goes on. In school, we can and must do better.

How should I teach this topic?

The 'Woke' debate is controversial at all three levels: behavioural, political, and epistemic. Somewhat akin to the Israeli-Palestinian conflict, any hint of the teacher showing their own perspective on the issue, especially if they take a side, will smack of bias and alienate students on the other side.

This is especially true as the concept of 'power' is central to the debate for many of those who consider themselves 'Woke.' The teacher-student relationship is inherently one of a power imbalance. Through the teacher disclosing their own perspective, it may be felt that this will inhibit students from speaking up, feeling fearful of their relative lack of power.

In turn, I would strongly recommend the teacher adopt the stance of 'neutral impartiality' and so not disclose his own view. Under the principle of charity, he will present the best versions of the competing viewpoints so that his students are empowered to decide for themselves. As ever, Socratic questioning is an excellent device to test student thinking and clarity of argument.

Key Terms and Necessary Knowledge:

A 'culture war' over 'Wokeness' may be seen in broad terms as a battle of ideologies: liberalism (as in 'liberty' not 'political leftism') vs critical race theory (CRT). By explaining the key terms below through these two lenses, you will help your students get to the heart of this fractious debate. In turn, your own ideological bent may well influence how you interpret many of these terms, sometimes impacting your evaluation of these concepts.

To help frame these two key schools of thought, let's draw on the opening definitions from Wikipedia to help us:

Liberalism is a political and moral philosophy based on the rights of the individual, liberty, consent of the governed, political equality and equality before the law... [Liberals] generally support private property, market economies, individual rights (including civil rights and human rights), liberal democracy, secularism, rule of law, economic and political freedom, freedom of speech, freedom of the press, freedom of assembly, and freedom of religion. Liberalism is frequently cited as the dominant ideology of modern history.

CRT is a cross-disciplinary examination... of how laws, social and political movements, and media shape, and are shaped by, social conceptions of race and ethnicity... Scholars of CRT view race as a social construct with no biological basis. One tenet of CRT is that racism and disparate racial outcomes are the result of complex, changing, and often subtle social and institutional dynamics, rather than explicit and intentional prejudices of individuals [as liberals believe]. CRT scholars argue that the social and legal construction of race advances the interests of White people at the expense of people of colour, and that the liberal notion of U.S. law as "neutral" plays a significant role in maintaining a racially unjust social order, where formally colour-blind laws continue to have racially discriminatory outcomes. CRT began in the United States in the post–civil rights era [in the 1970s]... With racial inequalities persisting even after civil rights legislation and colour-blind laws were enacted...

Racism:

The online Merriam-Webster Dictionary provides two definitions of racism, which can be broadly categorised according to the liberal outlook and the CRT outlook.

The liberal understanding of racism:

1: a belief that race is a fundamental determinant of human traits and capacities and that racial differences produce an inherent superiority of a particular race.

also: behaviour or attitudes that reflect and foster this belief: racial discrimination or prejudice.

The CRT understanding of racism:

2 a: the systemic oppression of a racial group to the social, economic, and political advantage of another.

b: a political or social system founded on racism and designed to execute its principles.

Note that while the liberal understanding is more about how each of us behaves and thinks about race, the CRT understanding is focused more about the systemic oppression of a racial group. So, liberals think primarily in terms of individual people, while CRT followers think more in terms of the structures that are said to shape us and our society.

Affirmative action/positive discrimination: According to Cornell Law School, affirmative action is defined as a set of procedures designed to eliminate unlawful discrimination among applicants, remedy the results of such prior discrimination, and prevent such discrimination in the future. Applicants may be seeking admission to an educational programme or looking for professional employment. In modern American jurisprudence, it typically imposes remedies against discrimination on the basis of (at the very least) race, creed, colour, and national origin. However, at the time of writing, the U.S. Supreme Court ruled that race can no longer be considered as a factor in university admissions, upending affirmative action.

Cultural appropriation: Susan Scafidi, a professor of law, defines cultural appropriation as:

> Taking intellectual property, traditional knowledge, cultural expressions, or artifacts from someone else's culture without permission. This can include unauthorised use of another culture's dance, dress, music, language, folklore, cuisine, traditional medicine, religious symbols, etc. It's most likely to be harmful when the source community is a minority group that has been oppressed or exploited in other ways or when the object of appropriation is particularly sensitive, e.g. sacred objects.

Nicki Lisa Cole adds:

> The adoption of the dominant culture by racially and ethnically marginalised groups is forced and required, in the sense that it is necessary for inclusion in society, and in some cases historically and today, physically forced.
>
>   Cultural appropriation, by contrast, is not required or forced. It is a choice, and as such, it is an expression of privilege. While people of colour are forced to adopt elements of mainstream white culture, white people can sample at the buffet of other cultures at their leisure, picking and choosing what they wish to consume.

Identity politics: coined in 1977 by a group of black lesbian militants, this describes how "political positions that are based on the social groups that people see themselves as belonging to, for example based on religion, race or social background, rather than on traditional political parties," according to the Oxford Learner's Dictionary.

Intersectionality: coined in 1989 by black feminist scholar Kimberlé Crenshaw to demonstrate "a multifaceted connection between race, gender, and other systems that work together to oppress, while also allowing privilege in other areas." For example, Crenshaw argued that law courts have tended to ignore black women's unique experiences by treating them as only women or only black, thus rejecting the notion of 'compound discrimination.'

Micro-aggressions: controversial term that describes "indirect, subtle, or unintentional discrimination against members of a marginalised group," according to the Oxford Language Dictionary. In school, this might include criticising a student's hair style which is associated with their race or culture. Ibram X. Kendi rejects the use of this term, preferring the word 'abuse.'

Presentism: the tendency to interpret past events in terms of modern values and concepts. Many argue this leads to unfair perspectives on our ancestors as we are judging them by today's standards.

Punching up and Punching down: taken from the world of comedy, some argue that while it is fine to mock and make fun of people in privileged positions ("punching up"), one shouldn't attack people who are already marginalised ("punching down"). *The Simpsons* thus found itself embroiled in controversy over jokes surrounding the Apu character, which many complained fed into Indian stereotypes. Others argue that in a free society, especially when it comes to satire, anyone may be the target of an 'offensive' comment.

Safe space: traditionally referred to refuges for women who may feel vulnerable to male attacks on them. This term has now extended to refer to a desired climate by some for a safe space on university or school campus that is free from bias or criticism, with conversations that could potentially offend some. For many liberals, the notion of a safe space, especially in university, is in tension with the notion of free speech and academic freedom.

Trigger warning: "a statement at the start of a piece of writing, video, etc. alerting the reader or viewer to the fact that it contains potentially distressing material" (Oxford Language Dictionary). As such, critics claim that trigger warnings have expanded to the classroom for seemingly innocuous reasons. Greg Lukianoff and Jonathan Haidt argue that trigger warnings are actually harmful for students, as such devices "coddle" them, leaving them unable to deal with real levels of threat or harm that may come their way in the natural course of life.

Virtue signalling: "the public expression of opinions or sentiments intended to demonstrate one's good character or social conscience or the moral correctness of one's position on a particular issue" (Oxford Language Dictionary). Often criticised as empty and insincere, virtue signalling is seen by some as a feature of 'cancel culture' whereby some may feel the need to 'virtue signal' so that they don't then face a backlash.

'Whiteness': a core concept of CRT, the Smithsonian's 'Talking about Race' series defines this term as follows:

> Whiteness and white racialised identity refer to the way that white people, their customs, culture, and beliefs operate as the standard by which all other groups of are compared. Whiteness is also at the core of understanding race in America. Whiteness and the normalisation of white racial identity throughout America's history have created a culture where nonwhite persons are seen as inferior or abnormal.

It is linked with the notion of 'white privilege':

> Since white people in America hold most of the political, institutional, and economic power, they receive advantages that nonwhite groups do not. These benefits and advantages, of varying degrees, are known as white privilege. For many white people, this can be hard to hear, understand, or accept - but it is true. If you are white in America, you have benefited from the colour of your skin.

Many liberals, such as John McWhorter, argue that such a term is in itself racist as it "essentialises" white people, claiming they are all guilty of some sort of 'original sin,' potentially belittle their own experiences, especially those from working class backgrounds.

Woke: a slang word that is said to be derived from the African-American Vernacular English (AAVE) meaning "alert to racial prejudice and discrimination." Although the phrase "stay woke" can be traced to the 1930s, the term has become much more widely used since the 2010s. As Aja Romano writes,

> 'woke' has evolved into a single-word summation of leftist political ideology, centred on social justice politics and critical race theory. This framing of 'woke' is bipartisan: It's used as a shorthand for political progressiveness by the left, and as a denigration of leftist culture by the right.

Socratic Questions and Critical Thinking:

Classroom Discussion:

To help frame a broad debate on 'Woke,' you may wish to begin by discussing the following sentence from Martin Luther King Jr., one of the most celebrated – yet controversial – lines in modern history:

"I have a dream that my four little children will one day live in a nation where they will not be judged by the colour of their skin but by the content of their character."

Of course, this vision is from the great civil rights leader's most famous public speech during the March on Washington for Jobs and Freedom on 28 August 1963. Yet how to interpret this passage has been hotly debated ever since.

For your students, you may wish to offer two broad approaches that we can label as follows:

- The Liberal 'colour-blind' approach
- The CRT 'structural racism' approach

Which approach is more consistent with MLK's struggle for civil rights?

Liberalism: 'colour-blind'	CRT: 'structural racism'
MLK meant that we should judge people on the merits of their individual character: who they are, not what they are. The aim is to reach a colour-blind society. As Morgan Freeman, the actor, responded when asked how we are going to get off racism: "Stop talking about it. I'm going to stop calling you a 'white man' and I'm going to ask you to stop calling me a 'black man'... You know me as Morgan Freeman."	MLK's speech recognises the intrinsic link between what people were marching for that day: 'jobs' and 'freedom.' As Martin Luther King III, MLK's son, put it: "I don't think we can ignore race. What my father is asking is to create the climate where every American can realise his or her dreams. Now what does that mean when you have 50 million people living in poverty?"
Thomas Sowell in 'A Poignant Anniversary' writes that: "Judging individuals by their individual character is at the opposite pole from judging how groups are statistically represented among employees, college students, or political figures." For Sowell, MLK's speech has been ironically championed by people opposed to its liberal message. Rather, it's original message needs to be adhered to. Indeed, Sowell has said this is important not just in principle but in practice: decades of progressive politics, he argues, has only worsened the lot of black individuals and communities in modern America.	MLK in his 1967 book, *Where Do We Go From Here*: "It is, however, important to understand that giving a man his due may often mean giving him special treatment. I am aware of the fact that this has been a troublesome concept for many liberals, since it conflicts with their traditional ideal of equal opportunity and equal treatment of people according to their individual merits." "A society that has done something special *against* the Negro for hundreds of years must now do something special *for* him, in order to equip him to compete on a just and equal basis."
Liberals like Sam Harris argue: "I want to live in a society where we care no more about skin colour and other superficial characteristics that are often attributed or ascribed to race than we care about hair colour... We're not living in a world where people are disposed to worry that a corporation like Apple isn't hiring enough blonds or brunettes. No one's checking." Therefore, in a liberal society we should pay no heed to so-called identity markers like race or gender. Rather, merit should win the day.	Followers of CRT like Reni Eddo-Lodge counter: "Colour-blindness is a childish, stunted analysis of racism. It starts and ends at 'discriminating against a person because of the colour of their skin is bad,' without any accounting for the ways in which structural power manifests in these exchanges." Thus, for champions of CRT, the focus isn't on individual racism but rather on structural racism and the history of white racial dominance. As Eddo-Lodge concludes: "Seeing race is essential to changing the system."

Follow-up questions for your students:

- *How might the above arguments impact our view on "affirmative action?"*
- *Which other groups might be said to have suffered so much historically that it is now right to do "something special" for them?*
- *Should we see each other primarily in terms of their individuality or more in terms of the group(s) they belong to? Why might others disagree with you?*

This broad debate impacts a whole host of related 'woke' controversies that have come to the forefront of society. Let's look at some of the most ferocious debates below:

Should countries like the United States or Britain make amends for historic injustices against other black and other ethnic minority groups?

Yes to reparations	No to reparations
It is a simple matter of justice: countries who benefitted from slavery, not least Britain and the United States, need to apologise and make up for the terrible injustices of slavery. We can't undo the past but we can try to make amends for what we as nations have done wrong.	It's surely unfair to make Western countries pay for historical injustices of slavery whilst so many other peoples benefitted from slavery too, e.g. Barbary pirates from North Africa who raided European coastal towns and villages to capture slaves for hundreds of years.
Just as we might be proud of British or American history and undoubtedly benefit economically from past injustices such as slavery, so too should we feel responsible for the wrongs committed in the past and continue to haunt the descendants of those slaves even today, not least through the terrible legacy of ongoing racism. Just because we can't make everything right, doesn't mean we should simply give up.	The passage of time means it's impossible to trace who should compensate who. Are today's descendants of slaves directly suffering due to those injustices? Even if so, can we say who exactly should pay for the crimes committed hundreds of years ago? Britain and America's outlawing of slavery and leading the fight against the slave trade is a legacy to be proud of – especially in comparison with how other nations were behaving at the time.
Reparations are part of 'restorative justice' and coming to terms with who we are as a society. It will help bring out into the open the terrible but undeniable aspects of who we are as a society and the resulting wealth gap which is surely a legacy of slavery that needs correcting.	Reparations will only divide us further – especially along ethnic lines. Is it fair that poor white people who are already struggling, are to pay for the past crimes of others? Will such moves really help heal our society or only exacerbate racial tensions?

- If we are proud of our collective British or American (or ......) identity, then should we also feel shame of those aspects which continue to impact on who we are?
- If we do feel shame, is there anything we should be doing in terms of 'restorative justice' and so assist those who have suffered and continue to suffer?
- Are we unfairly judging our ancestors of the past by the standards of today?
- Is it in fact racist to hold historically white nations to a higher standard than nonwhite nations who also practised slavery?
- Are reparations the fairest way to heal ongoing societal problems that can arguably be traced to the legacies of racism and slavery?

Can a white person write about black people? Can a heterosexual person act as a gay person?

Scenario 1: Dana Schutz's *Open Casket* Painting

In 1955, a black 14-year-old black boy called Emmet Till was lynched and murdered by two white men in Mississippi. It was a sickening racist crime that shocked much of America, especially when the all-white jury found the suspects not guilty of murder just a month later. Till's brave mother insisted on an open casket at the funeral so that the world should see what was done to her young son.

In 2016, an artist called Dana Schutz painted *Open Casket*, based on pictures of Till's mutilated body. The painting was included in the 2017 Whitney Biennial exhibition in New York – to much controversy. The reason? Shutz is white.

The artist Parker Bright protested in front of the work, wearing a T-shirt with "BLACK DEATH SPECTACLE" written on the back. He was reported to have said: "She has nothing to say to the black community about black trauma."

A British artist and writer called Hannah Black wrote an open letter that opens as follows:

> I am writing to ask you to remove Dana Schutz's painting 'Open Casket' and with the urgent recommendation that the painting be destroyed and not entered into any market or museum.
>
> As you know, this painting depicts the dead body of 14-year-old Emmett Till in the open casket that his mother chose, saying, "Let the people see what I've seen." That even the disfigured corpse of a child was not sufficient to move the white gaze from its habitual cold calculation is evident daily and in a myriad of ways, not least the fact that this painting exists at all. In brief: the painting should not be acceptable to anyone who cares or pretends to care about Black people because it is not acceptable for a white person to transmute Black suffering into profit and fun, though the practice has been normalized for a long time.

Dana Shutz responded as follows:

"I don't know what it is like to be black in America but I do know what it is like to be a mother. Emmett was Mamie Till's only son. The thought of anything happening to your child is beyond comprehension. Their pain is your pain. My engagement with this image was through empathy with his mother. [...] Art can be a space for empathy, a vehicle for connection. I don't believe that people can ever really know what it is like to be someone else (I will never know the fear that black parents may have) but neither are we all completely unknowable."

- Shutz has been accused of 'cultural appropriation.' Do you agree? Why might others disagree with your viewpoint?
- Shutz's defence is similar to the following quote by Terence, a Roman playwright: "I am human, and I think nothing human alien to me." Was he right? Can we empathise with other people no matter how different their experiences are from our own?
- Bob Dylan wrote 'The Ballad of Emmett Till' and many other protest songs that were celebrated throughout the world by peoples of all cultures. Many have described him as the voice of the Civil Rights Movement. Should Dylan's work be re-evaluated in light of claims of 'cultural appropriation?' Does it make a difference that Dylan is Jewish and so belongs to a historically persecuted group?
- Hannah Black urged for the painting to be destroyed. Is it ever right to destroy works of art, however much we may disagree with them?

Scenario 2: Anthony Horowitz including a black character in one of his novels

In 2017, the author Anthony Horowitz said he was "warned off" including a black character he had written into his new book as it was "inappropriate" as a white author. He explained that people felt that "it is not actually in our experience" and so white people shouldn't be writing about the experiences of black people. Horowitz himself complained that this view was "disturbing and upsetting."

Horowitz, the author of the popular Alex Rider teenage spy novels, said: "Taking it to the extreme, all my characters will from now be 62-year-old white Jewish men living in London."

- Where (if anywhere) do we draw the line on who can write about what?

  - The male Thomas Hardy created one of the great literary female heroines in Tess in *Tess of the D'Urbervilles: A Pure Woman Faithfully Presented*
  - The non-Jewish William Styron wrote *Sophie's Choice*, one of the finest novels about the Holocaust.

Scenario 3: Eddie Redmayne acting as Lili Elbe, a trans woman in *The Danish Girl*

In an interview with The Sunday Times, Eddie Redmayne regretted his participation in the film, saying: "No, I wouldn't take it on now. I made that film with the best intentions, but I think it was a mistake." He added: "The bigger discussion about the frustrations around casting is because many people don't have a chair at the table. There must be a levelling, otherwise we are going to carry on having these debates." At the time of its release, the trans writer Carol Grant described as the film as "regressive, reductive, and contribut[ing] to harmful stereotypes," whilst slamming the decision to not cast a trans actor in the leading role.

- Redmayne won an Oscar for playing Professor Stephen Hawking in *The Theory of Everything*. If he was wrong to play a trans woman, was he wrong to play a disabled man who suffered from motor neurone disease?
- Isn't the point of acting to play someone else, irrespective of who they are?

Should we knock down statues of controversial figures?

On 7 June 2020, anti-racism protestors in Bristol toppled the statue of Edward Colston, a British-born trans-Atlantic slave trader and philanthropist. The protests were part of the global outcry over the murder of George Floyd in My 2020, with other monuments and memorials also vandalised and removed due to alleged associations with racism.

In the ensuing trial of four people charged with criminal damage for tearing down the Colston statue and throwing it into the harbour, the jury decided to acquit the defendants. Professor David Olusoga told the BBC: "An English jury... has come to the conclusion that the real offence was that a statue to a mass murderer was able to stand for 125 years, not that that statue was toppled in the summer of 2020. That is enormously significant and we are on this very long and difficult journey in this country of acknowledging all of our history, the bad as well as the good and I think this is a landmark in that difficult, tortuous journey." It should be noted that there was a long-standing campaign to remove the statue or at least add a plaque to acknowledge and explain how Colston profited from slavery.

- If you were a member of the jury, what would have been your verdict for this trial? Explain your arguments. (See Sources and Resources below for research links into the story)

In the United States, the George Floyd protests involved people protesting statues in honour of:

- Christopher Columbus
- Thomas Jefferson
- Robert E. Lee
- Abraham Lincoln
- George Washington

Students can research into why these leaders were targeted, evaluating each case.
Arguments on both sides of the divide include:

For toppling the statues	Against toppling the statues
The statues honour people who did terrible things, such as owning slaves and fighting against the United States in the Civil War.	People are complex: no one is without fault. We are honouring people for specific things they did; we can still condemn any other negative aspects of their lives.
For descendants of slaves and others still feeling the pain of racism and oppression, such statues are antagonistic and humiliating.	Rather than topple the statues, add plaques with explanations to give the full picture of what the person did and so help understand our own history better.
Surely such statues can be replaced with other more worthy people who deserve to be honoured.	Just as people in the past built statues to people they celebrated, we can simply build more statues and memorials for people we wish to honour.

- A major argument against toppling statues is the idea of 'presentism': the danger of un-fairly judging past generations by today's standards? Discuss this argument.

Dilemma: Topple Mahatma Gandhi's Statue?
The social media hashtag #GandhiMustFall arose in 2019 to protest statues and memorials dedicated to the legendary founder of modern India, Mahatma Gandhi. Protestors described Gandhi as "a fascist, racist and sexual predator," pointing to his reference of Africans as "sav-ages," "uncivilised" and "dirty." Rajmohan Gandhi, his grandson and biographer, accepted that Gandhi was "at times ignorant and prejudiced about South Africa's blacks," but the "imperfect Gandhi was more radical and progressive than most contemporary compatriots."

Of course, for many around the world, Gandhi is seen as an icon of peace and pioneer of non-violent protest. In India, he is seen as the father of the modern country and a Hindu leader. In turn, many supporters of Gandhi counter that removing the statues would be tantamount to anti-Asian racism.

- Should statues of Gandhi be reconsidered? Explain your arguments. (See Sources and Resources below for research links into the story)
- Who should decide which statues remain and which should be removed?

'Cultural appropriation': Can white people wear dreadlocks?

The philosopher Kwame Anthony Appiah criticises the concept of 'cultural appropriation':
"We should resist using the term 'cultural appropriation' as an indictment. All cultural practices and objects are mobile; they like to spread, and almost all are themselves creations of inter-mixture. Kente in Asante was first made with dyed silk thread, imported from the East. We took something made by others and made it ours. Or rather, they did that in the village of Bonwire. So did the Asante of Kumasi appropriate the cultural property of Bonwire, where it was first made? Putative owners may be previous appropriators.

"The real problem isn't that it's difficult to decide who owns culture; it's that the very idea of ownership is the wrong model...

"...Unfortunately, the vigorous lobbying of huge corporations has made the idea of intel-lectual property go imperial; it seems to have conquered the world. To accept the notion of cultural appropriation is to buy into the regime they favour, where corporate entities acting as cultural guardians 'own' a treasury of intellectual property, extracting a toll when they allow others to make use of it.

"This isn't to say that accusations of cultural appropriation never arise from a real offense. Usually, where there's a problem worth noticing, it involves forms of disrespect compounded by power inequities; cultural appropriation is simply the wrong diagnosis. When Paul Simon makes a mint from riffing on mbaqanga music from South Africa, you can wonder if the rich American gave the much poorer Africans who taught it to him their fair share of the proceeds. If he didn't, the problem isn't cultural theft but exploitation. If you're a Sioux, you recognise your people are being ridiculed when some fraternity boys don a parody of the headdress of your ancestors and make whooping noises. But, again, the problem isn't theft, it's disrespect. Imagine how an Orthodox Jewish rabbi would feel if a gentile pop-music multimillionaire made a music video in which he used the Kaddish to mourn a Maserati he'd totalled. The offense isn't appropriation; it's the insult entailed by trivialising something another group holds sacred. Those who parse these transgressions in terms of ownership have accepted a commercial system that's alien to the traditions they aim to protect. They have allowed one modern regime of property to appropriate them."

Appiah makes three arguments against the claim of 'cultural appropriation':

1. All cultures borrow and exchange ideas from each other: this may be seen by some as 'cultural appreciation' and makes our world that much richer
2. 'Owning' culture is the wrong way to look at it: this is a capitalist, Western model that CRT activists have unwittingly appropriated
3. Rather, what people are justifiably upset about is 'exploitation,' 'trivialisation,' and 'disrespect' of their culture.

Questions:

- Is Appiah right that terms like 'exploitation,' 'trivialisation,' and 'disrespect' better capture the problem that 'cultural appropriation' seeks to diagnose?
- Who, if anyone, gets to speak on behalf of a group in terms of its identity? What if there are real differences of opinion within such groups?
- When does 'cultural appreciation' turn into 'cultural appropriation' – if at all? Consider the following case studies to help illustrate your thinking:

  - White people with dreadlocks? (Whilst the term 'dreadlock' is Rastafarian, scholars suggest many ancient cultures – from India to Egypt to the Vikings – had such hairstyles.)
  - Black people with Jewish names like Elijah or Isaiah? (Although these Hebrew names are from the Bible, the spread of Christianity and biblical teachings has led to these names becoming common throughout the world.)
  - American Football teams using Native American iconography?
  - White English people cooking and enjoying Indian food?

Black Lives Matter: Should sports teams 'take the knee?'

In 2016, American footballer Colin Kaepernick 'took the knee' during the national anthem, saying he could not take pride in a country that oppressed black people. Some saw the gesture as symbolic of Martin Luther King Jr who took the knee in prayer with a group of civil rights activists in 1965. It has since grown into an anti-racist symbol in sport and during protests throughout the world, including in the United Kingdom where the English team has often taken the knee before international matches.

However, others have argued that 'taking the knee' isn't about anti-racism but about supporting the Black Lives Matter movement, which took on the symbolic protest since the murder of George Floyd in 2020. With Black Lives Matter, a political and social movement very much framed by CRT thinking, critics believe the gesture to be divisive. Indeed, when English players have taken to the knee, some fans have booed while others have clapped in support. Defending his players taking the knee, the English manager Gareth Southgate said: "I think we have got a situation where some people seem to think it is a political stand that they don't agree with. That is not the reason the players are doing it. We are supporting each other."

For taking the knee	Against taking the knee
Racism and oppression are ongoing. By famous sportspeople – many of whom are role models for young fans – taking the knee, they highlight the continuing injustices against black and other minority groups.	Taking the knee is classic 'virtue signalling.' It hasn't actually reduced racism and is an easy, cheap way for people with high public profiles to increase their standing with the public without actually doing anything meaningful.
Martin Luther King took the knee, and this gesture is part of many sporting protests against ongoing oppression. The claim that it is linked with specific political movements is disingenuous and side-lines the real issue at hand which is fighting against racism.	Taking the knee is bound up with Black Lives Matter in the public imagination. It is therefore a political act which is divisive and alienates those who reject CRT approaches towards racism, including campaigns such as 'defund the police.'
Players and teams have the right of free speech: just because some people may find it offensive to take the knee during the national anthem, the players have the right to freely express themselves in a democratic society. As Rio Ferdinand, the ex-England captain, put it: "I think that the current players, the England manager have explained on many occasions now as to why they're taking the knee. I think that the fans should respect that."	There are many less divisive ways to show solidarity in the fight against racism. Fans had no problem with anti-racism armbands or public messages. It is specifically taking the knee that is politically problematic and so just as players have the right of free expression, so too do fans who boo and jeer. Also, 'cancel culture' means many players feel they have no choice but to take the knee for fear of a backlash on social media.

Some Theory:

This is a fierce debate that often has people speaking past each other rather than to each other. A major reason for this is that although people on either side of the debate will be speaking about concepts like racism and anti-racism, these words mean very different things depending on whether one takes a liberal or CRT stance on the issue.

When Martin Luther King Jr made his 'I have a dream' speech in 1963, many liberals look back at this landmark moment as symbolic of the seismic legal reforms that matched huge cultural and societal changes in attitudes towards racism in America and the West. Perhaps no one articulated this idea better than Barack Obama, the first black U.S. President and, indeed, the first black leader of any major Western democracy. In celebrating the 1964 Civil Rights Act under President Johnson's presidency, Obama rejected the notion that there was no progress made. "I reject such a thing," Obama said. "Not just because Medicare and Medicaid have lifted many from poverty... I reject such cynicism because I have lived out the promise of Lyndon Baines Johnson's efforts." However flawed things might still be, Obama argues, "the story of America is the story of progress."

Yet critics of Obama, like Ta-Nehisi Coates, point out that the Obama story is an exceptional one. The reality for millions of black Americans is that they are still paying the price both for historical injustices and continued structural racism. As Ibram X. Kendi has argued, even Martin Luther King was deeply distressed by the lack of real progress in race relations up until his assassination. As King observed in 1967: "the doctrine of white supremacy was embedded in every textbook and preached in practically every pulpit," entrenched as "a structural part of the culture." In turn, King argued, "justice for black people cannot be achieved without radical changes in the structure of our society."

This belief that "American racism was systemic and demanded systemic remedies," as Kendi puts it, helps explain the rise of CRT in the 1970s. Few were more influential in its development than the Harvard legal academic, Derrick Bell. Deeply pessimistic about any progress in racial justice, Bell argued that racism "is an integral, permanent and indestructible component of this society" and that black people "will never gain full equality" as "those herculean efforts we hail as successful will produce no more than temporary 'peaks of progress,' short-lived victories that slide into irrelevance as racial patterns adapt in ways that maintain white dominance." Bell maintained that even supposed landmark cases like *Brown vs Board of Education 1954*, which ruled that racial segregation in public schools are illegal, only occurred when it was to advance white interests too, in this case, to raise America's standing in the world during the Cold War.

In turn, Richard Delgado, another pioneer of CRT, has written that "Enlightenment-style Western democracy [i.e. liberal democracy] is... the source of black people's subordination. Racism and enlightenment are the same thing." Delgado and Jean Stefancic are clear in their opposition to liberalism: "Unlike traditional civil rights discourse, which stresses incrementalism [i.e. evolutionary reforms] and step-by-step progress, critical race theory questions the very foundations of the liberal order, including equality theory, legal reasoning, Enlightenment rationalism, and neutral principles of constitutional law."

If the system is rigged, with racism woven into the very fabric of society, claims of neutral principles of law become farcical and simply entrench the current inequalities. This is why writers such as Reni Eddo-Lodge see the liberal aim of a 'colour-blind' society as missing the point. Rather, the aim should be to "deconstruct racist structures" and "materially improve the conditions which people of colour are subject to daily." In complete opposition to the liberal approach to fighting race, Eddo-Lodge concludes: "In order to dismantle unjust, racist structures, we must see race. We must see who benefits from their race, who is disproportionately impacted by negative stereotypes about their race, and to who power and privilege is bestowed upon – earned or not – because of the race, their class, and their gender." In this small passage, Eddo-Lodge captures the need for concepts like intersectionality, power structures, and white privilege that have become central to CRT thinking.

For liberals, of course, the CRT approach is in itself racist. As John McWhorter, an American academic has argued, such "woke racism" is itself the barrier for social progress and racial harmony. Concepts such as 'white privilege' are akin to Christian 'original sin,' with white people having to accept "themselves as inherently complicit in a profoundly racist system of operation and thought." And there is no way out: for anyone who denies they are racist simply proves that they are. Indeed, critics of CRT point out, such racial essentialism, that lumps white people together on one side and black people on another, is precisely racist in itself. As Jordan Peterson has written, the very definition of racism is "the ascription of the hypothetical characteristics of a given racial group to all the individuals within that group."

Moreover, scholars such as Kenan Malik argue that "Our preoccupation with race frequently hides the realities of injustice." By seeing race in terms of colour, Malik observes, means that anti-Semitism, for example, may be overlooked as Jews are seen by many as "white" and "privileged." Decrying "the dominant social justice ideology," leading American Jewish thinkers wrote an open letter claiming that "critical social justice ideology fuels antisemitism," as it "holds that individuals bear collective moral guilt or innocence based on the current conception of group identity." They go on to explain: "Because this dominant narrative creates a worldview in which groups are only oppressors or oppressed, it encourages pernicious notions of 'Jewish privilege,' even implicating Jews in 'white supremacy.'

As most analysts agree, these debates are primarily American. However, they have and will continue to influence other countries around the world in terms of how we see the ongoing cleavages and fractures in our own societies. While all good people of conscience can subscribe to opposing racism, there are real divides now over what 'racism' even means and how we can get to live in a more harmonious and just society.

Beware!

Sweeping generalisations: This chapter has focused on specific debates that are prominent in today's society. Draw your students away from unhelpful sweeping generalisations that pit sides against each other in all-too easy straw man arguments: "being woke means being over-sensitive" or "not being woke means you're a racist." Rather than indulge in such unhelpful chatter, ensure the discussion among your students point to real issues that cause them to think critically and in a targeted manner.

Name calling: Similarly, this is a debate that will tempt many to go for the *ad hominem*: playing the person, rather than playing the ball. It is really important to lay out the ground rules that such name calling will not be tolerated as you wish to stick to the issues. We have seen that both liberals and CRT followers understand racism in very different ways. This crucial difference leads each side to say that the other side is missing the point, often falling into the trap of racism, even with good intentions. It is fine for students to point this out with the necessary justification, but this is very different from name calling "you're a racist" in order to score points and avoid the actual arguments at hand.

It's personal: school is about pursuing truth and also about nurturing core moral virtues for children in our care. Sensitivity for students' own personal circumstances is especially important in a topic like this where some will have experienced discrimination, whether along racial or gender lines, or for any other reason. There is a high potential for students to get very emotional when discussing these related topics and so teachers should plan ahead to ensure they are well-prepared to prevent such a fall out or be able to deal with adverse reactions if and when they occur.

Sources and Resources:

Aja Romano (2020), 'A History of "Wokeness,"' *Vox*. Retrieved from: https://www.vox.com/culture/21437879/stay-woke-wokeness-history-origin-evolution-controversy.

Alex Greenberger (2017), '"The Painting Must Go": Hannah Black Pens Open Letter to the Whitney About Controversial Biennial Work.' Retrieved from: https://www.artnews.com/artnews/news/the-painting-must-go-hannah-black-pens-open-letter-to-the-whitney-about-controversial-biennial-work-7992/.

BBC News (2019), 'Manchester Students Want Statue of "Racist" Gandhi Rejected.' Retrieved from: https://www.bbc.co.uk/news/uk-england-manchester-50062791.

BBC News (2022), 'Colston Statue Verdict 'Landmark' in Britain's Slave History.' Retrieved from: https://www.bbc.co.uk/news/uk-england-bristol-59892211.

CBS News, 'MLK's "content of character" Quote Inspires Debate.' Retrieved from: https://www.cbsnews.com/news/mlks-content-of-character-quote-inspires-debate/.

David Olusoga (2023), 'The Ties That Bind Us,' *The Guardian*. Retrieved from: https://www.theguardian.com/news/ng-interactive/2023/mar/28/slavery-and-the-guardian-the-ties-that-bind-us.

Derrick Bell (2018), *Faces at the Bottom of the Well: The Permanence of Racism*. London: Basic Books.

Emmanuella Grinberg (2016), 'Dear White People with Dreadlocks: Some Things to Consider,' *CNN*. Retrieved from: https://edition.cnn.com/2016/03/31/living/white-dreadlocks-cultural-appropriation-feat/index.html.

Greg Lukianoff and Jonathan Haidt (2015), 'The Coddling of the American Mind,' *The Atlantic*. Retrieved from: https://www.theatlantic.com/magazine/archive/2015/09/the-coddling-of-the-american-mind/399356/.

Ibram X. Kendi (2021), 'The Second Assassination of Martin Luther King Jr.,' *The Atlantic*. Retrieved from: https://www.theatlantic.com/ideas/archive/2021/10/martin-luther-king-critical-race-theory/620367/.

Jewish Institute for Jewish Values (n.d.), 'A Letter to Our Fellow Jews on Equality and Liberal Values.' Retrieved from: https://jilv.org/be-heard/.

Kwame Anthony Appiah (2018), *The Lies That Bind*. London: Profile Books.

Nadra Kareem Nittle (2021), 'A Guide to Understanding and Avoiding Cultural Appropriation.' Retrieved from: https://www.thoughtco.com/cultural-appropriation-and-why-iits-wrong-2834561.

Nicki Lisa Cole (2018), 'Definition of Cultural Appropriation.' Retrieved from: http://writingtheother.com/wp-content/uploads/2018/08/Definition-of-Cultural-Appropriation.pdf.

Nigel Biggar (2019), 'Cambridge Is Lost in a Cloud of Leftist Virtue-Signalling,' *The Times*. Retrieved from: https://www.thetimes.co.uk/article/cambridge-slave-inquiry-rewrites-history-with-leftist-virtue-signalling-nv2xhd63q.

Richard Delgado and Jean Stefancic (2017), *Critical Race Theory: An Introduction*. New York: New York University Press.

Smithsonian National Museum of African American History and Culture (n.d.), 'Whiteness.' Retrieved from: https://nmaahc.si.edu/learn/talking-about-race/topics/whiteness.

Soutik Biswas (2015), 'Was Mahatma Gandhi a Racist?' *BBC News*. Retrieved from: https://www.bbc.co.uk/news/world-asia-india-34265882.

Ta-Nehisi Coates (2014), 'The Case for Reparations,' *The Atlantic*. Retrieved from: https://www.theatlantic.com/magazine/archive/2014/06/the-case-for-reparations/361631/.

Thomas Sowell (2011), 'Twisted History.' In *The Thomas Sowell Reader*. New York: Basic Books, pp. 18–19.

Thomas Sowell (2013), 'A Poignant Anniversary,' *National Review*. Retrieved from: https://www.nationalreview.com/2013/08/poignant-anniversary-thomas-sowell/#pq=PKnYWG.

Wikipedia (2023), 'Intersectionality.' Retrieved from: https://en.wikipedia.org/wiki/Intersectionality.

Links to other controversies:

Are transwomen, women?
Should there be any limits to free speech?

You don't really believe what the government / media is telling us...?

9/11 was an 'inside job.'
The Americans faked the moon-landings.
JFK was killed by the CIA working with the mafia.
Vaccinations are a cover to implant trackable microchips.
QAnon: Groups of Washington and Hollywood elites are really satanic paedophiles.
Coronavirus emerged from a government-controlled laboratory in China.
Social media companies suppress free speech for their political agendas.

Age group: *11-18*

How explosive is this topic?

Conspiracy theories are by definition controversial. This is because they seek to undermine the mainstream or official approach on any given topic. For many, this is what is so dangerous about them; for others, this is why they are necessary and natural in any given society. And so, despite those who wish to dismiss conspiracy theorists as dangerous cranks or gullible simpletons, belief in conspiracies remain pervasive, with recent surveys showing that "over half of the American population consistently endorse some kind of conspiratorial narrative about a current political event or phenomenon." In the United Kingdom, just over half of the British public think that, despite being officially a democracy, Britain is really run by a few people with power. It is therefore likely that on any given conspiracy theory, you will have real differences of opinion in the classroom. Make no mistake, passions are bound to rise. Much like Holocaust denial, a most pernicious example of an 'unwarranted' conspiracy theory, teachers must be aware that the considerations here aren't just epistemic in nature. Rather, conspiracy beliefs will often go to the heart of moral and civic concerns too.[6]

How should I teach this topic?

There are two major approaches as to how to approach conspiracy theories in the classroom. The 'generalist' school sees conspiracy theories as typically irrational, and so the teacher should model a default scepticism that aims to debunk them as a class of explanation. In their excellent guide that supports this 'directive' approach, Jeremy Hayward and Gemma Gronland also caution against simply dismissing a conspiracy theory as false without consideration: we should always model good thinking and appreciate that not taking a belief seriously can further strengthen that very belief. In turn, for when conspiracy theories are raised, the following type of response is recommended:

Yes to directive teaching: "It's good to question things but do make sure you follow what the evidence is saying. In this case, there is simply no evidence to support the idea that Covid vaccines are a cover to implant trackable microchips."

No to non-directive teaching: "There are many people who believe that 9/11 was an 'inside job.' Let's look in to why they think this and whether there is any substance to their claims."

However, the 'particularist' school believes it's too simplistic to class all conspiracy theories together. Simply look at the examples I have offered above – can you notice any key differences between them?

Just as many conspiracy theories have proven false, so too have many proven true. Think about Watergate, Wikileaks, and the Volkswagen emissions scandal. Like it or not, people in powerful positions sometimes really do conspire! Rather, it's a case of examining conspiracy theories case by case and seeing where the evidence lies. This is easier to do with 'mature' conspiracy theories (those that have been around for a while), but more difficult with recent, 'immature' ones, where there are still so many unknowns.

As we will see, there are helpful rules of thumb – like the maturity of a conspiracy theory – to help the teacher decide whether a conspiracy theory might be considered 'warranted' and so worth debating or 'unwarranted' and so rejected on epistemic grounds.

For an 'unwarranted' conspiracy theory, yes to directive teaching: "There is simply no evidence to suggest 9/11 was an 'inside job.' It's also highly insulting to the victims of the terrorist attack as well as many Americans when you are laying the blame at their own government rather than those who actually carried it out. Let's talk after the lesson; I'd like to know how you came to think such things."

For a 'warranted' conspiracy theory, yes to non-directive teaching: "How Covid began is still not fully known. Why might people believe that the Chinese government is culpable for starting and spreading Coronavirus? What arguments would undermine such a view?"

Key Terms and Necessary Knowledge:

Conspiracy theories cause a lot of teachers to panic, with many opting not to deal with the claims made altogether. "Not for now," is a favoured response. A major reason for this is that when a student takes to a conspiracy theory, they may well know far more than the teacher on the given topic. This can be very uncomfortable, especially if the conspiracy in question is sensitive – which it usually is. Nevertheless, by building up your knowledge of the key issues surrounding conspiracy theories, you will be able to deal with them successfully in the classroom. Again, considering how contested the terms are, I provide what I believe are mainstream and helpful explanations together with the source for further research.

Conspiracy theory: A conspiracy theory is a proposed explanation of an historical event, in which conspiracy (i.e. agents acting secretly in concert) has a significant causal role. Furthermore, the conspiracy postulated by the proposed explanation must be a conspiracy to bring about the historical event which it purports to explain. Finally, the proposed explanation must conflict with an "official" explanation of the same historical event.
Source: David Coady (2006)

- **Event conspiracy theory:** in which a secret organised group stands behind a single event such as the assassination of U.S. President John F. Kennedy, or the faked landing of humans on the moon. The conspiracies imagined in this case are usually short term, plotted over just a few weeks or months or, at the most, a couple of years.
  Source: Richard Evans (2020)
- **Systemic conspiracy theory:** in which a single conspiratorial entity carries out a wide variety of activities with the aim of taking control of a country, a region, or even the whole world. Often, according to the theory, the conspiracy is hatched over a long period of time, even centuries, and spreads over a very wide geographical area, in some instances virtually the entire globe, propagated by some kind of universal organisation like the Illuminati, the Freemasons, or the Communists, or a racial or religious group such as the Jews.
  Source: Richard Evans (2020).

- **Unwarranted conspiracy:** a conspiracy theory that 'particularists' think is *prima facie* epistemically not worth investigating into. In contrast, 'generalists' would argue that conspiracy theories are prima facie unwarranted as a class of explanation, without the need to consider the particulars of individual conspiracy theories.

- Helpful rules of thumbs to suggest a conspiracy theory might be unwarranted include:

  - it is a systemic conspiracy, e.g. a New World Order, perhaps the Illuminati, secretly controls the world powers or is seeking to do so
  - it is mature, e.g. conspiracies surrounding the assassination of U.S. President John F. Kennedy in 1963
  - it would involve a relatively large number of people being involved in the conspiracy, e.g. the faked moon-landings would have involved some 415,000 NASA employees.

- **Warranted conspiracy:** a conspiracy theory that 'particularists' think is *prima facie* epistemically worth judging on its own merits. Helpful rules of thumbs to suggest a conspiracy theory might be warranted include:

  - it is an event conspiracy, e.g. Watergate
  - it is immature, e.g. at the time of writing, there are debates over whether Twitter did suppress free speech to support its own political agenda
  - it would have relatively few people being involved in the conspiracy, e.g. some Wikileaks revelations involved conspiracies that only people with highly classified clearance would have been party to.

Echo chamber: a social structure from which other relevant voices have been actively discredited. An echo chamber brings its members to actively distrust outsiders.
Source: Nguyen (2018)

Epistemic bubble: an informational network from which relevant voices have been excluded by *omission*. That omission might be purposeful or can also be entirely inadvertent.
Source: Nguyen (2018)

Disinformation: false information that is deliberately created – usually to harm an individual, social group, organisation, or nation. Often presented as news or made to look 'authentic.'
Source: Haywood and Gronland (2021)

Misinformation: false information that is accidentally shared or created. There is no intention of harm, but may cause harm. These could be rumours that spread on social media groups, or well-meaning but false information.
Source: Haywood and Gronland (2021)

'Generalism': school of thought that views conspiracy theories pejoratively and holds that they can be dismissed as a class of explanation without considering the particulars of individual conspiracy theories. It is the view that conspiracy theories are typically irrational.
Source: Buenting and Taylor (2010)

'Particularism': school of thought that holds that the rationality of belief in conspiracy theories can only be assessed by considering the evidence for and against individual conspiracy theories.
Source: Buenting and Taylor (2010)

Socratic Questions and Critical Thinking:

In broad terms, a Socratic question to get your students thinking hard about conspiracy theories is:

Why do so many people take to conspiracy theories?

Most specifically, for conspiracy theories that aren't morally sensitive, there is good scope for developing critical thinking skills and civic virtues through examining the rationale behind people's beliefs in these controversial claims. These might include:

- Faking the moon-landings: an event conspiracy
- Flat-Earth theory: a systemic conspiracy
- Watergate: a conspiracy that turned out to be true
- Twitter cover-up: an immature conspiracy theory.

For any of these case studies, one might wish to apply our rules of thumb for differentiating between 'warranted' and 'unwarranted' conspiracy theories. Thinking tools from our Mental Toolkit in Chapter 4 may also be helpful to employ when considering different conspiratorial claims:

- *Why do you think a systemic conspiracy theory is so unlikely to be true?*
- *How does the passing of time impact the plausibility of a conspiracy theory?*
- *Is it likely for a conspiracy theory to be true if it requires thousands of people to keep a secret?*

  (For example, we can compare the moon-landings and the U.S. National Security Agency's surveillance programme known as PRISM. Both involved thousands of people but while we still don't have a magic bullet to prove the moon-landings were fake over 50 years later, Wikileaks uncovered the NSA's surveillance programme in 2013, after five to six years. What does this suggest about the moon-landings?!)

- *How can we apply the following thinking tools for Conspiracy theories:*

  - *Ad hominem: do we have a prejudice against the people we are suspicious about, e.g. the U.S. government? Big business?*
  - *Occam's Razor: is a conspiracy theory the likeliest explanation here?*
  - *Occam's Broom: what information might be withheld that would be crucial to our proper understanding of the issues?*

Some Theory:

In the sections above, we have employed the thinking tools necessary for teaching and learning about conspiracy theories in a nuanced manner. These rules of thumb can ensure that teachers are in a position to conceptualise conspiracy theories effectively and so guide their students in how to think about them in epistemic terms. This includes "presuading," "prebunking," or inoculating students against particular mature conspiracy theories that have been shown to be false such as Holocaust denial and anti-vaccination conspiracies.

To be clear, the epistemic criterion should primarily frame any discussion of conspiracy theories. We want to ensure that our students are following the evidence and displaying critical thinking skills when considering the issues at hand. At the same time, we should be realistic about the limitations of a typical classroom: will any of the participants – teachers and students alike – have enough knowledge to fill in the 'epistemic gap' and get to the truth behind the decision-making of governments and global corporations? As Lee Basham has concluded, "the proper epistemic reaction to many contemporary conspiracy theories is (at best) a studied agnosticism. Typically, we are not in any position to seriously credit or discredit these conspiratorial possibilities." This is why our Mental Toolkit is especially important to help us think about what the most rationally cogent explanation for any controversial event is.

Nevertheless, when it comes to conspiracy theories, it would be naïve to think in thinking terms alone. Recent ground-breaking studies explain that people are drawn to conspiracy theories when they satisfy important psychological motives that can be characterised as:

- epistemic, e.g., the desire for understanding, accuracy, and subjective certainty
- existential, e.g. the desire for control and security
- social, e.g. the desire to maintain a positive image of the self or group.

And so where epistemic reasons are left wanting for any given conspiracy theory, there may still be powerful existential and social reasons that pull people into believing in them. For example, Joseph Uscinski describes how QAnon has gained traction in parts of American society:

> As wacky as the QAnon conspiracy theories sound, there's nothing new to them, and in fact, it's just a bunch of other long-standing conspiracy theories mushed together into one... What Q has done is to galvanise people around a set of ideas and weaponise [them] in a way that we haven't normally seen... because Q is a cult. They have a sense of group belonging, and even though they're decentralised because they're online, they have catchphrases, [a] sense of destiny, [and] they lean on each other.

These considerations call for a much broader educational and pastoral response. Where conspiracy theories grow out of hatred or racism, e.g. Holocaust denial, it is obvious that the epistemic vices are secondary to the existential and social problems. Where this is the case, the curriculum must be designed to take into account how best to incorporate the study of particular conspiracy theories that would "presuade" and inoculate students from accepting them by carefully weighing up the virtues and vices behind them before students develop a conspiracist mindset. For once a conspiracy theory matures within a person's worldview, it is notoriously difficult to counter: think Holocaust deniers, 9/11 truthers, anti-vaxxers, and QAnon followers.

Indeed, Dan Kahan's 'cultural cognitive thesis' suggests that a narrow focus on the epistemic issues will only serve to reinforce the conspiracist worldview. As Kahan so powerfully warns, people are more likely to accept the facts if their values are not threatened. And so, if a student is in your classroom with a conspiracist mindset, teaching directively will more likely reinforce his worldview that the gatekeepers of knowledge – including teachers – are not to be trusted. To deal with this scenario, I offer three nudges that may help make the decisive difference:

1. Teachers should make use of experts who can be trusted. A conspiracist is more likely to hear the truth from someone he deems 'on side.'

2. Teachers should use the language that would speak to conspiracy theorisers. For example, religious climate change sceptics may be more susceptible to think about environmental harm in the context of Genesis Chapter 1 and the concept of stewardship over God's creation.

3.   Build links with representatives of the local community and provide educational and social liaison groups to help overcome the local background conditions that may be epistemically harming the student. For example, if a student's conspiracist beliefs are influenced by his family, a teacher would do well to try and provide adult education opportunities, such as parental webinars, with the aim of families working in harmony with the school ethos.

Beware!

Down the Rabbit Hole:

Research into conspiracy theories in the classroom suggests that many teachers face a sense of panic when conspiracy theories are raised by students. It is understandably tempting to opt for 'exclusive neutrality' in the classroom and simply say "not for now."

Of all topics though, if schools aren't willing to face up to the challenges – and opportunities – that conspiracy theories may afford, then we really will be facing what Barack Obama called an "epistemological crisis." Schools are precisely the place to deal head on with conspiracist beliefs whether in reaction to a student question or as part of a critical thinking course as outlined in Part I.

Crucial for teacher success is to remember to stick to our rules of thumb about conspiracy theories in general rather than get into the nitty-gritty detail of a specific conspiracy theory. The chances are that a student will know that much more than you the teacher on the specifics and so it will be difficult to maintain control of the classroom if the discussion is played on that student's terms. Rather, as our Socratic Questioning and Thinking Skills section has shown, providing students with a mental toolkit to think rationally about any given conspiracy theory will help them follow the evidence and debate reasonably about the issue at hand.

Virtue Theory:

We have seen that a limitation of the epistemic criterion is that for controversies like conspiracy theories there are often existential and social considerations. There is little doubt that many conspiracies have an air of toxicity about them – even when they are true. For example, discussion about the allegations of sexual abuse in the Catholic Church in a Boston classroom in the 1990s would have been nigh impossible to manage in terms of ethics and safety. Any talk of 9/11 conspiracy theories shortly after the terror attacks in a New York school would be nothing short of grotesque, irrespective of truth claims.

Conspiracy theories therefore require 'polarity management' in the classroom. This means aiming for *both* the truth and for moral virtues, including compassion, kindness, and respect. This doesn't mean we can't promote intellectual virtues such as critical thinking and sound judgement at the same time. Remember, disagreement needn't mean disrespect. Indeed, the civic virtues of civility and awareness sum up well the character traits that bring together the ideals of responsible citizenship at the heart of character education. These should be our guiding principles for healthy student learning about conspiracy theories in the classroom. Such a topic helps us realise that our goal of nurturing the virtues of our students stands alongside the worthy aim of pursuing epistemic truths in the classroom.

Sources and Resources:

C. Thi Nguyen (2018), 'Escape the Echo Chamber.' Retrieved from: https://aeon.co/essays/why-its-as-hard-to-escape-an-echo-chamber-as-it-is-to-flee-a-cult.

Dan Kahan et al. (2012), 'The Polarising Impact of Science Literacy and Numeracy on Perceived Climate Change Risks,' *Nature Climate Change* 2(10): 732–735.

David Coady (2006), 'An Introduction to the Philosophical Debate about Conspiracy Theories,' in *Conspiracy Theories: The Philosophical Debate*, ed. David Coady. Farnham: Ashgate, pp. 1–11.

Glenn Bezalel (2022), 'Of Conspiracy and Controversy: A Pedagogy of Conspiracy Theories,' *Educational Theory*. Retrieved from: https://onlinelibrary.wiley.com/doi/epdf/10.1111/edth.12529.

Jeremy Hayward and Gemma Gronland (2021), *Conspiracy theories in the Classroom: Guidance for Teachers*. Retrieved from: https://www.teachingcitizenship.org.uk/resource/conspiracy-theories-in-the-classroom-guidance-for-teachers/.

Joseph Uscinski, interviewed by Anthony Brooks, 'QAnon: A Look Inside The Online Conspiracy,' On Point (radio), August 4, 2020: 25:44-27:46. Retrieved from: https://www.wbur.org/onpoint/2020/08/04/qanon-what-to-know-online-conspiracy.

Karen M. Douglas, Robbie M. Sutton, and Aleksandra Clchocka (2017), 'The Psychology of Conspiracy Theories,' *Current Directions in Psychological Science* 26(6): 538–542.

Lee Basham (2006), 'Living with the Conspiracy Theory,' in *Conspiracy Theories: The Philosophical Debate*, ed. David Coady. Farnham: Ashgate, pp. 61–76.

Peter Moore, 'Little British Belief in Outlandish Conspiracy Theories,' May 27, 2016. Retrieved from: https://yougov.co.uk/topics/politics/articles-reports/2016/05/27/conspiracies.

Pew Research Center, 'Americans, Politics, and Science Issues,' July 1, 2015. Retrieved from: https://www.pewresearch.org/internet/wp-content/uploads/sites/9/2015/07/2015-07-01_science-and-politics_FINAL-1.pdf.

Quassim Cassam (2015), 'Bad Thinkers,' *Aeon*. Retrieved from: https://aeon.co/essays/the-intellectual-character-of-conspiracy-theorists.

Links to Other Controversies:

Is the Holocaust a hoax?
You don't really believe in climate change? It's obviously a hoax!

Is the Holocaust a hoax?

Age group: 10-18

How explosive is this topic?

If a student asks a question or makes a statement that seeks to deny or distort the Holocaust, then alarm bells should be ringing immediately. Whether the question is a result of ignorance or malice, this is a really depressing educational and moral situation for any teacher to face. Nevertheless, at a time when a music artist as prominent as Kanye West talks openly about admiring Hitler, Holocaust revisionism is sadly all too real.

How should I teach this topic?

Yes to directive teaching: "Of course the Holocaust isn't a hoax. The Holocaust is the most well documented genocide in world history. You must understand that suggesting that the Holocaust didn't happen is not only factually incorrect but also deeply insulting and upsetting. Can we meet after the lesson? I'd really like to understand what led you to ask such a question?"
Absolutely no to non-directive teaching: "This is an issue over which people disagree. Let's explore why and weigh up which approach might be correct."

Key Terms and Necessary Knowledge:

There is a huge amount of educational material available to provide detailed and precise definitions of these terms. At the same time, online critical thinking skills are paramount for students undertaking research into the Holocaust as there will be many accounts, often seemingly authoritative, that are fronts for extremist and racist propaganda. In turn, I am providing mainstream definitions and guides from respected educational organisations and experts, with links included below for further research.

Anti-Semitism:

Anti-Semitism is a certain perception of Jews, which may be expressed as hatred towards Jews. Rhetorical and physical manifestations of anti-Semitism are directed towards Jewish or non-Jewish individuals and/or their property, towards Jewish community institutions and religious facilities.

Source: https://www.holocaustremembrance.com/resources/working-definitions-charters/working-definition-antisemitism

For an excellent guide on the different forms or 'mutations' of anti-Semitism, see this educational video from Rabbi Jonathan Sacks: https://www.youtube.com/watch?v=3UAcYn4uUbs

Genocide:

Genocide is an internationally recognised crime where acts are committed with the intent to destroy, in whole or in part, a national, ethnic, racial, or religious group. These acts fall into five categories:

1.   Killing members of the group
2.   Causing serious bodily or mental harm to members of the group
3.   Deliberately inflicting on the group conditions of life calculated to bring about its physical destruction in whole or in part
4.   Imposing measures intended to prevent births within the group
5.   Forcibly transferring children of the group to another group.

There are a number of other serious, violent crimes that do not fall under the specific definition of genocide. They include crimes against humanity, war crimes, ethnic cleansing, and mass killing.

The word "genocide" did not exist prior to 1944. It is a very specific term coined by a Polish-Jewish lawyer named Raphael Lemkin (1900–1959) who sought to describe Nazi policies of systematic murder during the Holocaust, including the destruction of European Jews. He formed the word genocide by combining *geno*-, from the Greek word for race or tribe, with -*cide*, from the Latin word for killing.

On 9 December 1948, the United Nations approved a written international agreement known as the Convention on the Prevention and Punishment of the Crime of Genocide. This convention established genocide as an international crime, which signatory nations "undertake to prevent and punish." Preventing genocide, the other major obligation of the convention, remains a challenge that nations, institutions, and individuals continue to face.

Source: https://www.ushmm.org/genocide-prevention/learn-about-genocide-and-other-mass-atrocities/what-is-genocide

The Holocaust Memorial Day Trust (HMDT) provides comprehensive resources to learn about more recent genocides: https://www.hmd.org.uk/learn-about-the-holocaust-and-genocides/

The Holocaust:

The Holocaust was unprecedented genocide, total, and systematic, perpetrated by Nazi Germany and its collaborators, with the aim of annihilating the Jewish people. The primary motivation was the Nazis' anti-Semitic racist ideology. Between 1933 and 1941, Nazi Germany pursued a policy that dispossessed the Jews of their rights and their property, followed by the branding and the concentration of the Jewish population. This policy gained broad support in Germany and much of occupied Europe. In 1941, following the invasion of the Soviet Union, the Nazis and their collaborators launched the systematic mass murder of the Jews. By 1945, nearly six million Jews had been murdered.

Source: https://www.yadvashem.org/holocaust/about.html

Holocaust Denial:

Holocaust denial is discourse and propaganda that deny the historical reality and the extent of the extermination of the Jews by the Nazis and their accomplices during World War II, known as the Holocaust or the Shoah. Holocaust denial refers specifically to any attempt to claim that the Holocaust/Shoah did not take place.

Holocaust denial may include publicly denying or calling into doubt the use of principal mechanisms of destruction (such as gas chambers, mass shooting, starvation, and torture) or the intentionality of the genocide of the Jewish people.

Holocaust denial in its various forms is an expression of anti-Semitism. The attempt to deny the genocide of the Jews is an effort to exonerate National Socialism and anti-Semitism from guilt or responsibility in the genocide of the Jewish people. Forms of Holocaust denial also include blaming the Jews for either exaggerating or creating the Shoah for political or financial gain as if the Shoah itself was the result of a conspiracy plotted by the Jews. In this, the goal is to make the Jews culpable and anti-Semitism once again legitimate.

The goals of Holocaust denial often are the rehabilitation of an explicit anti-Semitism and the promotion of political ideologies and conditions suitable for the advent of the very type of event it denies.

Source: https://www.holocaustremembrance.com/resources/working-definitions-charters/working-definition-holocaust-denial-and-distortion

Holocaust Distortion:

Distortion of the Holocaust refers, *inter alia*, to:

1. Intentional efforts to excuse or minimise the impact of the Holocaust or its principal elements, including collaborators and allies of Nazi Germany;
2. Gross minimisation of the number of the victims of the Holocaust in contradiction to reliable sources;
3. Attempts to blame the Jews for causing their own genocide;
4. Statements that cast the Holocaust as a positive historical event. Those statements are not Holocaust denial but are closely connected to it as a radical form of anti-Semitism. They may suggest that the Holocaust did not go far enough in accomplishing its goal of "the Final Solution of the Jewish Question";
5. Attempts to blur the responsibility for the establishment of concentration and death camps devised and operated by Nazi Germany by putting blame on other nations or ethnic groups.

Source: https://www.holocaustremembrance.com/resources/working-definitions-charters/working-definition-holocaust-denial-and-distortion

For a helpful guide summarising the different forms of Holocaust denial and distortion, see this video from Professor Deborah Lipstadt: https://www.ushmm.org/antisemitism/holocaust-denial-and-distortion/explaining-holocaust-denial

Conspiracy Theories:

Holocaust denial is inescapably tied in with the worst of conspiracist beliefs. It is not only an example of bad thinking but also of bad character. Whilst all responsible teachers recognise this, some may feel they don't have the expertise to counter these vices in the classroom. To help teachers navigate their way through the considerations that conspiracy theories raise in the classroom, it is important to understand exactly what a conspiracy theory is.

David Coady, a prominent scholar of conspiracy theories, provides a helpful three-part definition of conspiracy theories that I think articulates how most of us think about conspiracy theories and can frame our discussion:

A conspiracy theory is a proposed explanation of an historical event, in which conspiracy (i.e., agents acting secretly in concert) has a significant causal role. Furthermore, the conspiracy postulated by the proposed explanation must be a conspiracy to bring about the historical event which it purports to explain. Finally, the proposed explanation must conflict with an "official" explanation of the same historical event.

Of course, conspiracies do happen! History is full of them. In fact, the first two parts of Coady's explanation aptly relate to the Nazi conspiracy to exterminate the Jewish people. Leading Nazis met at the Wannsee Conference on 20 January 1942 to conspire and coordinate the 'Final Solution to the Jewish Problem.'

However, it is the final part of Coady's definition that describes the sort of conspiracism that we're concerned about: a proposed explanation that conflicts with the official – or, I would add, mainstream – explanation of the same historical event. In other words, claiming the Holocaust was a hoax or minimising its significance, is a conspiracy *theory*, which goes against the overwhelming evidence. Deborah Lipstadt, a leading Holocaust historian, puts it very powerfully:

> Think about it. For deniers to be right, who would have to be wrong? Well, first of all, the victims - the survivors who have told us their harrowing stories. Who else would have to be wrong? The bystanders. The people who lived in the myriads of towns and villages and cities on the Eastern front, who watched their neighbours be rounded up - men, women, children, young, old - and be marched to the outskirts of the town to be shot and left dead in ditches. Or the Poles, who lived in towns and villages around the death camps, who watched day after day as the trains went in filled with people and came out empty. But above all, who would have to be wrong? The perpetrators. The people who say, "We did it. I did it." Now, maybe they add a caveat. They say, "I didn't have a choice; I was forced to do it." But nonetheless, they say, "I did it." Think about it. In not one war crimes trial since the end of World War II has a perpetrator of any nationality ever said, "It didn't happen." Again, they may have said, "I was forced," but never that it didn't happen.

Socratic Questions and Critical Thinking:

The default position should be for teachers to only deal with Holocaust denial or distortion when raised by a student. Teachers should never initiate this conspiracy theory for discussion in the classroom. Although some educationalists have suggested employing Holocaust denial as a case study for critical thinking, I would argue that this would be inappropriate and could backfire, not least in alienating many students, considering how sensitive and emotive the Holocaust is.

As we will see below, simply dismissing such a question may be counterproductive. Admittedly, if the student is openly racist and seeking to provoke the teacher and his peers, then there may be no option but to close down the discussion and even remove the student. The correct response will depend on establishing the student's motive and the classroom context. Ultimately, the teacher's goal when dealing with Holocaust denial will be to direct students towards intellectually honest thinking and promoting moral character.

The Holocaust Memorial Day Trust has a helpful four-part model on how best to respond to Holoaust denial:

1.   Establish motive:
     • Genuine curiosity/disbelief about the topic and how the Holocaust could happen?
     • A form of rebellion against authority/attention seeking?

- Testing you for a reaction?
- Intended to provoke an argument?
- Expressing their own view, or the view of someone else?

2. Assert the historical authenticity of the Holocaust
3. Question the claim and/or open discussion of why the claim has been made
4. Follow up

With Holocaust denial or distortion bound to shock, here are some immediate responses that you can use to take control of the situation.

Where you think the motivation is anti-Semitic or aiming to provoke:

This school doesn't tolerate racism. Tolerance and respect are key virtues that underpin what we're about. Denying/distorting the Holocaust is a dreadful example of intolerance and disrespect towards Jewish people, known as anti-Semitism. It is really important that we think about our speech so that we are always mindful of others.

Where you feel the student is genuinely curious or hasn't come to terms with the scale of the atrocity:

Professor Deborah Lipstadt, a leading expert on the Holocaust, points out that the Holocaust has the dubious distinction of being the best documented genocide in world history. If you don't accept the overwhelming evidence surrounding the Holocaust, then what can you possibly believe in?

Where you sense that the student is unthinkingly expressing views they have heard elsewhere:

We value critical thinking and evidence. As the Holocaust is so well documented, think about where you heard such extremist and unsupported ideas from and question how reliable your sources are.

Some Theory:

When confronted with Holocaust denial or distortion, you must immediately assess whether the student is coming from a place of ignorance, malice or possibly both. The context will determine the correct pedagogical response.

In the United Kingdom, a 2019 poll carried out by the HMDT found that 5% of U.K. adults don't believe the Holocaust really happened and one in 12 (8%) say the scale of the Holocaust has been exaggerated. Yet the data suggest that this is more to do with ignorance than anti-Semitism. For example, 64% of people polled either do not know how many Jews were murdered or grossly underestimate the number, while one in five (19%) believe fewer than two million Jews were murdered. At the same time, the HMDT reported:

> the vast majority (83%) of respondents say it's important to know about the Holocaust and that we can all learn lessons for today from the past (84%), while over three quarters (76%) believe more needs to be done to educate people about what happened.

In other words, education about the Holocaust is key to raising awareness and an understanding of what took place. In this vein, the teacher and her colleagues may think about Holocaust education within the school curriculum and question what gaps allowed for a student to come out with such a question in the first place. Educational pathways that 'presuade,' 'prebunk,' and inoculate students against historical revisionism and distortion will be paramount and can be achieved through age-appropriate materials. Of course, assemblies, workshops, and other activities can help support formal classroom lessons.

The Holocaust thus serves as the prime reason for understanding controversy through an epistemic lens. In this sense, claiming the Holocaust didn't happen is on the level of claiming that 1 + 1 = 3 or that planet Earth is flat. Such claims are simply wrong and must be taught as such. Just as no maths teacher would give credence to different opinions on basic mathematical truths, so too must teachers in other disciplines not indulge 'alternative facts' and allow room for disinformation in the classroom.

But of course, beyond the epistemic, there is most likely to be something sinister when it comes to Holocaust denial or distortion. It's often not just about bad thinking. In turn, where such views are apparent in the classroom, simply presenting the facts and offering evidence may not work. Indeed, such an approach may even be counterproductive as the question is motivated by anti-Semitism or other nefarious motives. Research by Dan Kahan, a professor of law, shows how people's personal or social values shape their understanding of the facts. The 'cultural cognitive thesis' posits that "individuals, as a result of a complex of psychological mechanisms, tend to form perceptions of societal risks that cohere with values characteristic of groups with which they identify." This means that people are less likely to accept the facts if they feel their values are threatened.

If a teenager enters the classroom with a value-laden perspective that denies the Holocaust, simply dismissing his question will more likely reinforce his view that you the teacher, a gatekeeper of knowledge, cannot be trusted. In such a scenario I would suggest two educational responses, depending on what is really motivating the student's question:

i   Where Holocaust denial is a result of an 'echo chamber' in which the historical facts have been purposely excluded, the student will be more resistant to hearing from anyone he considers an 'outsider.' This means that schools should aim to forge links with trusted authorities. For example, if the student comes from a religious background, he is more likely to believe a leader of his own faith community confirm the Holocaust as historical fact.

ii Where Holocaust denial is a result of an 'epistemic bubble' in which the student has simply lacked exposure to other perspectives, then it may be easier to shatter such a worldview through learning the relevant arguments and information that they may have missed. For example, listening to a Holocaust survivor or their descendant may have a profound impact that pops the bubble the student has been living in (without unduly exposing the speaker to a disrespectful audience).

Either way, as Jeremy Hayward and Gemma Gronland write, it is important to get the manner and tone right:

> Simply dismissing as false, without consideration, any claim that is not received wisdom or goes against an official explanation does not model good critical thinking. Also, dismissing a point in a cursory manner can lead to a sense of grievance, which can further strengthen the determination to prove a belief and even add to a conviction that there is a conspiracy.

Modelling key virtues such as critical thinking, sound judgement, and justice must be front and centre of a teacher's response. This means having the confidence to advance the truth on the one hand, whilst showing compassion and respect on the other.

Beware!

Anti-Semitism, Racism, and Extremism

As a rule of thumb, such a question should lead the teacher to report the student to the school leadership and raise concerns about possible anti-Semitic, racist, and extremist beliefs. In many countries, there may well be a legal duty to report the student to the relevant authorities.

From the outset, it is really important to understand where the student is coming from and so be sure to follow up after the lesson with a member of your school's pastoral team.

Remember though, Holocaust denial is specifically anti-Semitic in nature. Even if there is no sense of a broader racist tendency on behalf of the student, it doesn't mean they aren't specifically anti-Semitic. The 'oldest hatred' – racism against Jews – is often viewed differently to other forms of prejudice. This is in part because Jews are stereotypically seen as white, powerful, and wealthy, and so can't possibly be victims. Holocaust denial is the ugly manifestation of this type of (non-)thinking which perversely attempts to transform the victims into the perpetrators. David Baddiel, a British author and commentator, has labelled this phenomenon 'Jews don't count': while racism is roundly condemned by all decent and fair-minded people, anti-Semitism somehow stands apart.

'Multidirectional Memory' vs 'Competitive Memory'

Holocaust denial in the classroom can be particularly jarring and difficult to deal with when it comes from a student who belongs to another minority group; even more so if the represented minority group has itself suffered persecution. Michael Rothberg, a memories studies scholar, insightfully points out that Holocaust denial or distortion from minority groups may be a result of what he calls "competitive memory." This is based on the logic of a zero-sum game whereby it is felt that remembering the Holocaust crowds out other genocides and traumas. For example, even subconsciously, an African American student may resent the emphasis on Holocaust education as it marginalises the horrors of slavery, undermining his own identity. In contrast, Rothberg proposes that we understand Holocaust education and commemoration through the lens of "multidirectional memory." Far from marginalising other collective trage-dies, the Holocaust actually serves as a vehicle to learn about them and increase our memory of other traumas.

In the United Kingdom, for example, Holocaust Memorial Day (HMD) is marked to "remem-ber the six million Jews murdered in the Holocaust, *and* the millions of people killed under Nazi persecution of other groups, and during more recent genocides in Cambodia, Rwanda, Bosnia, and Darfur." As Rothberg puts it, rather than being separate and distinct histories, such collective memories emerge dialogically because memory works productively through negotiation, cross-referencing, and borrowing. Precisely by remembering the Holocaust, do we turn to other genocides like those mentioned here. At the heart of the Holocaust Memorial Day Trust is its call of, "Learning from genocide – for a better future." The universal, multidi-rectional message is explicit:

> The Holocaust was a terrible and defining episode of the twentieth century, which un-doubtedly changed the course of history.
>
> After the Holocaust, the international community adopted a legal definition of the crime of 'genocide'. They wanted to make sure that never again would the crimes of the Holocaust be allowed to happen.
>
> However, in the years following the Holocaust, genocide has continued to be carried out. On Holocaust Memorial Day we remember all those who were murdered or affected by the genocides in Cambodia, Rwanda, Bosnia and Darfur.
>
> Subsequent genocides represent a failure of humanity to learn from the Holocaust and are a reminder for all of us that we must be prepared to guard against genocide happening again in the future.

Indeed, as Lipstadt warns: "In almost every society where they've gone after Jews first, they've gone after other people after that. Prejudice has to be fought and amongst those prejudices, anti-Semitism has to be fought."

Sources and Resources:

For Holocaust Education research:

Deborah Lipstadt, 'Behind the Lies of Holocaust Denial.' Retrieved from: https://www.ted.com/talks/deborah_lipstadt_behind_the_lies_of_holocaust_denial.

Holocaust Educational Trust. Retrieved from: https://www.het.org.uk/.

Imperial War Museum. 'The Holocaust Galleries.' Retrieved from: https://www.iwm.org.uk/events/the-holocaust-galleries.

International Holocaust Remembrance Alliance. Retrieved from: https://www.holocaustremembrance.com/.

UCL Centre for Holocaust Education. Retrieved from: https://holocausteducation.org.uk/.

United States Holocaust Memorial Museum. Retrieved from: https://www.ushmm.org/.

Yad Vashem – The World Holocaust Remembrance Centre. Retrieved from: https://www.yad-vashem.org/.

For wider issues:

C. Thi Nguyen (2020), 'Echo Chambers and Epistemic Bubbles,' *Episteme* 17(2): 141–161.

Dan Kahan et al. (2012), 'The Polarising Impact of Science Literacy and Numeracy on Perceived Climate Change Risks,' *Nature Climate Change* 2(10): 732–735.

David Baddiel (2021), *Jews Don't Count*. London: TLS Books.

David Coady (2006), 'An Introduction to the Philosophical Debate about Conspiracy Theories,' in *Conspiracy Theories: The Philosophical Debate*, ed. David Coady. Farnham: Ashgate, pp. 1–11.

Michael Rothberg (2014), 'Multidirectional Memory.' Retrieved from: https://journals.openedition.org/temoigner/1494?lang=en.

Links to Other Controversies:

Who's to blame for the Israeli–Palestinian conflict?
You don't really believe what the government/media is telling us...?

You don't really believe in climate change? It's obviously a hoax!

Age group: 10-18

How explosive is this topic?

Poll after poll shows that climate change is the major concern for young people today. Imperial College London reported that a majority of young people are distressed by climate change, feel guilty about their own contribution to environmental damage, and believe that they are "less capable of acting on climate change and less sure their actions around climate change would have an effect." Indeed, for many, feeling distressed and having a sense of agency appear to go hand in hand. This can lead to students feeling overwhelmed by the problems of climate change. The pastoral concerns are obvious for school leaders.

How should I teach this topic?

The scientific community is clear about the evidence behind anthropogenic climate change, and so this is an epistemically uncontroversial topic and should be taught in terms of the facts and the evidence in a directive manner.

Nevertheless, there is certainly much reasonable and exciting debate about the possible solutions for tackling climate change.

It is important to distinguish these issues clearly when teaching about this topic.

In turn, on the question of whether climate change is a hoax:

Yes to directive teaching: "Your claim that climate change is a hoax doesn't have the scientific evidence to support what you're saying. I'd be interested to follow up with you afterwards to hear why you think this."

No to non-directive teaching: "Well there are many people who think climate change is a hoax so let's explore the different viewpoints and vote on which we think is most plausible."

However, on the question of how best to tackle climate change:

Yes to non-directive teaching: "There are major scientific, political, and economic debates about how governments, organisations, and society should best respond to environmental concerns. Let's discuss the pros and cons of the major approaches as a class."

No to directive teaching: "Only renewable energies such as solar and wind should be used going forward. The move towards nuclear energy is highly dangerous and irresponsible, and so should be opposed."

Of course, the debate over climate change is highly controversial in behavioural terms. In 2021, Newsweek reported that although 75% of Americans believe that climate change is happening, 10% don't believe in it, with another 15% unsure. The issue is partisan for Americans in that 89% of Democrats accept climate change vs 57% for Republicans.

In contrast, the environment is not a 'culture war' issue in the United Kingdom, with the British Social Attitudes Survey 2019 showing both Labour party and Conservative party supporters are concerned about climate and the environment. The Progressive Policy Think Tank reports that:

The UK has some of the highest levels of concern regarding the climate emergency in the world with 81 per cent of people 'believing' in the climate emergency, with over three-quarters (77 per cent) saying we must do 'everything necessary, urgently as a response'.

For the minority of students believing climate change is a hoax, their view may well be seen in terms of being an 'unwarranted' conspiracy theory and so needs to be taught in a directive way - albeit sensitively - that this is wrong. As the 'Some theory' section discusses, research suggests that a narrow epistemic teaching style that only focuses on the facts may actually backfire when dealing with climate change sceptics, and so teachers need to be aware of what may be motivating the student who claims climate change is a hoax.

Key Terms and Necessary Knowledge:

Here I'll offer the background concepts relevant for climate change discussion specifically. Researching different forms of energy and their role in climate change is an excellent starting point to help build up student knowledge of this subject. (Please see the Conspiracy Theories chapter for related concepts regarding climate change sceptics.)

Climate change realist: sometimes known as a climate change believer, this refers to someone who accepts the scientific facts and evidence that anthropocentric climate change is occurring. Climate change realists may debate the potential solutions for tackling climate change.

Climate change sceptic: sometimes known as a climate change denier, this refers to someone who doesn't accept the scientific facts and evidence, often pointing to alleged ulterior motives of those warning about the threat of climate change.

Energy Sources:

- **Fossil fuels:** According to the United Nations, "Fossil fuels - coal, oil, and gas - are non-renewable resources that take hundreds of millions of years to form. Fossil fuels, when burned to produce energy, cause harmful greenhouse gas emissions, such as carbon dioxide."
- **Nuclear energy:** According to the U.K. National Grid, "Nuclear fuels, such as the element uranium, are not considered renewable as they are a finite material mined from the ground and can only be found in certain locations. But nuclear power stations use a miniscule amount of fuel to generate the same amount of electricity that a coal or gas power station would (1 kg of uranium = 2.7 million kg of coal), so they're considered a reliable source of energy for decades to come. There are concerns around what to do with spent fuel from reactors, as there's still no definitive way to dispose of it indefinitely without risk. However, although the reactors and housing remain untouchable for considerable lengths of time when a nuclear site is decommissioned, a new reactor can be built on the site itself." Also note that "In an emissions sense, nuclear power is considered to be clean. It produces zero carbon emissions and doesn't produce other noxious greenhouse gases through its operation."
- **Renewable energy:** According to the United Nations, renewable energy is "energy derived from natural sources that are replenished at a higher rate than they are consumed. Sunlight and wind, for example, are such sources that are constantly being replenished. Renewable energy sources are plentiful and all around us." Common sources of renewable energy include: solar energy, wind energy, geothermal energy, hydropower, ocean energy, and bioenergy.

Cultural Cognitive Thesis (CCT): Cultural cognition refers to the influence of group values – ones relating to equality and authority, individualism, and community – on related beliefs. For example, if someone supports a team in a football match, they are more likely to side with their team on any controversial decision. Research by Dan Kahan concludes that this is because people deal with evidence selectively to promote their emotional interest in their group. So too, on issues ranging from climate change to gun control, from the culture wars to counter-terrorism, they take their cue about what they should feel, and hence believe, from the cheers and boos of the home crowd. Furthermore, and crucially for teachers, cultural cognition causes people to interpret new evidence in a biased way that reinforces their predispositions. As a result, groups with opposing values often become more polarised, not less, when exposed to scientifically sound information.

Science Comprehension Thesis (SCT): This approach suggests that the more scientifically literate people are, the more they will accept the science. This suggests an 'epistemic' educational response for people rejecting the science: bad thinking is down to a bad education. Simply teach students the science and provide them with the evidence in order to reduce climate change scepticism. The problem with this view is that Kahan's research suggests that climate change sceptics are no less scientifically literate than climate change realists. This is why Kahan, Steven Pinker, and others draw our attention to CCT.

Socratic Questions and Critical Thinking:

Steven Pinker, in his quest for greater rationality and sharper critical thinking, offers these questions which are an ideal starting point to help develop your students' intellectual virtues when it comes to thinking about climate change:

*   *Climate scientists believe that if the North Pole icecap melted as a result of human-caused global warming, global sea levels would rise. True or false?*

    *   Answer for the teacher: False! As Pinker points out, "if it were true, your glass of Coke would overflow as the ice cubes melted. It's icecaps on *land*, such as Greenland and Antarctica, that raise sea levels when they melt."

*   *Global warming is caused by a hole in the ozone layer which can be reduced by cleaning up toxic waste dumps.*

    *   Answer for the teacher: False! As NASA explains: "While some extra ultraviolet (UV) rays slip through the ozone hole, their net effect is to cool the stratosphere more than they warm the troposphere. So, this increase in UV rays cannot explain the warming of the planet's surface."

*   *What is the safest form of energy that humanity has ever used?*

    *   Answer for the teacher: Nuclear energy! As Pinker explains, "Mining accidents, hydro-electric dam failures, natural gas explosions, and oil train crashes all kill people, sometimes in large numbers, and smoke from burning coal kills them in enormous numbers, more than half a million per year."

These questions are interesting as they help get to the heart of reasoned thinking. Importantly for educators, research shows that climate change sceptics are no more likely to get such questions wrong than climate change realists. Knowledge and belief come apart, suggesting that whilst we may be clued up on the science intellectually, our gut feeling about issues like climate change are much more aligned with our social or cultural ties. Like many of the controversies we teach and learn about, emotional attachments often get in the way of clear thinking. For climate change, if I'm a libertarian sick of government rules and regulations, I am simply much more likely to align with those cynical of government interference. I will feel an intuitive repugnance at the thought of yet more government regulations as the answer for climate change problems. Yet if I align myself with left-wing causes, I'm certainly going to side with those going after the likes of C. Montgomery Burns (owner of Springfield Nuclear Power Plant in *The Simpsons*) and be enthusiastic about challenging corporate greed in the name of our beautiful planet. For me, the government may well be the solution. Thus, while the left may enjoy riling some on the right as being unscientific for their climate change scepticism, those on the right may rib parts of the left as being irrational for not giving nuclear power a chance.

Of course, it is to be hoped that such starter questions (and many more like them) will instil a sense of intellectual humility into our students. If your students are getting pretty basic – yet purposely misleading – questions wrong, then perhaps they need to question their other assumptions about this complex topic.

With anthropogenic climate change itself epistemically uncontroversial, this topic should be taught in science lessons in a directive manner, much in the same way that smoking kills or that $E = mc^2$, however people might think or feel. Nevertheless, if students feel 'their side' isn't 'on side' with the science, it will be very difficult to win them over existentially. One possible nudge worth considering is to cite unlikely leaders of different camps whom students may look up to. For example, which political leader said the following at the United Nations?

> The environmental challenge that confronts the whole world demands an equivalent response from the whole world. Every country will be affected and no one can opt out. Those countries who are industrialised must contribute more to help those who are not.

- Answer for the teacher: Margaret Thatcher (of course) way back in 1989. The Conservative chemist clearly took conservation very seriously and was arguably the first world leader to do so. (If you wanted to be a little cruel to your students, you could pretend it was Al Gore and see if students will be intellectually consistent when you reveal it was Thatcher.)

Which future U.S. President signed a full-page advert in *The New York Times* in 2009 supporting "meaningful and effective measures to control climate change" arguing that "If we fail to act now, it is scientifically irrefutable that there will be catastrophic and irreversible consequences for humanity and our planet."

- Answer for the teacher: Donald Trump (of course). Admittedly, his view on the matter has been somewhat more ambiguous since he became president.

Religious texts and pronouncements on the environment will be important for 'presuading' students belonging to religious groups. Perhaps most famously, the pioneering Assisi Declarations in 1986 saw leaders from Buddhism, Christianity, Hinduism, Islam, and Judaism come together to voice declarations on humanity and nature based on their own religious texts and beliefs. These statements (link in 'Sources and Resources') would be especially helpful for classes in religious studies or sociology dealing with climate change.

Nevertheless, there are areas of epistemic controversy within the topic of climate change. For example, Greta Thunburg, perhaps the world's best known climate campaigner, may be clear on the urgency required for dealing with climate change, but at the same time she has avoided getting into the detail of what action should be taken, saying "it is nothing to do with me." This is because she appreciates that this is an area of epistemic controversy that scientists, economists, politicians, and others are all arguing about. So yes, let's get your students in on the argument, researching and debating the following question:

•   *What are the most effective ways of combatting climate change?*

This is an excellent opportunity for students to carry out a research project in the form of a Knowledge Organiser or class presentation.

If William MacAskill, an ethicist at Oxford, is right, many of your students will focus on their personal behaviour or consumption decisions. And so just as organisations like the United Nations and Greenpeace helpfully recommend, many people might think about sustainable transport options or recycling more. Yet MacAskill argues that "this emphasis, though understandable, is a major strategic blunder for those of us who want to make the world better."

As one of the originators of the 'effective altruism' project, MacAskill supports "using evidence and reason to figure out how to benefit others as much as possible, and taking action on that basis." As a consequence, although there have been massive campaigns to reduce the use of plastic, MacAskill warns that "the total impact this has on the environment is tiny." A statistic that will be sure to deflate some: "You would have to reuse your plastic bag eight thousand times in order to cancel out the effect of one flight from London to New York." And the effect on our oceans? It turns out that for those living in wealthy countries with effective waste management – like the United States and much of Europe – their plastic waste rarely ends up there.

Yet MacAskill writes that the personal consumption choice to go vegetarian really does make an impact for climate change: "By going vegetarian, you avert around 0.8 tonnes of carbon dioxide equivalent every year. This is a big deal: it is about one-tenth of my total carbon footprint."

Even here though, if people were to dedicate 10% of their annual income to the most cost-effective clean-energy organisations, such as the Clean Air Task Force in the United States, this would have a far greater impact than going vegetarian for your entire life. A helpful rule of thumb for MacAskill is that "donations are more impactful than changing personal consumption decisions" – whether for combatting climate change, reducing global poverty, or dealing with other pressing global problems.

Perhaps the most controversial 'effective altruism' argument with regard to climate change is the support for nuclear energy as part of the solution. An interesting 'effective altruism' story your students may wish to research is that of Isabelle Boemeke, a former fashion model, who now campaigns under the slogan of "nuclear energy is clean energy" after learning of the need for nuclear energy to help tackle climate change. Recognising its unpopularity, she decided to use her social media presence to advocate for this issue.

Perhaps the most well-known supporter for nuclear energy as part of the solution for climate change is Steven Pinker. The extract below provides a welcome starter for your students to debate, putting their thinking skills to the test:

The availability bias may affect the fate of the planet. Several eminent climate scientists, having crunched the numbers, warn that "there is no credible path to climate stabilisation that does not include a substantial role for nuclear power." Nuclear power is the safest form of energy humanity has ever used... Yet nuclear power has stalled for decades in the United States and is being pushed back in Europe, often replaced by dirty and dangerous coal. In large part, the opposition is driven by memories of three accidents: Three Mile Island in 1979, which killed no one; Fukushima in 2011, which killed one worker years later (the other deaths were caused by *the tsunami and from a panicked evacuation); and the Soviet-bungled Chernobyl in 1986, which killed 31 in the accident and perhaps several thousand from cancer, around the same number killed by coal emissions **every day**.*

- *What is 'availability bias?' Explain how, according to Pinker, it has affected our thinking on climate change?*
- *What is 'Occam's Broom?' Can you think of any other reasons many authorities have been reticent to invest in nuclear power plants?*
- *Do you find Pinker's argument convincing? Why might others disagree with you?*

To help your students think more sharply in terms of behaving effectively, Peter Singer's TED Talk on 'The why and how of effective altruism' will be sure to trigger healthy debates.

Some Theory:

Although young people are especially concerned about climate change, there are still likely to be some climate change sceptics in your classroom thinking it is a hoax. Such climate change scepticism falls into the category of an 'unwarranted' conspiracy theory. The evidence from the scientific community clearly opposes such a viewpoint and so the teacher is left with the pedagogical question of how best to educate about such conspiracism.

Intuitively, many teachers will hold what Professor Dan Kahan has called the "science comprehension thesis" (SCT), which suggests that "[a]s members of the public do not know what scientists know, or think the way scientists think, they predictably fail to take climate change as seriously as scientists believe they should." The SCT approach is clear that climate change scepticism is the result of poor education and bad thinking. For supporters of the epistemic criterion, the solution is simple: educate through the force of evidence and argument.

However, the evidence demonstrates that climate change sceptics are no less scientifically literate than climate realists. Tellingly, additional 'education' will only serve to reinforce the sceptical worldview! Rather, the data supports the "cultural cognitive thesis" (CCT), which posits that "individuals, as a result of a complex of psychological mechanisms, tend to form perceptions of societal risks that cohere with values characteristic of groups with which they identify." Rather than 'bad thinking,' CCT shows that the range of approaches to climate change are intuitive and highly linked to a person's overall worldview. As Kahan warns, people are more likely to accept the facts if their values are not threatened.

As we noted above, it is now understandable that climate change is a partisan issue in the United States. Democrats are much more likely to be concerned about environmental concerns than Republicans. Interestingly, Steven Pinker traces this back to former Vice President Al Gore becoming a champion for environmentalism. By taking up the environmental cause, Pinker argues, Gore "may have done the movement more harm than good, because as a former Democrat vice-president and presidential nominee he stamped climate change with a left-wing seal."

CCT is thus instructive when thinking about how to teach about climate change in the face of unwarranted scepticism. Where teenagers enter the classroom with value-laden perspectives, teaching as-settled will more likely reinforce the sceptic's view that the gatekeepers of knowledge, including their own teachers, are not to be trusted as they are simply trying to brainwash them.

Here are three nudges that could make the decisive difference for those teaching this topic:

1.   Teachers should make use of experts who can be trusted by the students. As Pinker advises, climate realists would be better off "recruiting conservative and libertarian

commentators who have been convinced by the evidence and are willing to share their concern... than recruiting more scientists to speak more slowly and more loudly." Simply presenting data from scientists who are known to be 'on the other side' will only reinforce the sceptic view that this is all a hoax.

2.   Teachers should use the language that would speak to sceptics, affirming their values, rather than threatening them. For example, when teaching sceptical students from a traditional culture, environmental protection may be couched in terms of the importance of conserving the environment and the duty of stewardship in looking after God's creation.

3.   Teachers are all too aware of the social structures in which their students are embedded: "But my dad says..." or "My priest argues that..." It really does take a village to raise a child, so building links with representatives of the local community and providing educational and social liaison groups will be vital in attempting to overcome the local background conditions that may be epistemically harming the student.

Beware!

Climate change and culture wars: In the United Kingdom, beliefs in the threat of climate change are pretty consistent across political lines. Yet in the United States, the issue has become highly partisan with left-leaning liberals often seeing it as the key issue of the day, and many on the right sceptical both about how serious the issue really is and perhaps even more cynical about government policies on renewable energy.

The reason for the discrepancy might be because in the United Kingdom, Margaret Thatcher, doyen of the right, was one of the first world leaders to actually draw attention to threats to global warming. As Jonathon Porritt, head of Friends of the Earth in the late 1980s, said:

> Thatcher... did more than anyone in the last 60 years to put green issues on the national agenda. From 1987-88 when [she] started to talk about the ozone layer and acid rain and climate change, a lot of people who had said these issues were for the tree-hugging weirdos thought, 'ooh, it's Mrs Thatcher saying that, it must be serious'. She played a big part in the rise of green ideas by making it more accessible to large numbers of people.

In other words, in true CCT fashion, she gave the green light for conservatives to be concerned about, well, conserving.

In the United States, however, the political champion for climate change has been Al Gore, darling of the liberal left. He went on to win the Nobel Peace Prize, a Grammy, an Emmy, and was the subject of an Oscar winning documentary for his work on climate change. Whilst this galvanised the American left – already receptive to environmental values – Gore's campaigning had the unintended consequence of alienating much of the right. For Americans, the issue has become political.

In such a contentious climate, teachers need to be extra cautious. On the one hand, this doesn't mean they should give way to viewpoints that simply go against the evidence. As Ben Shapiro, the Conservative commentator, likes to say: "Facts don't care about your feelings." On the other hand, schools should think strategically about how their pedagogical approaches and teaching materials are inclusive to help win over climate change sceptics rather than alienate them.

Sources and Resources:

Assisi Declarations (1989), 'Messages on Humanity and Nature from Buddhism, Christianity, Hinduism, Islam & Judaism.' Retrieved from: http://www.arcworld.org/downloads/THE%20ASSISI%20DECLARATIONS.pdf.

Daniel Kraemer (2021), 'Greta Thunberg: Who Is the Climate Campaigner and What Are Her Aims?' *BBC News*. Retrieved from: https://www.bbc.co.uk/news/world-europe-49918719.

Dan Kahan et al. (2012), 'The Polarising Impact of Science Literacy and Numeracy on Perceived Climate Change Risks,' *Nature Climate Change* 2(10): 732–735.

Emma L. Lawrance (2022), 'Psychological Responses, Mental Health, and Sense of Agency for the Dual Challenges of Climate Change and the COVID-19 Pandemic in Young People in the UK: An Online Survey Study,' *The Lancet* 6(9). Retrieved from: https://www.thelancet.com/journals/lanplh/article/PIIS2542-5196(22)00172-3/fulltext.

Glenn Bezalel (2022), 'Of Conspiracy and Controversy: A Pedagogy of Conspiracy Theories,' *Educational Theory*. Retrieved from: https://onlinelibrary.wiley.com/doi/epdf/10.1111/edth.12529.

Greenpeace (n.d.), 'What Are the Solutions to Climate Change?' Retrieved from: https://www.greenpeace.org.uk/challenges/climate-change/solutions-climate-change/.

Luke Murphy and Becca Massey-Chase (2022), 'As Some Politicians Seek to Divide on Climate Change, the Public Remain United', *IPPR*. Retrieved from: https://www.ippr.org/blog/as-some-politicians-seek-to-divide-on-climate-change-the-public-remain-united.

National Grid (n.d.), 'What Is Nuclear Energy (and Why Is It Considered a Clean Energy)?' Retrieved from: https://www.nationalgrid.com/stories/energy-explained/what-nuclear-energy-and-why-it-considered-clean-energy#:~:text=Is%20nuclear%20energy%20renewable%3F,be%20found%20in%20certain%20locations.

Peter Singer (2013), 'The Why and How of Effective Altruism,' *TED*. Retrieved from: https://www.ted.com/talks/peter_singer_the_why_and_how_of_effective_altruism.

Sam Crawley et al. (2019), 'Public Opinion on Climate Change: Belief and Concern, Issue Salience and Support for Government Action,' *The British Journal of Politics and International Relations* 22(1). Retrieved from: https://journals.sagepub.com/doi/10.1177/1369148119888827.

Steven Pinker (2018), *Enlightenment Now*. London: Allen Lane.

Steven Pinker (2021), *Rationality*. London: Allen Lane.

The Grantham Institute (n.d.), '9 Things You Can Do about Climate Change.' Retrieved from: https://www.imperial.ac.uk/stories/climate-action/.

UN Environment Programme (2022), '10 Ways You Can Help Fight the Climate Crisis.' Retrieved from: https://www.unep.org/news-and-stories/story/10-ways-you-can-help-fight-climate-crisis.

William MacAskill (2017), 'Effective Altruism: Introduction,' *Essays in Philosophy* 18(1). Retrieved from: https://commons.pacificu.edu/work/sc/a3bc869a-d6aa-4bb4-837b-3dcf6847199e.

William MacAskill (2022), *What We Owe the Future*. London: Oneworld.

Zoe Strozewski (2021), '10 Percent of Americans Don't Believe in Climate Change, 15 Percent Unsure: Poll,' *Newsweek*. Retrieved from: https://www.newsweek.com/10-percent-americans-dont-believe-climate-change-15-percent-unsure-poll-1642747.

Links to Other Controversies:

You don't really believe what the government/media is telling us...?

Notes

1. If a student asks outright about the transgender issue, then I would certainly not pursue the Jaffa Cake analogy: many students might feel that you're belittling the issue. However, if you're brave enough to raise this most controversial of issues, then this route that I'm sharing certainly works for me and leads to high level debate that fulfils both our epistemic and virtue aims.
2. Drawn from: http://www.timcrane.com/jaffa-cakes.html.
3. At the time of writing, Scotland has found itself in the eye of a media storm on trans policy for female prisons. In a masterclass of Socratic questioning, an interviewer for ITV tested Scotland's First Minister Nicola Sturgeon's view that while on the one hand trans women are women, on the other hand, for the purpose of prison, they may be treated differently to born women: https://www.youtube.com/watch?v=5fSEVUMGIKY

   As teachers and students of controversy, we can critically assess whether Sturgeon is being logically consistent. My sense is that both sides of the debate might feel frustrated with her answers...
4. See Chapter 1 for a full explanation.
5. If you're unsure what any of the words are, then perhaps you're better off! However, if champions of free speech like Chimamanda Ngozi Adichie are right, banning words and books will simply cause us to search them out, and so the chances are you've Googled or asked a more 'worldly' friend for their meaning by the time you've finished this footnote!
6. Considering the gravity of Holocaust denial, this book treats this issue elsewhere. Moreover, because climate change is such a major concern for young people, I have also offered a separate guide on this too. Nevertheless, there are overlapping features with conspiracy theories in general and so helpful rules of thumb can be applied where relevant.

AFTERWORD

Relationships First

When I told an old friend I was writing a book on **con**troversy, his immediate reply was, "Don't you mean con**trov**ersy?" After the initial chuckle, I felt a little apprehensive as I realised that people could and probably would gripe about my pronunciation, let alone the content of what I was writing.[1] But I remain hopeful that teachers and students alike are in a unique position to model the art of disagreeing well.

Rather than shy away from controversy, a key argument of this book has been that schools are precisely the place to confront the challenges of the day. Unlike the university lecturer and researcher whose worthy goal is educating for the truth, the whole truth, and nothing but the truth, the schoolteacher has broader aims. Yes to pursuing truth but also yes to nurturing the broad moral, civic, and performance virtues that help develop students into well-rounded adults. Being smart isn't good enough. This is why the finest of teachers recognise that before we teach our 'subject,' we teach our 'students.'

Relationships come first. This is because, as the behavioural sciences show us, it is difficult to learn from someone you don't particularly like or trust. Where there is no rapport, the barrier is up and negative emotions block the learning process. Just as many of us close our ears when the opposition speaks up, teenagers with the whole sweep of emotions running through them, will do the same. The relationships we form in our classroom will be elemental for success.

For this reason, I have long been inspired by Ludwig Wittgenstein's decision to become a schoolteacher. Ray Monk in *The Duty of Genius*, his magisterial biography of perhaps the greatest philosophical mind of the 20th century, cites Wittgenstein's explanation of choosing his vocation to his disapproving sister:

> You remind me of somebody who is looking out through a closed window and cannot explain to himself the strange movements of a passer-by. He cannot tell what sort of storm is raging out there or that this person might only be managing with difficulty to stay on his feet.

As teachers well know, no class is alike, and no two students are the same. The struggles and quandaries each of our students are facing require open-minded teachers and peers to help reach the truth in a sensitive and nurturing manner. As the Bible (Deuteronomy 16: 20) puts it: "Justice, justice you shall pursue." In a text that spares no words, the repetition of 'justice' comes to teach us that the right ends must be reached through the right means. Intellectual virtues and moral virtues go hand in hand.

Two Types of Knowledge

Professor Rupert Wegerif at the University of Cambridge takes this idea further in a powerful observation of two types of knowledge.[2] As Wegerif writes, we in the West "now live in a world once dreamt of by Comenius." John Amos Comenius (1592–1670), a Dutch pedagogue, was a pioneer of universal education for boys and girls, organising an educational system from kindergarten to university now found throughout the Western world. As Wegerif writes:

> Comenius's vision included the need for feedback from students to show that they are now 'possessors of knowledge' and also the need for end of year examinations ensuring that 'subjects have been properly learned'. Comenius's model of nationally-based phases of schooling was adopted by the whole of Europe and the USA during the 19th Century.

Comenius's literacy-based educational model centred on gaining 'knowledge' in the sense of 'representation.' By learning facts from books in the classroom, we commit ourselves to learning images or representations of "the real thing." Of course, this kind of learning has paved the way for the modern educational system which provided for the basic skills of literacy and numeracy that could be extended to everyone. Yet, as Wegerif suggests, perhaps there is something we have lost in this model of education.

For there is a second type of knowledge which is centred on 'relationship.' Rather than learning *about* a subject matter in a purely epistemic manner, this is where I seek to *experience* that very thing I am interested in. This model of education was championed by Socrates and the ancient Israelites through their oracy-based educational cultures. In contrast to Comenius's knowledge as 'representation,' the Bible uses the word 'to know' in reference to relationships, often describing an act of intimacy between two people. Think back to Genesis Chapter 4, which opens as follows: "And Adam *knew* Eve his wife; and she conceived, and bare Cain, and said, I have gotten a man from the Lord." Of course, Adam didn't pass a factual Couples Dating Quiz about the details of Eve's life. If he 'knew' her just before she conceived, the text is telling us that he knew her intimately (Figure A.1).[3]

Wegerif writes:

> Tracing the roots of the Hebrew word for knowledge found in the Bible, Da'at (דעת) from the verb Ya'da (ידע), to know, we find that the original pictographs behind the two letters used in these words, dalet and ayin, combine the image of a tent door flap (Dalet) with the image of an eye (Ayin).
>
> To know, for the ancient Hebrews, apparently involved moving a seeing eye through the tent door flap to enter inside a previously hidden space. Knowing, on this metaphorical imagery, involves the difference between an outside view and an inside view, not just, for example what someone looks like from the outside but also effectively 'moving inside' them to know what it feels like to be them. Knowing as the eye passing through a tent door flap to see inside the tent.

This book is a plea for education to combine knowledge as 'representation' with knowledge as 'relationship.' Just as Wittgenstein calls for us to 'open the window' to fully engage with our students and help them weather the storms they are battling, so too do our students need to see through the tent door flap and experience the other side. On all too many issues, we are living in 'epistemic bubbles,' hardened against the possibility that others who think differently from us may be decent people with cogent ideas that we ourselves would do well to learn from. In Jonathan Sacks' pithy phrase, our students must learn that "honest doubt can be more powerful than dishonest faith."[4]

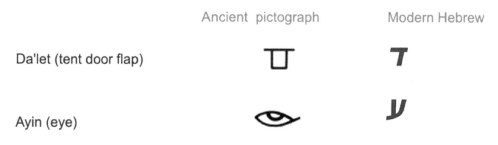

Figure A.1 Knowledge in the Biblical Sense

'Nudgeucation': Change the Environment, Not Your Students

So how do we pop those 'epistemic bubbles?' How do we get our students to be more open to learning from those unlike themselves?

In one of the most insightful messages for all in education, Daniel Kahneman provides a key principle that should revolutionise our schools: "The easiest way to change people's behaviour is to change their environment; it's to create conditions in which the behaviour that you consider desirable will be easier, will be more natural than it is now."[5] It is up to school leaders and teachers to think about the 'choice architecture' in each of our schools to ensure that we are creating the right conditions for learning about issues of controversy.

Taking up Kahneman's sound advice, here are my favourite educational 'nudges' – small differences that can make the world of difference – for teaching controversy effectively.

Classroom Layout

Teacher at the front with students in rows facing you makes sense for a 'convergent' teaching style. So when you're teaching the facts or offering the evidence, stick to this traditional classroom set-up.

However, when you want to pursue a 'divergent' teaching style, inviting many possible responses and ideas, ensure your classroom layout is more democratic. Two examples:

- Philosophy circles: simply arrange the chairs in a large circle so everyone is included, no one is at the 'front' or 'back.' The sense of equality and fair exposure means all are welcome to participate.
- Harkness tables: an oval boardroom-style table is ideal but putting some tables together with everyone sitting around to discuss ideas with targeted teacher intervention is fine too. For a bigger size class, simply have two or three tables set up in different parts of the room. The table is helpful for reviewing and writing notes, and helps model the sort of discussion meetings your students may well have when they get older.

Embed Oracy into the Curriculum

Remember, the foundation of a classical education was the trivium: grammar, logic, and rhetoric. Whilst literacy and numeracy reserved their places on the modern curriculum, oracy got shoved to the side. Time to bring it back:

- Oracy for everyone: every subject can embed oracy into their core curriculum rather than as an add on or as part of a co-curricular club for the few. One forward looking headmistress has put oracy into her Year 7 curriculum (for 11–12 year olds) – which she teaches! That way she gets to know all of her students and they get to practise their public speaking skills in front of the most intimidating person they know. If they can do that at just 11 years of age, imagine what they'll be able to achieve as they get older.
- School debating chamber: every school has classrooms and so every school should have a debating chamber. This can of course be a decent size hall with the right props, including a lectern for your students.

Embed Thinking Skills into the Curriculum

Whether as part of specific subjects' curriculum or as standalone courses, thinking skills are crucial life skills. These ideas need to be taught explicitly rather than hoping that through some sort of magic, our students will somehow acquire them. This book has a suggested course for thinking skills for controversy. It's time to get interested teachers on board and design a course that will work for your students.

Co-teach for Other Perspectives

Teaching is for the most part a very solitary job: it's just you and your students. Oracy, thinking skills and collaboration go together. Bringing a co-teacher into your class can add so many dimensions. This is especially true if you have wildly differing views on a topic of controversy that you'd like to present to the class. Model the 'principle of charity' by inviting in your opponent to share their perspective. If you are a science teacher discussing climate change, welcoming in the art teacher or humanities teacher can help enrich the learning experiences for your students.

'Bridging'

Get your students to meet peers unlike themselves. This could mean in terms of background. For example, if you live in a homogeneously ethnic community, taking your students on a visit to meet students from other ethnicities will be eye opening for them. Students from different socioeconomic backgrounds rarely mix: this is not healthy for an inclusive society. Simply seeing how others live their lives is a value in itself.

But don't stop there. Diversity, especially in the area of controversy, means cognitive diversity too. Meeting people who *think* differently from you is a real lesson in intellectual humility. It is so easy to stereotype and demean others when we have never met them or really listened to them. In Israel-Palestine, one of the most worthy projects is for schoolchildren on each side of the divide to meet up and discuss the conflict, play football with each other, and ultimately appreciate that there may be more that unites them than divides. Each half-term schools can arrange for students to meet peers from other schools – unlike their own – to discuss key topics of controversy. Students (and teachers) will find they have a lot to learn from others unlike themselves.

Questions, Questions, Questions

Socratic questioning works! Since the great pedagogue went around making trouble in ancient Athens thousands of years ago, skilful questioning gets to the heart of every topic. Continuing professional development for teachers in this area should be a priority for schools. Knowing how to get your students thinking hard through the challenging questions you can pose for them is the key ingredient for any successful lesson on controversy.

We know that pretty much any reasonable teaching intervention will have some impact. But teachers have little time and so the concept of 'opportunity cost' becomes all important. What small differences can I make that will bring about a real difference? As the experts in the behavioural sciences remind us, for success,[6] nudges must be:

- Easy
- Attractive
- Social
- Timely.

So there's your challenge: as you head EAST, what easy, attractive, social, and timely nudges can you implement for your students so that teaching controversy is no longer controversial but simply part of what you do?

Notes

1. For the record, I stand by the emphasis on the first syllable, refusing to give way to my friend's pretentious stress on the second syllable.
2. Rupert Wegerif. (2022) 'Two Kinds of Knowledge: "Representation" or "Relationship"?' Retrieved from: https://www.rupertwegerif.name/blog/two-kinds-of-knowledge-representation-or-relationship.
3. Even today, to 'know someone biblically' is a euphemism for sleeping with them.
4. Jonathan Sacks. (2019) 'Honest Doubt Can Be More Powerful than Dishonest Faith.' Retrieved from: https://www.rabbisacks.org/archive/honest-doubt-can-be-more-powerful-than-dishonest-faith/.
5. Daniel Kahneman. (2021) 'Changing Behavior by Changing Environment.' Retrieved from: https://www.youtube.com/watch?v=pbSzjWaC1pc.
6. Owain Service et al. (2015) 'EAST: Four Simple Ways to Apply Behavioural Insights.' Retrieved from: https://www.bi.team/wp-content/uploads/2015/07/BIT-Publication-EAST_FA_WEB.pdf.

ACKNOWLEDGEMENTS

I count myself lucky that I was brought up in a culture which values questions more than answers. Arguing, debating, and discussing "for the sake of Heaven" are at the core of my identity. And every Friday night, together with the compulsory challah bread and chicken soup, our family characteristically argues about the timely and timeless issues of controversy facing us.

Isidore Rabi, winner of the Nobel Prize for Physics in 1944, was once asked why he became a scientist. He replied: "My mother made me a scientist without ever knowing it. Every other child would come back from school and be asked, 'What did you learn today?' But my mother used to say, 'Izzy, did you ask a good question today?' That made the difference. Asking good questions made me into a scientist."

Indeed, asking good questions makes us all good students of life.

As Richard Feynman, winner of the Nobel Prize for Physics in 1965, put it: "I would rather have questions that can't be answered than answers that can't be questioned." This book is written very much in this spirit, championing the virtue of enquiry – wherever it may lead us.

Life is complex and often requires out of the box thinking. This means taking risks and being prepared to get it wrong. If we truly care about pursuing the truth, we need intellectual humility as we remain open to other perspectives. Just as we don't wish to be humiliated for getting it wrong, so do we need to be forgiving of others too.

As a schoolteacher for some 15 years, my sense is that these virtues for intellectual enquiry are eroding. Teachers are more afraid to teach, justifiably worried that they'll be called out in this new age of orthodoxy that has answers that can't be questioned. There is almost a secular blasphemy growing around us as certain topics are considered off-limits. This has a chilling effect for many. Understandably, an increasing number of teachers and students alike feel they don't want to speak up or discuss issues of real controversy lest they become the new heretic and social outcast.

I hope this handbook of controversy gives teachers both the theory and practice required to reintroduce the issues that matter to the next generation. As a teacher of Religion, Philosophy, and Ethics, I am lucky that my typical lesson will be controversial. I have found that students do want to engage and that it is precisely in the warm and safe environment of the classroom that they feel most comfortable to speak up and debate. Schools have a unique role to play but this unapologetically means pushing the boundaries, sometimes requiring our students to feel uncomfortable, questioning themselves and the ideas they hold sacred. But it's worth it: not only in pursuit of the truth but also to help nurture the moral and civic virtues that we wish to see in our students – helping us to develop in kind.

At the same time, I have had the good fortune to have taught with outstanding colleagues over the years who have helped me think that bit better about the issues we all love to discuss and debate. A special thank you to Alan Bird, Alice Lucas, and Mary Short for providing outstanding models of educational leadership that help students thrive. In particular, my work with Alice on 'Nudge for Learning,' thinking about how to bring the behavioural sciences into the classroom, as discussed in Chapter 4 of this book, proved hugely exciting, much due to Alice's inspirational mentorship, effortless charm, and loyal friendship. Teaching with the likes of Hannah Williams and Sophie Hussey, as well as my brilliant colleagues at City of London School, has not only been entertaining but also proves how cognitive diversity really does strengthen our own thinking.

I have been so fortunate to pursue my interests in all things controversial at the incomparable Faculty of Education at the University of Cambridge. Learning from a community of the finest scholars in the world has been a real privilege and there has been no better guide in helping me think about these issues than Professor Jo-Anne Dillabough. As my long-suffering PhD supervisor, she is not just the most brilliant and insightful person, she is also particularly lovely and caring.

It was during my Master's in Education at UCL that I came across the inspiring Jeremy Hayward who got me thinking seriously about issues of controversy. A master pedagogue, Jeremy is the teacher's teacher who has influenced me hugely. Thank you, Jeremy.

As a teacher, one of the most pleasurable things I can do is thank my own schoolteachers who, in their distinctive ways, modelled for me what outstanding teaching is all about. I look back at my own school days with much fondness and the teachers that really stood out for me were Nick Calogirou, Pat Glynn, Sharron Krieger, Kathy Schindler, and Peter Williamson.

I want to thank Annamarie Kino, my thoughtful and ever wise editor at Routledge, for her enthusiasm for this project throughout and for making me feel uncomfortable on occasion to help deliver a much better book than I could have done otherwise. I am also grateful to Annamarie's team at Routledge – including Sophie Ganesh and Paige Loughlin – and all the reviewers whose feedback on the book has been so generous. Of course, I take full responsibility for any remaining errors.

In thinking about and writing this book, I have drawn on my wonderful and large family, who have been forever patient in indulging my thought experiments and perennial desire to play devil's advocate. Huge thanks to Zoe, my gorgeous sister-in-law, for letting me have endless phone conversations with my brother, Ariel. Just about the kindest person I know, Ariel also has a matchless ability to "say it how it is," often forcing me back to the drawing board to sharpen my argument or simply ditch it altogether.

As a firm believer that you get the in-laws you deserve(!), I couldn't have done better than the Levy clan that I married into. Moshe and Viv, Darren and Mira, Dov and Sara, Ari and Natalie, you and your families mean everything to me. Not least because you gave me my better half (as she would be the first to admit) in my darling wife, Shuli. There are no issues of controversy between us as we both know you're always right. My sense is that most happy marriages are based on this principle and I'm more than happy to keep it that way.

This book is ultimately for the next generation of young people to learn about issues of controversy in a more sophisticated and nuanced manner. I therefore dedicate this book to my own children who I love more than I can say: Hannah, Shayna, Akiva, Jemima, and Tamara.

ABOUT THE AUTHOR

Glenn Y. Bezalel is Deputy Head (Academic) at City of London School, where he teaches Religion & Philosophy. Glenn is also researching the pedagogy of conspiracy theories and controversy at the University of Cambridge and has written numerous articles on a range of educational topics for both academic and professional publications. He lives in London with his wife and five children.

INDEX

Note: *Italic* page numbers refer to figures and page numbers followed by "n" denote endnotes.